Wow! What a remarkable seri
qualified, reflective practitione
"Living Well" to "Finishing Wel
transform their world for Jesus, both in the marketplace and in the world around us.

Rev Edmund Chan
Leadership Mentor, Covenant EFC;
Founder, Global Alliance of Intentional Disciplemaking Churches

Living an authentic Christian life is often challenged by the complexities of our contemporary world. This collection recounts faithful men who seek to live out what their relationship with Christ means for each of them. They share their thoughts, struggles, convictions and moments in life that formed an integral sum of answering God's call through varied stations in society and faith communities. The prophet Joel declared that in the last days God shall pour out His Spirit to all flesh, enabling young men to see visions and old men dream dreams (Acts 2:17). May the sharing in these pages rejuvenate the visions and dreams of all men, both young and old, whom God calls in this age before Christ returns.

Dr Chew Wee
President, Graduates' Christian Fellowship, Singapore

A book of rich tapestry — the insights and real-life accounts will widen your perspective, inspire you to follow after Jesus and stir both your faith and hunger to live well for God. *Men for Christ* is a timely call to all men, whatever our life stage or domain, to arise and fulfil our calling in these unchartered times.

Rt Rev Rennis Ponniah
Bishop of Singapore, The Anglican Church;
President, National Council of Churches of Singapore

Christians often ask for resources to help them live out their faith in down-to-earth, real world situations. They look for help in making connections between their Sunday faith and the rest of their lives. This book is a marvel of practical, godly wisdom to help people looking for support in living a deeper, more meaningful Christian life. Each chapter offers an honest, heartfelt exploration of how a Christ-centred faith makes a difference in everyday life. It is a valuable contribution to the cause of making disciples in Singapore and beyond.

Professor Jeffrey P. Greenman
President, Regent College, Canada

The struggles we face as Christians are real. Hence, there is immense value whenever a brother shares his life experiences and faith journey, through a men's fellowship like Carmel Men for Christ, to offer insightful and practical guidance on embracing right Christian thinking and to finish well for Christ. I have benefitted so much, learning from the personal sharing from the more senior band of brothers-in-Christ, which is now compiled in this book. This book would certainly help younger men like myself better relate to issues and strengthen our Christian worldview and walk, so that we will "not conform any longer to the pattern of this world, but to be transformed by the renewing of your mind" (Romans 12:2). May the sharing of these leader-writers inspire all men for Christ, to step forward to serve our true and living God with greater clarity and conviction, wherever God has purposed us to be.

Benedict Leow
Participant, Carmel Men for Christ Ministry;
Co-founder, Soup Spoon

The writers bring much wisdom in addressing some of the most critical and contemporary issues concerning our lives and society today. The outcome is an accessible, trenchant and thoughtful reflection that will greatly clarify and challenge all readers.

Rev Dr Oh Boon Leong
Senior Pastor, Mount Carmel Bible-Presbyterian Church

Men for Christ: Living Out Our Faith is a seminal practitioner's contribution on Christian engagement that richly contributes to our nation building in the civic and political public square and the marketplace. This well-respected, erstwhile and responsible band of 21 brothers speak frankly and humbly of their challenges, experiences and journeys. Their sharings will be an inspiration for the next generation.

Listen to the spirit behind their stories and you will hear and see the living hand of the Lord. I am reminded of Oswald Chambers in *My Utmost for His Highest*, where he reminds us: "The one mark of a saint is the moral originality which springs from abandonment to Jesus Christ ... The saint realizes that it is God Who engineers circumstances ... He is with you".

Here, 21 passionate saints moved by the Spirit of God tell us their stories. How can we not follow their examples?

Richard Magnus
Former Senior District Judge;
Chancellor, Anglican Church of Singapore;
Vice Chair, UNESCO Bioethics Domain

This collection of talks from the Carmel Men for Christ is a gift. These 21 essays, compiled as *Men for Christ: Living Out Our Faith*, provide a valuable, inspirational and provocative resource for men (and women). With honest assessments, men from politics, various professions, businesses and churches reflect on the successes and failures of their journeys through life, articulating from diverse perspectives how their faith have been, is now, and will be lived out. Throughout the book we are reminded that God's call is for life. One's calling does not end with retirement or any life transition. This volume ignites our thinking about who we are and who we intend to be in the places where God has us now. And in sharing their stories, the writers invite us to ponder our own.

Dr Walter C. Wright, Jr.
Senior Fellow, Max De Pree Center for Leadership, USA

I applaud this effort to put together the various nuggets from talks given at Carmel Men's Ministry. Every effort adds to the development of such a man as described in the Bible:

For the eyes of the LORD range throughout the earth to strengthen those whose hearts are fully committed to him.
(2 Chronicles 16:9a)

[The LORD looks] for a man who would ... stand before [him] in the gap on behalf of the land ... (Ezekiel 22:30)

Such a man finds his significance in his relationship with God. He is secure with a band of brothers, defined as those he can call at 3 a.m. for help and vice versa. Such a band of brothers support each other on this journey to be godly men, godly husbands and godly fathers.

The good Lord multiply His wisdom and favour, peace and strength to all men reading this book, for such a time as this!

Rev Daniel Foo
Senior Pastor, Bethesda (Bedok Tampines) Church, Singapore

This is a helpful collection of essays by men who have made life-changing discoveries about themselves, their realities and God. Their self-realization encourages readers to reimagine themselves, discern God's purposes and make a difference in their world at every stage of life. The writers distill wisdom from their life journeys, with compelling yet compassionate, inspiring yet practical reflections. Written from the vantage point of experience, this collection will inspire readers who desire to live meaningfully and purposefully. It is a thought-provoking and action-inspiring collection for all who desire a focused life.

Peter Chao
Founding President, Eagles Communications, Singapore

By men, for men. This book is a compilation of 21 talks at the Mt Carmel's Men's Ministry over the past few years. These talks were delivered by men of great spiritual stature and high distinction in society.

Men for Christ is especially attractive and relevant because it is written from a Singaporean setting with a lot of local flavour in it. I found it to be very inspiring. The insights and issues raised are extremely pertinent and relevant in an Asian context. There is so much to glean from the experiences of these men of God who have been tested in their various fields of ministry, especially in the marketplace.

All these men have not only emerged unscathed but came through with great honour and distinction. What a testimony to the goodness and glory of God! That's why this book is well worth your reading.

Dr Chew Weng Chee
Senior Pastor, SIBKL, Malaysia

It was my joy to read every one of the submissions. I found many of them gripping, enthralling, written from the heart, brutally frank and honest, insightful, provocative and deeply enriching. I could identify with many of the joys and struggles mentioned in the testimonies. It was helpful as the stories parallel the struggles that I faced and continue to grapple in my own life. I warmly commend this book. This book is important for Christian men to read and ponder over real-life situations that they face in their lives.

Rev Dr Quek Swee Hwa
Founding Principal Emeritus, Biblical Graduate School of Theology;
Senior Pastor, Emmanuel Bible-Presbyterian Church, Singapore

MEN *for* CHRIST

MEN *for* CHRIST

LIVING OUT OUR FAITH

Edited by
Ho Peng Kee, Lim Kheng Hai, Siew Kim Siang, Yeo Siew Yam

GRACEWORKS

Men for Christ: Living Out Our Faith

Published by
Graceworks Private Limited
22 Sin Ming Lane
#04-76 Midview City
Singapore 573969
www.graceworks.com.sg

ISBN: 978-981-09-8884-5

A CIP record for this book is available from the National Library Board, Singapore.

2 3 4 5 6 7 8 9 10 • 25 24 23 22 21 20 19 18 17

To the many men and women, especially Uncle Robert Ong, a pioneer Man for Christ, whose faithful service over the years have made it possible for Mt Carmel BP Church to joyfully anticipate its Jubilee Year Celebration in 2017.

Uncle Robert Ong, a young deacon from Life Bible-Presbyterian Church, started a Sunday School for some neighbourhood kids living in the Redhill/Bukit Merah area in1958. Initial attendance fluctuated between 6 and 12. Undeterred, he persevered. By 1963, the class had grown into a youth worship service as the kids grew older and brought their friends along. In May 1967, Mount Carmel Gospel Mission was officially inaugurated at Lengkok Bahru. Uncle Ong went home to be with the Lord in May 2012. Till the very end, he was a Man of Prayer. He finished strong and well! Praise the Lord.

"Their light must shine before men, that they may see your good deeds and praise your Father in heaven."

(MATTHEW 5:16)

CONTENTS

CONTRIBUTORS

DAVID ANG, PBM
Chairman, Local Church Executive Committee, Kum Yan Methodist Church; Councillor, Northeast Community Development Council; Honorary Treasurer, Trinity Theological College.

AW SWEE ENG
Adjunct Associate Professor, Duke-NUS Medical School.

ERNEST CHEW
History Consultant, Findings Education; Chairman, Singapore History Museum; Founding Chairman, University Staff Christian Fellowship; Elder, Bethesda (Frankel Estate) Church.

JOHN CHEW
Bishop, Anglican Church of Singapore; Advisor, Chinese Church Committee of the National Council of Christian Churches of Singapore; Member, United Bible Societies Global Council.

ANDREW GOH
Honorary Editor, *Impact* Magazine; Founding Elder, RiverLife Church.

HO PENG KEE
Associate Professorial Fellow, Law Faculty, National University of Singapore; Elder, Mount Carmel Bible-Presbyterian Church; Chairman, Home Team Volunteer Network Steering Committee, Ministry of Home Affairs; Advisor, Biblical Graduate School of Theology.

HSIEH FU HUA
Chairman, United Overseas Bank; Chairman, Tiger Airways Holdings; Advisor, Prime Partners Group.

LEE HAN KIAT
Halftime Certified Coach and Roundtable Facilitator.

LEE SOO ANN
Senior Fellow, Department of Economics and Lee Kuan Yew School of Public Policy, National University of Singapore; Preaching Elder, Prinsep Street Presbyterian Church; President, Bible Society of Singapore; Advisor, Presbyterian Community Services.

PATRICK LIEW
Founder, Success Resources; CEO, HSR International Realtors; Chairman, Junior Achievement; Co-chairman, Responsible Gambling Forum; Co-founder, Worldwide House of Prayer.

LIM HUA MIN
Executive Chairman, PhillipCapital Group of Companies; Elder, Covenant Evangelical Free Church.

TIMOTHY LIU
Founder, Ministry for Marketplace Christian Network; Senior Associate for Marketplace Ministry, Lausanne Committee for World Evangelism; Council Member, Biblical Graduate School of Theology; Deacon, Mount Carmel Bible-Presbyterian Church.

PHILIP NG
Chief Executive Officer, Far East Organization; Chairman, Singapore University of Technology and Design Board of Trustees; Advisor, Biblical Graduate School of Theology.

JOHN NG
Chief Passionary Officer, Meta Consulting; Honorary Chairman, Eagles Communications Board of Governance; Founder, Eagles Mediation and Counselling Centre.

ROBERT SOLOMON
Bishop Emeritus, The Methodist Church in Singapore.

TAN LAI YONG
Lecturer, National University of Singapore; Director of Outreach and Community Engagement, College of Alice and Peter Tan, National University of Singapore.

TAN SOO INN
Founding Director, Graceworks Private Limited; Adjunct Lecturer, Biblical Graduate School of Theology.

GREGORY VIJAYENDRAN
Partner, Messrs Rajah & Tann LLP; Chairman, Law Christian Fellowship; Vice President, Law Society of Singapore; Honorary Secretary, Prison Fellowship Singapore.

WILLIAM WAN
General Secretary, Singapore Kindness Movement; Pastor Emeritus, Hope Presbyterian Church; Chairman, Prison Fellowship Singapore.

WONG KAR FATT
Elder, Mount Carmel Bible-Presbyterian Church.

DAVID W. F. WONG
Senior Pastor, Zion Bishan Bible-Presbyterian Church; Founder, Finishing Well Ministries; Advisor, Men's Ministry Network.

FOREWORD

Over the past 50 years, profound changes have taken place in Singapore. To begin with, the physical landscape of today would not have been recognized by our forefathers. A new city has emerged onto the world scene. The population has grown from two million in 1970 to our present 5.5 million. In the 1960s, most people lived in squalid shophouses in the central town area and in outlying squatter farmlands. Today, 85 per cent of people reside in neat, affordable government-built apartments. From the beginning, Singapore's economic well-being has always been dependent on trading activities. Today, the city has become a key financial, educational and communications hub.

What is striking is that the church scene has also changed. In the 1960s, those professing the Christian faith numbered about seven to eight per cent; today it is 18 per cent. These believers then worshipped in some 80 churches; today, there are over 600 churches. Furthermore, these churches manifest a vitality that would have been unthinkable. They are active in community service, marketplace ministries and overseas missions. Bear in mind too that much of that growth took place among young people. The 1957 census revealed that 42 per cent of the population were below 15 years old. It was these young lives that active Christian youth organizations were able to draw to the faith. Today, many church leaders can trace their conversion to the hard work put in by church schools, the Interschool Christian Fellowship, Youth for Christ, Navigators and others.

The contributors to this book have lived through this period of change. Some have been active in the academic world, others in marketplace ministry, and yet others in public life. They have also been part of the growing church. As first-generation Christians, many have had to grow their faith amidst a multicultural and multifaith society. This has not always been easy. A number have had their ups and downs in life but they have always learned to recognize the sovereign hand of God at work. It is out of their varied journeys in life that they now share the lessons they have learnt with others.

Shortly before Jesus went to the cross, He uttered a prayer to the Father, expressing two compelling truths. Firstly, Christians are to have a Scripture-based worldview: "I have given them your word and the world has hated them, for they are not of the world any more than I am of the world" (John 17:14). At times, this worldview compels us to take a position that is contrary to that of the secular world. Secondly, we have a God-given mission in the world: "As you sent me into the world, I have sent them into the world" (John 17:18). Christians have lives that need to be lived out. Earlier, Jesus had told the disciples that they were to be the salt of the earth and light to the world (Matthew 5:13–15). Their light must "shine before men, that they may see your good deeds and praise your Father in heaven" (Matthew 5:16).

The contributors in this book have sought to do just that. In their journeys through life, they have sought to understand what it means to be a Christian in the world, amidst its many complexities. It is their prayer that as a younger generation of believers journey through life, they too will discover for themselves what it means to be "sent … into the world" (John 17:18).

Dr Bobby Sng

Advisor and Past President (2002–2012), Bible Society of Singapore

General Secretary, Fellowship of Evangelical Students (1969–1993)

PREFACE

Carmel Men for Christ (CM*f*C) was launched in June 2012, ten months after I had stepped down from political office. During this time, as I prayed and sought God's guidance on how I could add value wherever He had put me, I felt a conviction that we should restart our men's ministry in Mount Carmel Bible-Presbyterian Church. I then surveyed other churches' men's ministries.

For Carmel, I felt that we should help our brothers forge a solidly-grounded Christian worldview. Romans 12:2 exhorts us to "not conform any longer to the pattern of this world, but be transformed by the renewing of your mind". To do this, I felt that we should adopt a three-prong approach, that is, (1) study what God has to say in His Word on the various roles of men in society — as fathers, spouses, workers, co-labourers in God's Kingdom, etc.; (2) be encouraged and inspired by men who have striven to live by His standards wherever He has put them, especially in the workplace and marketplace; and (3) examine, as guided by the Holy Spirit, how God is working in the world — in history, business, missions, world events, etc. This is how I put it when I launched the ministry in June 2012:

> *Dear brothers, let us be a band of brothers, an army for God! We are all here because we believe that as men, God has a purpose for us. There is potential in us, whatever stage of life we are in, whether we are at the beginning of our careers or already retired. The fact is, whatever our station or age, God has a purpose for us. And God, in His Word, has determined the various roles that men should play. As a band of brothers in Carmel, we prayerfully seek His will for us, individually and corporately. Please remember that we do this not for ourselves, but because we believe that God can use us. We are all instruments for Him to be used.*

Indeed, God has put us in different settings. Many of us are fathers and husbands. We either are or have been in the workplace or marketplace. We are also members of the community where He has put us. This can be a neighbourhood, church or para-church organization, voluntary welfare organization or grassroots body. We are also citizens of Singapore and the world. That is the larger context. This Men's Fellowship will meet monthly to hear a brother-in-Christ share his walk with God, including his struggles. No man is perfect, so it is important that we do not put anyone on a pedestal. Our speaker will share from the perspective that God has given him the opportunity to walk his walk and run his race in a certain arena of life.

As men, it is good for us to share some of the problems we face in life. Any of us can fall anytime, as we are subject to many temptations — "the lust of the flesh, the lust of the eyes, and the pride of life" (1 John 2:16, NKJV). As we face these temptations and struggles, we should be mindful of God's Word and have the encouragement of godly men to keep us afloat. And as we are at different stages of our life, the old can share with the young and vice versa. We learn from one another."

Tapping my contacts from over 20 years in public life, I invited brothers from various sectors to come and share at our monthly men's ministry gathering. We thank God for the 35 brothers who have come over the past four years. Coming from diverse backgrounds, their talks have enriched our men, especially in helping us form a Christian worldview and encouraging us to finish well. This book captures 21 of these talks, up till December 2014. Some have been further refined. (Our thanks go to Soh Swee Peng and Joshua Yeo for patiently transcribing the bulk of the talks, and to Tien Li from Graceworks for painstakingly editing them.) If there is interest, God willing, we hope to publish another book setting out the later talks.

We have categorized these 21 talks under four headings, viz. (1) Living Well; (2) God in the Marketplace; (3) God in the World Around Us and (4) Finishing Well. God's Word exhorts us to "Love your neighbor as yourself" (Mark 12:31).

As men, how do we love ourselves? I believe that a key to doing this well is to be the best man that we can be, that God has made us. For this to happen, we have to know and understand ourselves. Part 1 seeks to achieve this purpose. Many of our readers will still be working. Some run their own businesses. Part 2 will be especially relevant to these brothers. How can they be his priests and ambassadors during the nine or ten hours every day that they are out there "in the world" (John 17:11)?

Matthew 28:18 states, "All authority in heaven and on earth has been given to (Jesus)". Our sovereign God manifests His presence in every field of human endeavour. In a limited way, we try to show this in Part 3, illustrating how God is in history, science, our churches and politics. Finally, our clarion call is for all our brothers in our churches (and readers who are sisters too) to persevere and run the race marked out for them (Hebrews 12:1). We must press on and fight the good fight, finish the race and keep the faith (2 Timothy 4:7). Indeed, by God's grace, we should try to finish the race of life strongly, with faith, determination and passion, always trusting in Him. This is what Part 4 seeks to move us to do.

Our intention in sharing the insights gleaned with a larger audience of men in Singapore churches island-wide is not to put the contributors on a pedestal. Rather, we hope that these testimonies and the issues raised will get men thinking and praying about their own walk with God, both individually and collectively. How can they be better men for Christ in the various settings God has put them? How can they live life fully and finish well? To stimulate thinking, each contributor has listed four to five questions for reflection. Indeed, the contributors form an informal faculty that our churches' men's ministries can tap. To facilitate this, their email addresses are listed at the end of their profiles in each chapter. Alternatively, you can email <enquiries@graceworks.com.sg>.

These talks are reproduced in the spirit in which they were given (as shared originally at CM*f*C) and not necessarily because they represent Mount Carmel's stand on particular issues. May God use them to enrich the men's ministries in our churches and inspire our men to live fully and finish well for Him. Amen.

Assoc Prof Ho Peng Kee
Elder, Mount Carmel Bible-Presbyterian Church
Chief Editor

"God saw all that he had made, and it was very good."

(GENESIS 1:31)

LIVING WELL

THE THREE CALLS OF LIFE: WHAT IT MEANS TO BE TRULY HUMAN

Tan Soo Inn

What is the purpose of life? I am 57 years old this year. Steve Jobs died when he was 56. What legacy did he leave behind? He founded Apple! Sometimes I ask myself, "What legacy will I leave behind?" I have not founded any multibillion-dollar company; does this mean I'm a failure? In three years I will qualify for senior citizen discounts. Life seems to flash by when you get older. It is good to ask periodically, "What is the purpose of life anyway?"

It's always good to go back to the beginning, to Genesis, which presents the picture of Man's condition as it was meant to be before sin entered the world. I believe that as humans we have three main callings.

Our First Call: To Co-labour with God and Care for Creation on His Behalf

The creation of mankind is recounted in Genesis 1:26. If we skip ahead a little, we read in verse 31 that God surveyed all He made and declared it was very good. When He created the fish and the animals, He considered all these "good". It is only when humankind was created that He declared it "very good". We are the pinnacle of God's creation! We see this in Psalm 8 as well.

As the peak of God's creation, we have been given the job of representing God to the rest of His creation and to each other. God is spirit so we cannot see Him, but if you want to catch a glimpse of what God is like, take a look at humanity. We are made in His image, and we represent Him through the things we do and the characters we display. And we have been given the job of caring for creation on His behalf.

Of course, God is God. He does not need us; He can do it on His own and better. Yet, in His love, He created us to manage His world, to rule and subdue it. In Genesis 2, we see that this injunction to rule and subdue more closely resembles a call to be a loving gardener than a call to bully and exploit.

For God's world to be managed, you need all sorts of people to do all sorts of things! Doctors, lawyers, bus drivers, cleaners ... Perhaps we should write down a list of every conceivable occupation the world needs to keep functioning. I wish I could sit down and ask each of you what you do. Whatever it happens to be, you are doing God's work!

Christians tend to divide the world into sacred and secular portions. If you are a pastor and missionary, you are in the "sacred" portion and you are doing God's work. If you happen to be a politician or a lawyer or a businessman, you are doing "secular" work. But God has created us differently to manage different things to keep His world going. If everybody became a pastor, the world would grind to an end. Who will cook your favourite chicken rice? So there is no sacred-secular divide.

I knew I was serving God when I was a dentist. I never saw myself as a kind of mechanic for teeth. Rather, I always kept in mind the patients I was treating, and endeavoured to show them Christ's love. I wish I knew what each of you is doing! Some of you are in vocational Christian work, and that is good, for we need our best people there.

We are all called to flesh out Kingdom values wherever we are. I might not have been a full-time church worker as a dentist, but I certainly hope that there was something about the values and love that I tried to put into my dental practice that intrigued my patients and led them to ask what made the difference. The work we do gives us opportunities to flesh out Kingdom values and point people towards Christ.

As I grow older, I find there is no retirement either. Retirement is not a word we see in Scripture. Some of us reach an age where we may not be on a payroll anymore, and I hope by then we have enough savings! We may reach a certain age where we are not employed. But work is not tied to paid employment. Work is an exercise of our gifts to bless people. In fact, society is asking us to work longer, so maybe we should stop thinking, "Well, when is my time to retire?"

There will always be groups that require volunteers — the church, for example. I am now caring for my mother back in Penang. She is 85 years old and in the early stages of dementia, while my father-in-law stays with us in Singapore and has Parkinson's and some degree of dementia. I do not know how to delay the onset of dementia but I do know I want to be engaged all the days of my life. I see some of my seminary professors who are now in their 80s and 90s still fully engaged in their work. I want to be like them.

So there's no retirement! We may retire from paid employment, but we will always want to be good stewards of our gifts and continue to bless people. We want to be engaged because we are called to do meaningful work. No matter our age, let us be involved in meaningful labour. What are our gifts? What are our passions? Let us find ways to express them. The context for our work may change as we move down the path of life, but there is no basis for the idea of retirement in Scripture.

Our Second Call: To Live in Communion with God

I see our second calling in Genesis 2:2 which says: "By the seventh day God had finished the work he had been doing; so on the seventh day he rested from all his work." Those of you who were at Mount Carmel's Church Camp in 2013 heard me making this point then.

I am somebody who cannot wait to get started whenever I am given an important assignment. I will always remember this incident. When I was a child, my family lived in Penang. The last thing my dad would do every night was to go around the house and make sure all the doors and windows were locked, to make sure the house was secure while we slept. A day came when my dad came to me and said, "My boy, I think you're old enough now, I can trust you with the job of locking the windows and doors at night."

This was a big deal indeed! Dad trusted me to lock all the windows and doors at night. He told me this in the daytime. I couldn't wait for night to come, because I could then go lock all the windows and doors! I really wanted to get going because it was such a big honour to lock all the windows and doors. When we are given an important job, we can't wait to get started.

On the sixth day of creation, Adam and Eve were created and were given a most important job. God tells them, "I want you to take care of the rest of my creation on my behalf." If I were Adam and Eve, I would definitely be very excited and want to get started. I can just imagine that on the seventh day, they woke up and asked God, "Where do we start! Which part of creation should we work on first? Give me my to-do list."

But as you know, there is no working on the seventh day! No work. So God tells them to relax, pull up a chair and probably asks them if they would like some waffles and coffee. The seventh day is a day to cease from work, to enjoy God's blessings, and to commune with God. God seems to be telling Adam and Eve, "Yes, I have created you for the most important work of all, but you are even more important to me than your work." Men, especially, sometimes find it hard to understand this because we are so defined by our work. While our work is important, we need to keep in mind that God loves us for who we are.

> "There is this deep need in all of us for intimacy with God."

If our first calling is to co-labour, our second calling then is for communion. Therefore, we need to carve out space in our lives to spend time with God. This is where we as men need to be extra careful. Relationships are not our strong point. Our weakness in connecting with others not only sabotages our relationship with one another, but it also often sabotages our relationship with God.

Indeed, even our time with God can be very functional — to prepare for next Sunday's lesson, etc., and not really to be quiet and remember who God is and to enjoy communion with our Abba Father. If we are made for communion, we simply have to carve out space for God. Call it "Quiet Time", call it whatever you want, but just make sure we have time to be quiet and hear God's voice say, "This is my Son, whom I love; with him I am well pleased" (see Matthew 3:17).

We may be most successful at whatever we do, but there will always be a dimension of life that is missing if we do not carve out space for God. This is because, just as there is a part of us that is meant to co-labour with God, there is also a part of us that is meant for communion with our Abba Father.

Do not forget, "Abba" is a very powerful word. It is not a childish word. It is a term of affection that even an adult may use to call his or her father. Think of the affectionate terms you use to address your parents. I called my father "Papa". (He has gone to be with the Lord. I still miss him.) There is this deep need in all of us for intimacy with God. I will say it again: as men, we have to be even more intentional and deliberate to carve out space and time for God. Our first calling is to co-labour with God and our second calling is to commune with Him.

Our Third Call: To Live in Community

Our third calling is found in Genesis 2:18. Here, for the first time, you encounter a negative in the Scripture, "It is not good for the man to be alone". We usually hear this passage preached on at weddings, perhaps even at your own. Certainly, having a good marriage is one way that this need for connecting is met, but obviously it's not the only way. Jesus was single and fully human. Paul was single as far as we know.

Single or married, we all need to have meaningful relationships with significant others. We must keep in mind that at this point in history, i.e. in Genesis 2, sin was not yet in the picture. Adam had perfect communion with God. Sin had not yet separated him from God. Yet it was not enough. We need communion with God, but we also need community with other human beings.

So this is what it means to be human: we are called to co-labour for God's purposes, we are called for communion with God and we are called for community with people. Marriage is one way this need is met, but as I found out, the Lord may take your spouse home to Him. (My first wife died of cancer.) So married or single, we need key relationships in our lives.

I always quote this study, so bear with me. In 1985, a survey was done in America, where participants were asked how many close friends they had. The answer was three. Most Americans in 1985 had three close friends. As a comparison, the same survey was conducted in 2004.[1] This time, a quarter of the respondents said none. One quarter of these Americans had no close friends at all! Perhaps you are thinking that this is America, not Singapore, but I suspect the proportions would be similar in any advanced urban society. When I teach about spiritual friendship, most people say, "That's all well and good, but I've no time." I hear this all the time, so I'm not sure Singapore is that far behind.

The study also found in that time frame that the proportion of people with depression and bipolar disorder had jumped to one in ten. The number of people indulging in binge eating and drinking also saw a rise. When your heart is empty and you are lonely, you turn to comfort food — things like chocolate and ice cream. When you are lonely, eating what you like gives you a temporary emotional boost. Similarly, why do people binge drink? When you are lonely, it is "Bottoms up!", and the warm liquid trickles down your throat and gives you a temporary boost. Then you get a headache afterwards (don't ask me how I know). Not being connected with others has direct negative consequences.

Indeed, many empirical studies have shown that the one key factor dictating whether or not one recovers strongly from serious illnesses or surgery is the strength of your relationships with others. That is the number one factor, even more important than exercise or diet. All these expensive studies only confirm what Genesis 2:18 tells us already! It is not good for man to be alone. I believe that if you wait long enough, empirical science will only confirm what the Bible tells us.

But this is a challenge for us guys. We often struggle to connect with others. Our conversations tend to be superficial, and focus more on work and sports. Often our conversations are competitive. "I made this much this month", "Oh, I made even more!" People you meet at the club can't wait to tell you about their fancy new car or some other new glamorous purchase. So we tend to speak competitively rather than open our hearts and our wounds to each other. The truth, however, is that we all need safe places where we can be ourselves and don't have to put up a front. I pray that your fellowship will lead to such safe relational places!

We all need two or three very close friends. Even Jesus had three close friends. He ministered to the masses, He had a social group called the 70 and He had the 12, but sometimes we forget the three! Peter, James and John were obviously His very close friends. He allowed them to see the transfiguration. He brought them to the Garden of Gethsemane. He was totally transparent with them, telling them, "My soul is overwhelmed with sorrow to the point of death" (Matthew 26:38).

Jesus too needed friends. Of course the friends fell asleep, but that's a different matter — even friends let us down. The point is Jesus, being fully human, also needed friends. Do we have one or two really close buddies we meet up with on a regular basis to share our lives?

One of the things I advocate is the 3-2-1 model: three friends meeting for two hours once a month. If you have no time, arrange to meet at mealtimes! I practise this. I have two buddies with whom I meet once a month over a meal. We have covenanted to do this. When we meet we share how we are doing in our family, marriage, kids, vocational life, the temptations we face, key decisions we have to make and other struggles.

We voluntarily share with each other. It is never forced. We have given each other the permission to speak into each other's life. Most of the time we know what to do because we know the Bible. But we need accountability to encourage us to do what we know we should. The 3-2-1 groups provide the relational accountability we need as we follow Christ.

Conclusion

So, what does it mean to be human? To sum up, we have three callings. First, we are called to co-labour with God, to do meaningful work. Second, we are called to live a life of communion with God. Finally, we are called to community. Co-labour, communion and community. These are the real three 'C's we cannot do without. May the Lord help us grow in all three areas at whatever stage of life we find ourselves.

■ ■ ■

Questions for Reflection

1

Do you agree that our daily work in the world is as important as any church-related work? How do you think your daily work is an expression of God's purposes?

2

Every relationship needs nurturing. How do you nurture your relationship with God? How could you do it better?

3

We need friends if we are to flourish. Do you have any close friends in your life? How about Christian friends? Are you following Jesus in the company of friends who encourage you in your discipleship?

4

To be human we need to attend to our three 'C's. We are called to co-labour with God, commune with God and have community with close friends. How are you doing in these three areas? Which one is the healthiest? Which needs work?

Rev Dr Tan Soo Inn is co-founder and director of Graceworks, a training and publishing ministry committed to promoting spiritual friendships in church and society. He has a BDS from the University of Singapore, a ThM in New Testament from Regent College and a DMin from Fuller Seminary. Soo Inn's primary passions include connecting the Word of God to the struggles of daily life and the promotion of the discipline of spiritual friendship. He has supported Arsenal Football Club since 1971 and his favourite movie is Star Wars 4.

MALE SPIRITUALITY: IMPLICATIONS FOR OUR CHURCH'S MEN'S MINISTRY

Robert Solomon

I find it very encouraging to see men's groups forming up in our churches. I myself have been involved in a men's group for 20 years now. It is very heartening to see God calling His men to come together in fellowship groups to encourage each other to rediscover the core of Christian discipleship that we are called to live out.

I would like to speak on the topic of male spirituality. We are a group of men here. So, my focus will be on how we can live as male disciples of Jesus Christ. In general, we live our lives just like our sisters. But there are some differences I would like us to understand. It is my hope that this will help us in two ways: one, that we will walk closer to God and two, that our ministries targeted at men can be more effective in speaking to their hearts.

Common Universal Aspects

What does it mean to be a male disciple of the Lord Jesus Christ? First off, I would like to state that there are many things common to us all regardless of gender, educational level or nationality. We can say that all of us have sinned and fallen short of the glory of God, as Scriptures tell us (Romans 3:23). So sin is not a problem peculiar only to certain groups of people. Sin is a really huge problem! It is a universal problem. In addition, all of us have physical needs, for example, food and rest, and the need to be loved. These are common needs in us all. And the call to Christian discipleship is the same: Jesus calls us to deny ourselves, take up our cross and follow Him. This is equally relevant to both men and women.

Some Differences Between Men and Women

What I propose to do first is to highlight some differences between men and women. One of the difficulties I have with Christian literature when it comes to gender is that our discussions often focus on relationships, roles and authority. Yes, they are important and we need to work those things out, looking to Scripture to answer questions about how a husband should relate to his wife and so on. But it seems to me we tend to focus too much on power and authority. We neglect the spirituality part of it. How has God made us differently, and what impact does this have on how brothers and sisters function in the church?

Biological differences

Let me begin by saying that there are biological differences. This is obvious — men are physically stronger. I remember back in medical school I once heard that women were marathon runners and men were sprinters. This is our old philosophy — we men run fast and die early! Women conserve their strength and outlive us by a few years. Everywhere in the world, the lifespan of women is longer than the lifespan of men. There are also slight differences in our brains. Take for instance the corpus callosum, which joins the left and right brain. This wiring is more pronounced in women than in men. Men have quite sparse wiring, and that is why we do not make connections quite as well as our sisters. They tend to be more holistic in their outlook.

Let me be quite frank. When it comes to sexual relationships with our wives, men compartmentalize and think, "The time has come, time to perform." For the sisters, the experience is linked with many other things: "He didn't wash the dishes, so I don't feel like it." And we men wonder, what has washing dishes got to do with this? Women are wired up differently. For us men, we focus on one thing at a time. We watch football and then say a prayer and have Quiet Time; it is compartmentalized. The other thing to mention when talking about wiring has to do with how our sexuality is connected. In men, the sexual responses are connected with the visual centres of our brain. This wiring is more pronounced, and that is why men are more visually oriented when it comes to sex, and why

Playboy is or was very popular. You do not have quite such an equivalent for women, because women operate differently. So, a lot of pornography is meant for men, because it appeals to our circuitry.

This has many implications for male spirituality, which we ought to look at. How do we overcome these temptations as Christians? In the Bible, lust is a big problem. You have several examples of even the greatest leaders who fell or could have fallen. David is a good example — it all started from one look (2 Samuel 11). Joseph is another leader, and he shows how to handle this sort of temptation (Genesis 39:6–12). Yes, we are wired in a certain way, but Jesus tells us that if you look lustfully at a woman, you have already committed adultery. Jesus traces the root of the problem, not just its effects. He tells us that unless we address the root of the problem, we are not going to have victory in our Christian lives. These are things we need to understand.

Psychological differences

Let us move now to some psychological differences. These differences have biological roots. Take for instance the observation that men are less verbal. We do not talk so much. Is that common in your family? If you count the number of words spoken by your wives and the number of words spoken by yourself, do the husbands lose out? In the New Testament, we meet a few characters who are called the strong, silent types. One example is Joseph, the husband of Mary. A lot is mentioned about him in the birth narratives of the gospels. But can you find any verse where he speaks a single word? The answer is "no". Very strange, is it not? Mary speaks, sings and prays, but Joseph? No, he does not say a single word. He acts to take his family to Egypt, but he does not speak.

Another silent New Testament character is Lazarus. Lazarus is mentioned in the Gospel of John, chapters 11 and 12. Luke 10:38–42 also mentions Jesus' visit to the home of Lazarus and his two sisters. If I compare the three of them, the most talkative among them was Martha. In John 11 where Lazarus dies (and of course he does not speak after that), when the Lord visits their home, Mary speaks a few measured words. So we have Martha who speaks very much, Mary who speaks a little and Lazarus who says not a word. In fact, some Bible scholars think that is evidence that Lazarus had a problem or a speech impediment of some sort. A few commentators note that it is very strange that where the three members of this family are described, one member does not speak even a single word.

Now, that may be one point of difference. Going back to the brain, the speech centre of men is less developed. (I would like to point out that there are no absolutes here, just that there are some differences.) Men usually do not fare as well at languages. Women tend to do better here. That is why we say "mother tongue", not "father tongue". "Fatherland" maybe, but not "father tongue". Because our mothers speak to us, not our fathers! Our fathers are strong and silent. This suggests to us that culturally we have understood this difference in genders. And because our speech centres are less developed, we sometimes have problems communicating. The classic example of a wife telling her husband, "You never say 'I love you.'" And the husband replies, "Why should I? Every day I show you I love you! I work and do this and that. What is there to say?" For the woman it is a little different. She likes to hear these words from her husband. She longs to hear these things. We men sometimes miss this. We have some difficulty communicating.

They also say that women have a better vocabulary of emotions than men. Women can articulate their anger or bitterness. Ask men to speak and they do not know what words to use. The old BOH tea advertisement is apt here. It features a person saying, "When I taste BOH tea, I feel ... Ummph!" That is men. We have to think of the implications. How do we get men to come together not only when there are issues to discuss? When men gather, it is because there are issues to sort out. When women gather there are tissues! They are able to share more deeply. They have the vocabulary to communicate their feelings more effectively. Their relationships are more important. So men have some deficits in that regard. We have to think about how we can resolve some of these deficits.

However, men are also blessed. God is quite fair in these things. While men have language limitations, we are good when it comes to space orientation. Which of the genders tend to be better map readers? Men or women? The typical scenario illustrates this point. A husband and wife are on a holiday. The man is driving. He asks his wife to take the map and guide him in turning right or left. A lot of women have problems with this! They end up going round and round, and the husband will be asking with great aggravation, "Do I turn right or left?" while his wife can only reply, "I don't know!" This again has biological reasons, because the centres dealing with space orientation are better developed in men's brains. I suppose for those reasons, men are also more fascinated with toys. This is a lifelong obsession. Manufacturers know this, so they keep bringing out new toys. Women are not as excited — I may be wrong, but I think women are not as excited by the latest technological toys or tools as men are. This may have to do with the way we are wired.

Differences in moral development

What about moral differences? Let me try to be brief here, though it is more complex. Many years ago, there was a Harvard psychologist called Lawrence Kohlberg. Kohlberg was an expert in moral development. He studied extensively how people think morally. He came up with six stages of moral thinking or moral development. I will not delve into that, but what happened was that one of his colleagues called Carol Gilligan who was involved in the same field challenged his findings. She asserted that his model described how white males functioned and was not universal. So what she did was to use the same instruments Kohlberg used to test moral thinking, but this time with women subjects. She then wrote a book of her findings, which became very popular.

What she tried to show was that whenever it came to a moral issue, men prefer to sit down and discuss it while women prefer to do something about it. Men are more justice-oriented — is it right or wrong? — while women veer towards compassion. They care less about whether it is right or wrong. The main issue for them is — what are we going to do about this? How do we help these people? We can think of this as the difference between practical and theoretical theodicy. Men like to discuss and talk. They may not come to any conclusion, but they enjoy just sitting and discussing things over coffee. Philosophers try to explain it this way. Women have been functioning as a group that has been marginalized, relatively speaking. They do not have the kind of privilege that men enjoy. So they are more aware of suffering, of deprivation. They connect with those who suffer better than men do, or at least this is one way of looking at the results.

This again poses very interesting challenges for us when we consider how we function morally. And I think here we greatly need women to lead us. The Bible tells us that the Lord created us male and female (Genesis 1:27), and the Lord is both holy and compassionate — holy and merciful, righteous and merciful (Psalm 116:5; Romans 11:22). So I find that the combined results of Kohlberg's and Gilligan's studies are very apt, for men and women come together to portray the character of God. On our own, we are a bit lopsided but together, we express the holiness of God better.

That is why it is good for us to connect with our wives, to observe how they feel and think, and also to learn or share from our perspective, so that as a couple, we reflect more deeply the very character and holiness of God. This is why a healthy marriage relationship is a great blessing. It helps you to connect and function better, to be more holistic in your approach to life. On the way here I heard something on the radio that went a little like this: "It is not so important to solve the problem, but to love the person." I am paraphrasing, but the point stands. That quote was probably by a woman. A man would say it is very important to solve the problem! And to solve it quickly, not let it simmer. Nip it in the bud! That is very male. We need reminders to love the people too as a response to some of the challenges we face.

Let me just make a few more comments about psychology and morality. Are you familiar with the MBTI? — the Myers-Briggs Personality Indicator and its four polarities. One of them has to do with Thinking/Feeling, or how we make decisions. There are some who make decisions based on logical thoughts, and others who tend to be more emotional. They make decisions with their feelings as a significant factor. Which sex tends to be more "feeling"? Well, 60% of men score 'T' and 60% of women score 'F'. It is not such a drastic polarity, but it does show some differences there.

A typical example, which may be exaggerated, comes when we go shopping. Your wife looks at a dress and she immediately says she wants it. How do you react? Most of us would keep silent, and then try to get closer and look at the price. If it is manageable, you tell her, "It's nice!" Otherwise, you just get a shock. Or you can say, "This same dress at the other place is cheaper. Why don't we go there? Similar material, better price." And of course your wife gets very upset. She says, "You don't love me." You say, "What does this have to do with love?" It makes no sense to us!

> "It is not so important to solve the problem, but to love the person."

So we find that we men really cannot see eye to eye with our wives in this regard. For us, it is not a matter of just the dress, it is about what is better value for money and makes more economic sense. For the wife, your refusal is simply evidence to her that "this man is terrible"! We come off as unromantic, unsentimental. This is not to say that all women are 'F's or all men are 'T's. There is always a mix. I just mention this to show some differences.

Spiritual differences

Are there spiritual differences? I think there are. In church meetings, which gender tends to predominate? In our churches, we tend to have more women than men. What about prayer meetings? Who likes to come? It is usually the women. Who in the family actually passes on the spiritual traditions? Who reads the Bible stories? Who prays for the children? It is the mothers; the men are watching football! I exaggerate, and I know many fathers who are exceptional in spiritual leadership, but the point is that there seems to be a greater spiritual depth or earnestness in women than in men.

I do not know if you have ever thought about what the population profile of heaven will be like. Have you ever thought of that? Will there be more women than men in heaven? If you have not thought about it, start thinking about it! Heaven may very well have more women than men. We do not know, but it should make us more evangelistic, reaching out to our male contacts and friends! Perhaps part of the problem lies with how men perceive the church, which does not attract them as much as it attracts women.

The other thing is that women are more spiritually sensitive, which can be a disadvantage — it can lead them to witchcraft and idolatry. In the Bible, we read about Jezebel (1 Kings 16; 19ff) and the book of Revelation names her again (Revelation 2:20). It appears that openness to spiritual realities can strengthen one's spirituality, but it can also lead to all kinds of disasters. This is something to think about. I am not going to delve too deep here.

Men, however, tend to need greater effort to be sensitive to spiritual things. Also, men live in a "fatherless generation" (Henri Nouwen) or a generation with a "father-wound" (Richard Rohr). We have few models on how to be a godly male.

Some Suggestions

Let me make some suggestions in the remaining time as to what we can do about our own spirituality and to make our ministry to men more effective.

Meeting the needs of men

First of all, we need to be better in our ministry to men. Some models of discipleship do not meet the needs of men. We have to explore and think about this more deeply. Some programmes we have in church actually repel rather than attract men.

Let me read something you might find controversial but I find important all the same. In his book *Money, Sex and Spiritual Power*, Keith Drury says,

> *The feminization of religion probably started in Sunday School for most of us. When you and I were in Sunday School, most men in the church refused to work with children as many still do. They figured children's work was women's work. So for most of us, men were absent during our earliest and deepest bonding with Bible stories.*[1]

The earliest impressions we would have if we grew up in church is the feminine input in our lives about God and the Bible and religion. We had few male models in our lives. So our understanding of God, the church, the Bible and Christian discipleship becomes skewed and a little distorted. It may not resonate with how we are made or how we function. This is something we need to consider. Perhaps Sunday School teaching needs to be open to the men too. There is a great need for male models of Christian discipleship. We should be teaching! Teaching is something men need to be involved because it involves mentoring — it involves raising a new generation in the faith. Men should rise up to meet these challenges!

Another point to consider is that there may be too much of spirituality going in the direction of interiority. From the perspective of men, there is a lack of action. Ask men to sit down for a few days and just talk about their relationships, and many men will run away. They find it very scary. For women it is fun — they sit together, cry together and connect relationally. For men, this is tough. They feel restless; they feel the need to do things together. This too requires thinking.

The songs that we sing in church may be too sentimental for men. Men like to sing, "Onward, Christian soldiers, marching as to war!" It stirs something within them. Action is called for. Enough of reflection, we need to get things done. Men get connected by tasks; women get connected through relational communication.

At the same time, we need to make sure not to create a spirituality based merely on our strengths. We also have to minister to our weaknesses, of which I have already mentioned a few. The Christian faith is about relationships, and if we have a weakness in that area we need to correct it. We need to find ways to get men to talk about their relationships. One of the things about men's meetings is that it is very difficult to make them talk about themselves. It is easy for men to talk about issues, but not to make them talk about their feelings, aspirations and struggles at a deeper level. This is something we need to look at if we want to minister to men.

Redeeming our maleness

We also need to redeem our maleness. There are certain things the Bible says about masculinity which are good. But there are also things that the Bible reveals about men that are weaknesses and need to be addressed. A reflection on the differences between the male disciples of Jesus and His female disciples can reveal some of these differences. The male disciples were constantly jockeying for position and privilege (Luke 9:46–48; Mark 10:35–37), something that we do not find among the women disciples.

There were also other major gender differences among the disciples. Take for instance the fact that men like tools and techniques better than women do. We are obsessed with tools — in fact, there is a saying that "the man who dies with the most tools is the winner". A lot of us operate on that basis. Every morning we get up and get into our cars to aggressively acquire more tools. The man who dies with the most tools is the winner! That's how many men function — or rather, dysfunction.

The other thing is technique, which men are fascinated with. "Let's sit down, let's sort it out and let's get it done." Techniques! Tools and techniques are not as useful when we suffer adversity. When things break down and we reach the end of our ropes, our tools and techniques do not help us enough.

Sheila Cassidy, a British doctor, served in Chile many years ago when it was ruled by a repressive regime. She was arrested on false charges and severely tortured but survived. Eventually, she ended up as the medical director of a hospice in Plymouth, England. She wrote a book called *Sharing the Darkness*.[2] In that book, she describes her experience as a medical director of a hospice. In a hospice, there are no superstar doctors, unlike famous surgeons who earn lots of money in hospitals. In a hospice, you cannot do very much except make people comfortable and minister to them in a humane way so that they die with dignity.

In her book, Sheila Cassidy has a series of cartoon drawings. The first one features a patient dying in the hospice bed. There is a priest with his elements. The doctor has his coat and stethoscope. In the second picture, some of the tools are missing. The stethoscope is gone, and so is the priest's stole. In the final picture, both the doctor and the priest no longer have anything — neither clothes nor tools, but they stand with the person. What she is trying to say is that when you approach a dying person with tools and techniques, it is not going to help very much. What is needed is that you give yourself. You are present with the dying person. Get away from the tools and techniques because they are not going to help.

This was demonstrated at the time when Jesus was arrested. When the Lord Jesus was arrested, what was the reaction of the disciples? We read that Peter took out his sword (John 18:10–11). That is a tool! That is the male response. Any problem, get a tool out! The next thing is technique. One swish and the ear of the servant of the High Priest is off. But the Lord rejected such actions. He said, "Enough of this." He healed the man's ear (Luke 22:51). The Lord was telling Peter to put his tools and techniques away because that was not the right answer to the crisis at hand. And when that happened, His disciples ran away (Mark 14:50). They were not comfortable. How could they face this kind of situation without tools and techniques? They ran away.

It is like at funerals. Back in the old days, funerals were a very communal event. Who would be nearest the dead body? The women! In most cultures, it is the women who get closest to the body. There are anthropological explanations for this, but it is usually the women who sit around and cry and comfort one another. What do the men do? Whatever it is we usually do — play cards or what not. Ask the men to get more drinks and they will gladly go, because men like to be useful. In situations such as a funeral or wake, we just do not know how to handle it. We cannot sit quietly and wait; we must act. So, ask us to do this or get that done and we men will be very happy to be useful.

I think it is precisely in such situations that we need to learn from women. At the cross of Jesus, who were gathered there? The male disciples or the female disciples? It was the women, and it is worth pointing out that women are used to facing crisis situations where they are helpless. At the foot of the cross they were indeed helpless. They had no tools or techniques, but they gave their presence (Luke 23:27; Mark 15:40–41). The women disciples were there at the foot of the cross. All the men, except John, were absent. In a sense Jesus had no one but John to offer as a new son to Mary (John 19:25–27).

On Easter morning, again note the devotion of the women to Jesus (Mark 16:1). I think this is a powerful lesson on differences, and why we need to let the Lord's grace redeem our fallenness. We cannot approach Christian discipleship with tools and techniques; we need to follow Christ intimately. Some men may have a problem with that. So think of this as a potential corrective for ministry among men.

Dealing effectively with male sins

What about men's sins? Are you familiar with the seven deadly sins? The chief one is pride. There are seven sins to correspond with the seven days of the week. Originally, it was eight but the church fathers decided seven was better. They meant it as a devotional aid for us to reflect on one of the sins each day. Not to do it, but to abandon it! And Sunday's sin was pride. We solve the sin of pride by starting the week in the presence of God. We begin the week by giving the first moments of the week to God in worship. It is a declaration that God is first in our lives and unless God works, all our work is wasted. That deals with the sin of pride. Monday's sin is envy, and so on. Saturday's sin is lust; Friday's sin is gluttony, and that is why the church historically had fasts on Friday.

Which of these — pride, envy, anger, sloth, greed, lust and gluttony — scored the highest for women in a survey?[3] And which came first for men? The number one sin for women was pride, and without any doubt, lust was the number one problem for men. It should not be surprising because that seems to be a basic problem. Remember that the Lord said, "If you look at a woman lustfully, you have already committed adultery" (see Matthew 5:28). Lust seems like a default position for men. Our eyes need to be forced to make a commitment, just as Job made a covenant with his eyes not to look lustfully at a young woman (Job 31:1).

This seems to be a major area for obedience in Christian discipleship. It is made all the more difficult today because of the Internet. In the old days, if you wanted to look at pornography, you had to steal some magazines or get them from your schoolmates and sneak it home. Today it is so simple. Even if you are a taxi driver, you have a smartphone or tablet, and who knows what can happen?

About two years ago, an American pastor confessed in writing how he became addicted to pornography. He said that his secretary worked half a day. For the first half of the day, he would go about his normal work. But when the secretary left for lunch and took the rest of the day off, he would turn on his computer and he would be surfing pornography sites the whole afternoon. He eventually became addicted and nobody knew it. Even on Sundays right before the sermon, he would have some time alone in his office and he would find himself surfing pornography sites. He did this even before worship services! When he did that, he realized he was really in deep trouble and decided not to go on in this manner. He ended up confessing to someone and sought help. Since then, he has written about his struggle.

I suspect that this is an increasingly common problem. This will be one of the hardest problems for men in their attempts to follow Jesus — the whole area of purity and clean thoughts. If you think that this gets better as you get older, go and talk to older men. I remember meeting a Youth for Christ worker from India many years ago. He was in his 60s at the time. We were at a meeting, and the congregation asked him about this particular problem. What he said was quite striking at that moment. He said, "The problem doesn't lessen as you age. In fact, the problem gets worse." I think this is an area that we also need to think about.

Fulfilling male roles

We have many roles, especially those in our families, to which we men have traditionally not given enough attention. The roles of husband, father, brother, son and so on need to be examined in the light of biblical teachings and pastoral insights, and strengthened through education, training and accountability relationships. Our families and the church will be so much stronger if we learned to be better and more godly husbands, fathers, sons and brothers. We will be better models of male discipleship to the next generation.

May God help us to take this calling seriously and seek to follow Christ wholeheartedly with the kind of robust discipleship that we see in some of the men in the Bible such as Moses, Joshua, Caleb, Elijah and Daniel. We have an advantage in that our Lord was a man — how much easier it would be for us to emulate Him in our daily lives! Let us do so and bring glory to Him.

■ ■ ■

Questions for Reflection

1

What are the emotional, social, intellectual, physical and spiritual needs of men that may be different (in measure or manner) from women? How can the church improve its ministry to men in terms of these needs?

2

What male Christian role models of godliness can you identify — in the Bible, in church history and in your current relationships? How do they inspire you and how can you emulate them? How can men be made to examine these role models?

3

In which areas of their spiritual lives do men have particularly great difficulties? Think of the deadly sins and the Christian virtues and disciplines. How can men help each other in these areas?

4

How can men improve their relationships — with God, spouse, family and friends?

5

What should a men's group focus on? How do you think a men's group can help men be better disciples of Christ?

For Further Reading

Mark Boyer, *Biblical Reflections on Male Spirituality* (Collegeville, MN: Liturgical Press, 1996).

John Carmody, *Toward a Male Spirituality* (Searcy, AR: Twenty-Third Publications, 1989).

Jim Fowler and Sam Keen, *Life Maps: Conversations on the Journey of Faith* (Waco, TX: Word Books, 1978).

James Nelson, *The Intimate Connection: Male Sexuality, Masculine Spirituality* (Philadelphia, PA: The Westminster Press, 1988).

Martin Pable (OFM Cap.), *A Man and His God* (Notre Dame, IN: Ave Maria Press, 1988).

John Ream, *Velvet & Steel: A Practical Guide for Christian Fathers and Grandfathers* (San Jose, CA: Resource Publications, 1997).

Bishop Emeritus Robert Solomon was Bishop of the Methodist Church in Singapore from 2000 to 2012. Previously a medical doctor and church pastor, he was Principal of Trinity Theological College and served for a time as President of the National Council of Churches of Singapore. He has degrees in medicine, theology, intercultural studies and a PhD in pastoral theology from the University of Edinburgh. A prolific writer, he has authored more than 20 books, including The Race, The Conscience, The Enduring Word, The Sermon of Jesus *and* Apprenticed to Jesus. *He has an active speaking ministry in Singapore and overseas. His email address is <rsolomon@methodist.org.sg>.*

YOUR PAST WILL ALWAYS HAUNT YOU, UNLESS YOU RECOVER!

John Ng

"Fear can retreat protectively into the darkness."
— Brian Muldoon

"I will never forget what the company did to me! The management is a bunch of crap!" screamed Dave, a former senior staff of a leading organization.[1]

He blurted out all his grievances to me for one long hour, after getting acquainted with one of my staff. Obviously he had been deeply hurt by some things the company had done.

When I asked him, "How long have you left the company?" his answer was, "Five years!" I was amazed that after such a long time, he still harboured such deep pain and grievances. I was told later that he could never hold a job for more than six months and his family life was breaking up as well.

Another woman, Lisa, had shared how her older brother Victor had abused her physically and emotionally when she was ten. When she was 35, at the peak of her career, I met up with her. After talking about her wonderful career journey, I affirmed her achievements.

After thanking me, she recalled her relationship with her brother and added, "I can never trust people again, especially men. I don't want to depend on others for my success. It's all my own hard work that I got to where I am." She confessed she was a taskmaster at work and drove her people that way as well. She also could not hold her marriage together. (If you have similar stories, please feel free to write and share your experience with me. I will be happy to respond to you.)

These stories are not uncommon. I have encountered many such individuals with past bad experiences. We all have bad experiences. When I was 12, I was attacked and bitten by an Alsatian. I was jogging around my neighbourhood when a dog came charging at me barking furiously, and bit me! It was a most frightening and painful experience, one that I have not forgotten till today. For many years after that, whenever I saw a dog, I would recall this experience vividly. I have an "instant replay button" to recall the visual images of that experience in my brain:

- The sight and smell of the huge brown-black Alsatian attacking me;
- The futile attempt to ward it off;
- The excruciating pain and the blood flowing out of my leg;
- The hospital visit where I was given an antibiotic injection.

For a long time, I hated dogs and dog lovers.

All of us have unpleasant experiences that continue to haunt us:

- Favouritism and unfair treatment by your parents;
- Emotional abuse by your siblings;
- Betrayal by trusted business partners;
- Constant insults and taunting by your co-workers;
- Failed business ventures;
- Abrupt removal by the board for your leadership failures.

Dr Daniel Siegel, one of the world's leading clinical psychiatrists at UCLA School of Medicine and Executive Director of Mindsight, has done much research and clinical work in this area of memory and the healing of memory. His exploration of the triad of the mind, brain and relationships, termed "Interpersonal Neurobiology", is unsurpassed. I consider him to be a thought leader in this field.

According to Siegel, the way to promote well-being and healthy interpersonal relationships is to have an integration of the mind, brain and relationships. He writes in *Mindsight: The New Science of Personal Transformation,* "Well-being emerges when we create connections in our lives — when we learn to use mindsight to help the brain achieve and maintain *integration*, a process by which separate elements are linked together into a working whole".[2]

This can be done in a practical manner, as "integration is at the heart of how we connect to one another in healthy ways, honoring one another's differences while keeping our lines of communication wide open".[3] The way to achieve this is through "mindsight", defined as a kind of focused attention that allows us to see the internal workings of your minds. It helps us to be aware of our mental processes without being swept away by them. It enables us to get ourselves off the autopilot of ingrained behaviors and habitual responses, and moves us beyond the reaction emotional loops we all have a tendency to get trapped in.[4]

In other words, mindsight helps us to step back to reflect on our thought processes. This enables us to respond more rationally and reflectively instead of merely reacting on the basis of our predisposed tendencies. I truly believe that understanding how our minds, brains and relationships interact will help us navigate many intractable conflicts.

Brain: Processing the Flow of Energy and Information

The brain is like the computer processing unit. For example, when I mention the word "dog", what comes to your mind?

- A pet?
- A puppy?
- Loyal?
- Cute?

It conjures up different images and words based on your past experiences. For me, it represents the ferocious Alsatian that bit me. And it has made me hate dogs and dog lovers!

The key fact is that the activation of neural pathways directly influences the way connections are made within the brain: "experience early in life may be especially crucial in organizing the way the basic structures of the brain develop", says Siegel.[5]

Allow me to share an example. Mui, an administrative executive and vivacious women in her thirties, reacted explosively when her supervisor, Peggy, remarked during a meeting, "You should learn from Lynn, she is so thorough in her reports."

Mui screamed at Peggy, "Don't you ever talk to me like that!" and stormed out of the room. Everyone was shocked. Through therapy, Mui discovered that her over-reaction was due to the unhealed memory of always being discriminated against and unjustly compared to her brother by her parents. This had become the mental model from which she operated. So when Peggy employed the comparative mode on her, albeit innocently, Mui's memory activated the painful encounters of her past with her parents.

In Asia, most would not have reacted as frightfully as Mui but instead would have stored Peggy's undiplomatic comments. The brain can become the breeding ground for bitterness, rage and revenge. In your brain, with repeated similar episodes and unresolved memories, your mental framework is formed. This contributes to the formation of "hot buttons" in your life. These connections are experienced in the brain, heart and gut, which are all part of the nervous system.

Hot button words or phrases include:

- "You stupid, idiot!"
- "Whatever!"
- "You are always late!"
- "You don't care about the family!"
- "You will never make it!"

Hot button episodes include:

- Walking out after a quarrel;
- Person with tattoos and earrings;
- Stonewalling expressions;
- Having an unkempt office desk;
- Writing a long, 20-page report;
- Slamming the door.

Neurons are fired in your brains every time you experience something in life. These fired neurons then create a pattern and memory.

Mind: Regulating the Flow of Energy and Information

The mind is where you regulate energy and information with the help of neurons in your brain. This flow of energy creates what you know as mental processes. The mind controls the flow of information and energy from your sensory system, which can respond to stimuli of sound, sight, touch and smell. Your mind creates representations of the various types of information it receives about the outer and inner worlds. For example, you decide what information you should accept and reject. As you are perusing this article, you can decide to continue or stop the reading. You regulate the flow of information. The mind can make the brain re-fire and rewire. Remember that what you fire, you wire.

Back to my dog-biting experience. Since that experience, whenever I saw a dog or hear a dog's yelp, I would be overcome with fear. I shun dogs. However, over the years, with fresh flows of energy and information, I began to realize that not all dogs are harmful. Some are really quite cute and loveable. I saw my friend playing with his Chihuahua, how he would cuddle the dog and how the cute, impish dog would frolic with him. My children were a nice key influence that chiselled away my fear of dogs. They loved dogs and had no fear because unlike me they did not have any bad past experiences. These different and healthy experiences of dogs slowly chipped away my bad memory of dogs.

Relationships: Sharing Energy and Information Between Two or More Parties

Dr Siegel's third piece in the healing of memory is relationships. Interpersonal relationships may facilitate or inhibit this integration. Some people are haunted by past bad experiences and relationships with their parents. The relationship between parents and children plays a critical role in shaping of memories. Their experiences of this significant relationship creates representations and directly influences how realities are mentally constructed. If you have parents who respond positively to you in your early childhood, you will have the basis for healthy interpersonal experiences. You will have good regard for authority and the word "parents" will come to symbolize love, kindness, care, etc.

Conversely, if your parents physically or emotionally abused you when you were young, you would form a very different image of people in authority. The word "parents" would represent injury, abuse or authoritarianism in your minds.

This shaping process occurs throughout life and is most decisive during one's early childhood.

Relationships can shape your minds and wire your brains. Relationship experiences have a dominant influence on the brain because the circuits responsible for social perceptions are the same as, or linked tightly to, the functions that create meaning, regulation of bodily states, modulation of emotion, organization of memory and capacity for interpersonal communication.

Siegel underscores the impelling significance of relationships: "Interpersonal experience thus plays a special organizing role in determining the development of brain structure early in life and the ongoing emergence of brain function throughout the lifespan."[6]

How you interact and communicate with each other makes a difference to your minds and brains. Just as the wiring in your brain affects your relationships, your relationships also affect the wiring. Using my dog analogy again: Because of the "dog fearing" wiring that was etched in my memory, I was not particularly fond of people who loved dogs. I could not understand why people kept dogs as pets. I thought they were weird, and I could not develop deep relationships with dog lovers. However, my children, who did not have my agonizing experience, were fond of dogs. Whenever they saw dogs, they would fearlessly stroke and cuddle them. They influenced my reaction to dogs and aversion to dog lovers. This relationship regulated the flow of information about dogs. I was more receptive to listen to them about dogs.

> "Relationships can shape your minds and wire your brains."

My mind — the regulation of energy and information — was slowly affecting the "dog fearing" wiring in my brain. However, when my daughters first tried to coax me to buy a Golden Retriever, I objected vehemently. The "dog fearing" rewiring had not completed. Unperturbed by my resistance, they pursued the idea of keeping a dog as a pet. They showed me articles and made me watch documentaries of how lovable dogs could be. They took me to Yan's (a good friend of my wife's) home, to experience the playful nature of dogs. She had eight dogs. One was a Golden Retriever. Yan managed to convince me that a Golden Retriever was one of the best dogs to keep as a pet for young children. She shared, "Dogs are good for kids. If they learn how to take care of dogs, they will learn how to take care of you when you grow old!" Alison and I were naïve enough to believe her. I found out later that taking care of dogs and older people are two different things!

As you can see, the relationship between my children and me affected the "dog fearing" wiring in my brain. The continuous flow of new energy and different information affected my brain and dislodged my previous dislike for dog lovers. Through these close relationships, a transformation was taking place in me. After some time, I ended up buying a cute, cuddly, baby Golden Retriever! This would have been totally inconceivable, even insane, a few years before! My family relationships literally and wholly rewired my brain and changed my mind. With new information and experiences, I overcame my fear of dogs. I could stroke a dog and it would wag its tail happily and harmlessly. My fear of dogs (a wiring of the past) has been rewired (new neuron-firing and circuits have emerged and reconnected). My fear is not completely gone though. Sometimes when I hear a dog bark, I still cringe.

So, having understood this three-part aspect of interpersonal neurobiology, the brain, the mind and the relationship, you can learn some principles about recovery. One of the key principles of recovery is this, "Unless you find meaning and value in past bad experiences, the past will always haunt you."

How then do you find meaning and value out of the past?

Implications for Leadership: Mind, Brain and Relationships

"If we can't put an end to the violence within us, there is no hope for putting an end to the violence without."[7]
— The Arbinger Institute

1. You are what you think: Watch what you feed your mind

This notion of the mind, brain and relationships helps in your understanding of your emotions like anger, resentment, lust, passion and jealousy. It is critical to get on the inside of your brains and view how you have been wired and which neurons have been firing.

Remember, GIGO (Garbage In, Garbage Out). What you feed your minds will influence and shape the way you think. Your bad memories will be reinforced if you allow the wrong information to be fed into your minds. Conversely, if you are fed with different and fresh information, it will also rewire the way you think. The implication for leaders in organizations is the need to constantly communicate the right message as many times as possible, with as many different channels and through different people. No communication is also communication and people will invent their own communication. Especially now with the dominance of social media, it is equally important for leaders to make use of this format for their messages.

2. Who determines what: Relationship determines what information is fed into your minds

You listen more to your friends and to people whom you respect. That's why some children don't listen to their parents — because they don't like them and they don't respect them. They may listen (if you are lucky) but will not act on what they hear. That's why bosses who are not credible and/or liked have a hard time motivating their staff. Credibility and likeability are strong attributes to help change the staff's mindset. Staff who have bad experiences and wrong perceptions will be more willing to change when their bosses are people they respect and like.

The implication for leaders is that you need to focus on building strong and healthy relationships with your staff. This demands effort and time. Today's leaders like to lead by remote: by SMS, WhatsApp and emails. Face-to-face interaction is kept to the minimal because of distance and space. As such, communication has become too formal and one-way. They are usually restricted to town hall meetings, report meetings and annual conferences, which are usually unidirectional and functional. That's why the staff are not engaged and their mindsets are not changed.

3. The heart is more important than the head: Emotional connection rather than functional connection

Most leaders are connecting functionally and not emotionally with their people. They do a lot of things for their staff — they pay them, give them bonuses, share vision and goals, demand reports and sales activities, etc. These are all functional.

What's missing in leadership is the emotional connection today. Staff need:

- Affirmation (not just correction),
- Encouragement (not just reprimand),
- Caring support (not just demands),
- Sharing with (not talking down to),
- Understanding (not just being given instructions),
- Celebration (not just discipline),
- Fun and laughter (not just failures and bad news) and most of all
- Integrity — do as I do and keep promises (not just "do as I say but not as I do").

Connecting emotionally with the heart will make staff more engaged, more motivated. What is missing in today's organizations is the heart-connection, not just the mind-connection. If you want to change your staff's negative mindsets, you need transformative leaders, not just transactional leaders!

Past negative experiences will haunt us unless we recover.

"This essential skill can help us build social and emotional brainpower, move our lives from disorder to well-being, and create satisfying relationships filled with connection and compassion."[8]

— Daniel Siegel

How Do You Recover?

1. Recognize your pains and emotions

Every one of us has what psychiatrists call "implicit memory" that is the result of unsettled and un-rehabilitated base memories, which have become your mental models. You need to come to terms with your feelings of anger, resentment, jealousy and hot buttons. This is especially difficult when you have experienced betrayal, abuse and trauma. Certain hot button words, pictures, people and situations will set off a most negative reaction in us. If this syndrome persists, professional help can help us recover by bringing meaning to those terribly painful episodes, experiences and memories.

It is important to acknowledge that what had happened is bad and painful. Some people try to suppress or repress it, pretending that what had happened is good and fine. The betrayal, the trauma, the unfair treatments, the business breakups are bad. It is all right to be angry, disappointed and bitter, and even revengeful. You must admit your hurts. That's part of your humanity.

2. Reflect on the experience

The next step to healing is important. You need to reflect on the experience. As humans, you will continue to have implicit-memory experiences that haunt you. But life is a process of perpetual learning. Turn these negative experiences into learning opportunities by rewiring the pathways in your brains and memories. When you are confronted by anger, resentment and jealousy that do not go away easily, you need to reflect and discover why you react negatively. When you find yourselves reacting unfairly and inappropriately to people and situations, it is time to dig deep into your implicit memories and rebuild your brain wiring, restructure your information flow and reconstruct your relationships.

Take time to pause and reflect on your behaviours. This is a strategic necessity. It is not navel-gazing or becoming self-absorbed. On the contrary, Siegel explains, it should make us less self-absorbed and self-obsessed. You should become more connected to others, show more interest in others and develop greater empathy for others. This, in turn, will make us more effective in our interpersonal relationships.

What has happened is bad and unhealthy, but you need to ask yourself:

- Do I want to continue to nurse the hurts?

  Sometimes, we even enjoy nursing these hurts because they make us feel justified and good about being angry and revengeful. But it has a boomerang effect. It keeps haunting us perpetually.

- Where will it lead me if I continue to nurse the pains?

  I am reminded of this beautiful poem by Robert Schuller, a churchman:

Every adversity is an adventure.
Every pain is a pilgrimage.
Every trial is a trail.
Every problem is a path.
Every load is a road.

Every hurt is on the move.
It's leading you somewhere.
Where is it taking you?[9]

- Do I want these bad experiences to continue to affect my present and future relationships?
  Unfortunately, your past bad experiences will not only haunt you but will affect your present and future encounters with people. Not unlike Dave, Lisa and Mui, whose three stories I shared in the beginning, they will continue to affect the way you treat people, the way you relate to them and the biases you have of them, through no fault of theirs. You begin to impute guilt and create prejudices on all these innocent victims.

3. *Reframe to find meaning and value*

Dr Siegel proposes that you develop this new competence called mindsight. This is the ability to focus your attention on the internal workings of your minds. You become more aware of your mental processes so that you can get rid of your reactionary, ingrained behaviours and habitual responses. Only then can you navigate the emotional loops that we all have a tendency to get trapped in.

Mindsight is also a way of helping us rewire our mental process. You will grow to become more aware of your impulses and make better choices in life. By doing this, you can change the physical structure of the brain, stimulating it to grow important new connections. Developing the reflective skills of mindsight activates the very circuits that create resilience and well-being and underlie empathy and sympathy. In so doing, you learn to create well-being in your mental life, in your close relationships and even in your bodies. This can be developed by choice, effort, time and practice.

As past experiences keep haunting and hounding us, each time it happens, you must continue to ask these questions:

- What new perspectives do I need to help me move forward?
  If you find yourself running in circles, thinking the same thoughts, justifying yourself or rationalizing your anger and revenge, it is time you seek different perspectives.

- Who can provide me the new perspectives and help me out of this?
  Finding the right friends and significant other to help is very important. The support system you have is critical to the success of your recovery. However, sourcing for the right people is even more critical. If you find your friends and relatives reaffirming your anger and revenge, you should intentionally move away from them because they are "firing" the same signals and "wiring" your mental model even more deeply. This is not in any way asking you to be naïve and continue in a bad, unhealthy relationship. If you have suffered abuse, you must move out of the abuse situations. The point is that you do not want to allow those experiences to continually affect your other relationships and create more pains.

- Finally, remember Paul McGee's advice: "How can I SUMO (Shut Up and Move On)?"
  Moving on is the decisive action that you should take. You can wallow in your hurts and pains for a while but after that, you need to start afresh.

4. Refer for professional support

If you can't recognize, reflect and reframe, you need to refer to professional help.

Conclusion: Never Too Late to Learn

The most powerful predictor of children's emotional and psychological development is how their parents make sense of life. Just as how our parents' unmitigated pasts have affected us, we too shape our children with ours. There is a generational impact. Hence, in finding resolution to our hurtful memories, we can bring new hope and fresh life to our children. Some of us may feel discouraged and depressed because we have allowed our implicit memories to invade our thoughts and affect our behaviours. The good news is that it is never too late to rewire — "it is never too late to stimulate the growth of the neural fibers that enable mindsight to flourish ... the brain never stops growing in response to experience".[10]

Dr Siegel gave an example of a 92-year-old man who, despite a painful and twisted childhood, emerged to be a mindsight maven. "It is never too late to teach old dogs new tricks" is the adage that this man personifies. There is hope even for the worst of us who have been pained by life's traumas and vicious parental behaviours.

Finally, I would like to close with another inspiring poem that is reportedly hung on a wall in Mother Teresa's home in Calcutta, entitled, "Anyway".

Anyway

People are often unreasonable, illogical and self-centered;
Forgive them anyway.
If you are kind, people may accuse you of selfish, ulterior motives;
Be kind anyway.
If you are successful, you will win some false friends and some true enemies;
Succeed anyway.
If you are honest and frank, people may cheat you;
Be honest and frank anyway.
What you spend years building, someone could destroy overnight;
Build anyway.
If you find serenity and happiness, they may be jealous;
Be happy anyway.
The good you do today, people will often forget tomorrow;
Do good anyway.
Give the world the best you have, and it may never be enough;
Give the world the best you've got anyway.
You see, in the final analysis, it is between you and your God;
It was never between you and them anyway.

▪ ▪ ▪

Questions for Reflection

1

What is one past experience that is haunting you today?

2

How are you feeding my mind with this unhealthy past experience?

3

Who can you seek support and help to get over this past experience?

4

Based on this article, what is one thing you can do differently to help you get over your past experience?

Dr John Ng is Chief Passionary Officer of Meta Consulting, providing consultation services to top international corporations. He is also the Honorary Chair of Eagles Communications' Board of Governance and founder of Eagles Mediation and Counselling Centre. John is deeply passionate about great marriages and families, peacemaking and leadership. A thought-leader on Asian leadership and conflict management, he directs the programme of Eagles Leadership Institute, including the highly successful biennial Eagles Leadership Conference (ELC), which will hold its eighth edition in 2017. Author of six books, his latest, Heart to Heart with Asian Leaders, *is a bestseller. His email address is <john@meta.com.sg>.*

MY HALFTIME JOURNEY

Lee Han Kiat

I want to speak to a feeling that all of us have, that is, a desire for our lives to count for something more. All of us, at one point in our lives, will reach the stage where we attain some measure of success. It could be in your career or it could be in your family, with your children all grown up and successfully married. You have amassed enough wealth, more than you would ever need. Despite that, we often feel something is missing. And if we are true to ourselves, in our honest moments, the prospect of amassing more wealth or to continue climbing the corporate ladder to secure another promotion does not seem that exciting anymore. Success seems to lose its meaning for us.

Peter Drucker, a well-known management guru, once said that a hundred years from now, when future historians write about our generation, they will not be writing about technology or the Internet. Instead, they will be writing about a very unique phenomenon that has occurred in this generation, which is many of us having choices. The challenge is we need to manage ourselves. But the honest truth is that we are very unprepared for that.

Can anyone guess what the life expectancy of a Singaporean was in 1957? It was 60 to 61 years. But every year the life expectancy increases. According to the statistics published by the government in 2014, our life expectancy has risen to an average of 82.7 years, with the ladies scoring a little higher. Every year the figure is rising! I will not be surprised if next year when the government publishes the statistics again, the figure will rise to 83 or something like that. Other than our life expectancy, we are progressing in many other aspects of our lives; for example, we are much healthier, better educated and wealthier than the previous generation.

My Halftime Journey

God has given much to you and me. The big question is, what do we do with all that God has given to us: our time, talents and treasures? Luke 12:48 reminds us that those of us who have been given much, much more will be demanded from us. Not "appreciated" or "requested", but "demanded". I hope that as I share my own halftime journey, it will help many of us with our struggles.

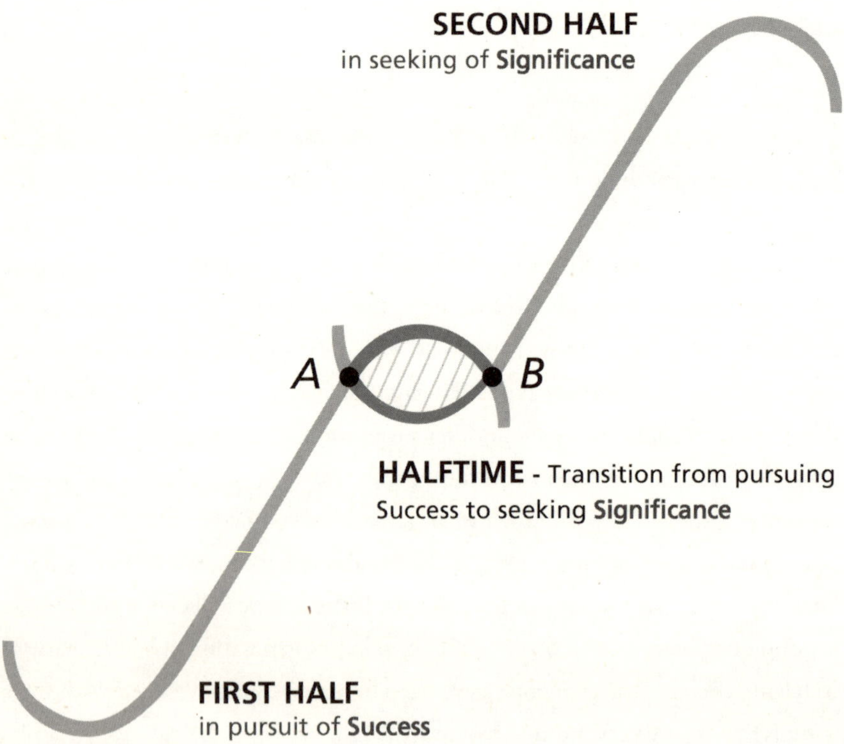

Look at the Sigmoid or 'S' curve above.[1] I would like to use it to introduce myself and share my halftime journey.

I accepted Jesus as my personal saviour at the age of 14 while I was studying at Raffles Institution. A close friend brought me to a student meeting where I accepted Jesus Christ as my Lord and Saviour. I completed my studies and when I first started working for a multi-national company in 1982, I was at the bottom of the curve like everybody else. School did not quite prepare me for work! I had no knowledge of computers, yet I joined an information technology company. Initially, I got knocked around in the company, until I found my place through help from mentors. And then all of a sudden, God decided to bless me. I was promoted to be a manager at a young age. I married a lovely wife and had three wonderful kids. Then, I was promoted to Vice President, the first person from an ASEAN country to reach that position.

> "What have you done with the time, talents and treasures that I have given you?"

In 2007, I celebrated my 25th year with the company, and there was a lot of fanfare. But a strange thing happened. I was not rejoicing as what many people would have expected. It was a troubling time for me. That year, if God had asked me two questions, I would only be able to answer the first but not the second. For the first question, "What have you done with the name of your Lord Jesus Christ?" I would have answered confidently, "I have accepted Him as my personal Lord and Saviour."

But if God had asked a second question, "What have you done with the time, talents and treasures that I have given you?" I would have really struggled to answer it. I felt ashamed for living selfishly. I felt that I had been given much but had given very little back. It was at this time that I asked myself how to transition from the stage of life I was then at. For two years, 2007 to 2009, I did not get much help although I read a lot of books and talked to a lot of friends. And then in 2009, I was invited by a friend to attend the Halftime Summit.

The Sigmoid or "S" Curve

Through the Halftime Summit, I discovered that I was not alone. More importantly, I learned the vocabulary to describe my feelings to others. Point A on the graph represents a healthy, curious point where we look up from our desk and wonder if there is more to life than this. Point B represents a typical mid-life crisis. When you push something good for too long, too hard, it always flips over. Perhaps you receive a very bad health report from the doctor. Maybe some of your friends pass away abruptly or your children move out and you now have an empty nest. Or closing the next deal or getting another promotion does not excite you as before. The new perspective of life is represented with a second U-shaped curve going upwards. It does not necessarily mean you need to leave your work or sell your company, although for some, it may come to that. What it represents is how you channel your extra capacity towards what God has placed in your heart.

At this point in time, you may feel the busyness of daily living crowding out the serious and sustained attention required to put strategic thought and action to realizing the more fulfilling life God intends for you. Your heart craves for greater meaning, joy and balance in life. Or you may be wondering what gifts God has given to you that you have failed to tap in your Christian ministry. Or you could be blinded by personal success such that you do not see creative and compelling options for living differently. Or you may be sensing that the do-it-yourself and self-help approaches to attempt a meaningful life change are difficult to implement. You lack a guide who can help you navigate foreign waters and is committed to enabling you to dream, be creative, commune with God, stay accountable and test your way into discovering your life purpose.

The shaded area, halftime, really signifies this very confusing period when we start to ask ourselves a whole list of questions that we have been processing internally, perhaps for some time. Questions that pop up include "Where am I on the S curve?"; "What are the things I would like to change about my life?" and "What is my biggest dream for the next season in life?"

For myself, I discovered that I should serve in the Halftime Ministry as a coach. This way, I could help my brothers and sisters to process their own struggles. No matter where you are on the curve, the good news is that there is a process whereby you can successfully transition into what is called the "second half". We can take inspiration from Ephesians 2:10 (NIV 2011), "For we are God's handiwork, created in Christ Jesus to do good works, which God prepared in advance for us to do." It is really up to us to find the work that God has prepared for us to do beforehand. This question itself can be very complex. So, let us try to unpack it and break it up into smaller bite-sized pieces.

Our Core, Capacity and Context

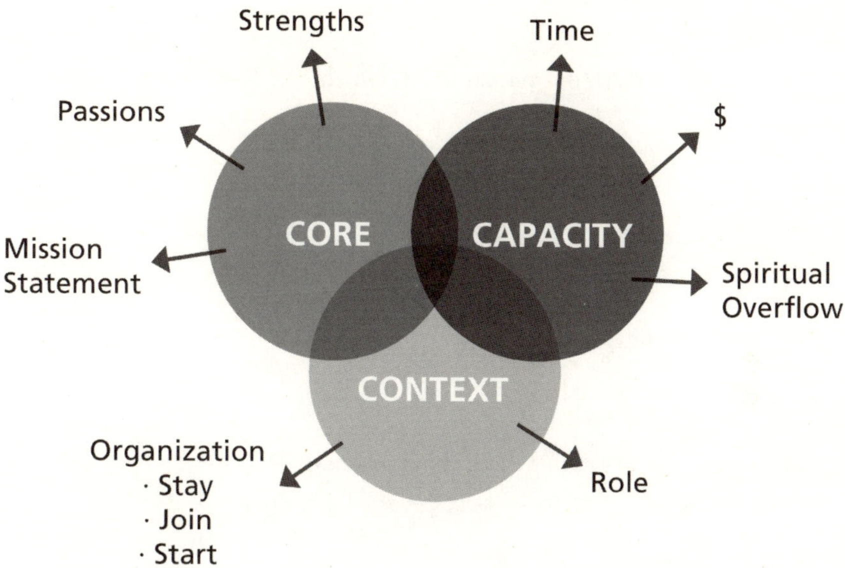

Diagram from *The Halftime Roundtable Member Guide*[2]

To answer the question of what God has prepared for us to do, we have to answer three questions. First, what is your "core"? This represents your passion, your strengths and your mission. The second is "capacity". Here, you think about the issues of money, time and spiritual overflow. The halftime journey is both head and heart, and our relationship with the Lord is the most important. We cannot love others in a sustainable way, even when it is in the zone of our strengths and passions, if we are not overflowing with God's love. The last question to answer relates to "context" — which platform or which organization can serve your calling best, and what is our role within it?

It is when we process these three questions, with all their sub-elements, that we will get in a sweet spot that represents our discovery of God's calling in our lives.

▪ ▪ ▪

Questions for Reflection

1

What do you want to be remembered for?

2

Where are you in your halftime journey?

3

If you were independently wealthy, how would you spend your days?

4

What is the most exciting thing about pursuing God's will for your life?

Lee Han Kiat spent a rewarding 32 years at IBM, where he was involved in business and technology development and various leadership positions across the Asia-Pacific region. While he enjoyed the work tremendously, he also pondered on what God had in store for him, desiring to maximize his gifts from God for His Kingdom's purpose. Today, Han Kiat is a Halftime Certified Coach and Roundtable Facilitator, and continues to work in the marketplace as a business coach and trainer. In his Halftime role, he journeys with those whom he has coached in their exploration of best-fitting roles. His email address is <hankiat.lee@halftime-asia.org>.

TURNING THE HEARTS OF FATHERS AND CHILDREN TOWARDS EACH OTHER

David Ang, PBM

I am a regular Singaporean male who has grown up in our highly competitive but thriving environment. I always endeavour to do and give of my best in light of the potential that my God has given me. The deep joy in my simple life is made up of a meaningful marital relationship with Amy, seeing the healthy and steady growth of my three children, and being a filial child to my parents and faithful friend to my friends. While fully discharging my responsibilities at workplace and communities (including church), I have come to see that a deeply satisfying life is a function of the depth and amount of meaningful relationships we have. One of the very fulfilling things I have done these past five years is to help promote the "Dads for Life" movement.

Malachi 4:5–6 has impacted me in a very real way, in terms of my relationship with my children, especially my eldest son, and also with my father.

> *See, I will send you the prophet Elijah before that great and dreadful day of the* L*ORD comes. He will turn the hearts of the fathers to their children, and the hearts of the children to their fathers; or else I will come and strike the land with a curse.*

Turning My Heart as a Father to My Children

In 2006, I had a big promotion, from finance director to CEO. I was excited — in finance, my job was very much constrained. I was then working in a large French multi-national corporation that had a top management of 12 persons, managing about a thousand people with an annual revenue of S$200 million. The promotion gave me a nice boost to my career and I felt that I was "arriving". I was in my mid-thirties and given a great responsibility. It felt really good. But I felt that I was growing distant from my family.

In covering Southeast Asia, my travels took me away 50 to 60 per cent of the time. The rest of my time, I was involved in church. From a very comfortable, stable family life, I had challenges in terms of meeting the needs of my wife, Amy. We had been married for 17 years then and had three children. While my career was taking off, the situation at home was in shambles. My eldest son showed his displeasure and even sadness at my frequent absence. He knew what it was like to be bonded with his father whereas my two younger children were not able to tell me what was in their hearts. My wife had to shoulder a lot of things at home as the kids were small and she had to look after the whole household.

One Saturday morning, I was leaving for a church meeting. I had just touched down from a business trip the night before. As I was walking out the gate, my eldest son asked, "Daddy, why are you abandoning me?" That really sobered me up. It hurt me. I started to ask myself if I had been abandoning my kids. Things in the office, things in church and what I was doing in the community and grassroots level were really taking off. I was being put in feted positions where I had a lot of influence and could make a lot of decisions. But I knew there was a crack in my home life, and that I had to get it right. I believe I was not driven by greed or pride, but responsibility to the different stakeholders I was working with. I had taken on too much to swallow!

My continual absences at home also meant there were tensions that my wife could not resolve. The previously intimate relationship I had shared with my son was reduced to a mere "hello" and "goodbye". It was a subtle change that I could not sense. In my mind, I was very much driven by what I needed to do in the office, church and grassroots. At the same time, I was thinking that given my active involvement in church, God would be very pleased with me! I was so active in serving and helping my brothers in different roles.

Two years later, things came to a head when the company decided to form a group of young leaders. I was selected for it and had to go through an internal MBA programme. This meant more travelling as well as having classes. This was a real dilemma as it meant that I would be away from home 75 per cent of the time. It was then that I really came to my senses about what was happening. It was really difficult. I was assured that after I had completed the course I would be the regional CEO of Southeast Asia. As men, we aspire to these positions. At the same time, I knew the repercussions it would have to my home life. It was a sobering time, and I had to come to terms with what was happening, seek the Lord and talk to Amy.

After a prolonged period of prayer and consultation with Amy, we decided to give it up and forego the possibility of my being a CEO. It was a fateful night in August 2008. We sought the Lord, and that very night I called my boss to say that I was sorry, but I could not take up the course on account of my family demands. I knew that I had given up one of the best career opportunities that came my way. But when I woke up the next morning I felt a huge stone lifted off my back. Sometimes when we make controversial decisions, we will never know if it was a right or wrong decision, but that morning when I woke up I knew that my decision had pleased the Lord. I had done something right for the family.

Soon after, I was able to stabilize things at home, have a better sense of prioritizing my values, and spend more time at home. At work, I had an understanding with my boss. He knew my heart's priorities, and we came up with a workable system that allowed me to be at home a lot more. At that time, I figured my highest priority was to restore the relationship between my son and me. We worked out a schedule that would allow us to spend time together. This included basketball matches in the evenings and overnight trips to Malaysia. We restored to some extent what was lost in those years I was very busy.

My eldest is a very bright boy, but in the intervening time he had deteriorated academically and had become downcast. His social life and self-esteem took a hit as well. Thankfully, as our relationship improved, these aspects also saw improvement. He has since done well in his studies and co-curricular activity, found a new direction for his life, and is serving in the church youth ministry. We find that God has restored not just our relationship but his whole person as well.

We spend a lot of time together. We pray together and have nightly chats. As a water polo player, his training is heavy and he gets aches quite frequently. One way I show love to him is by giving him a good massage. This is when he shares a lot of information about his personal life with me. It is a wonderful time of bonding. As fathers, it is a challenge for our sons to share private things with us. I really thank God for the rich relationship I enjoy with my son. I got my son back, or maybe he has found me back! It was a case of a "prodigal father".

I did not make it to the CEO position, but I have become my son's best friend. I forewent a promotion, but gained a son whose soul is uplifted. The first part of Malachi 4:5–6, where the father's heart is turned to his children, was being played out in my life.

Turning My Heart as a Child to My Father

Two years down the road, I was working at the then Ministry of Community Development, Youth and Sport (MCYS) and faced another challenge. My dad runs the family business in shipbuilding, but at his age, he has multiple chronic illnesses — diabetes, hypertension and high cholesterol. At one point, he was taking 19 different pills every night. Things boiled over around Chinese New Year, when he talked to me and confessed that he could not go on any longer. He needed me, not only to succeed him in the business, but also to be there for him. He did not use those words, but I could tell that he wanted his son with him. He asked me to consider joining the business with him. I was enjoying my work at MCYS and it was a difficult decision for me. But God reminded me again of Malachi 4:5–6, where the heart of the son turns back to the father. God told me that just as I had turned my heart towards my son, it was time to turn my heart to my own father.

"I forewent a promotion, but gained a son whose soul is uplifted."

I am not sure how many of you have worked in a shipyard. It is not a glamorous job. The sun beats down on you and you work long hours. I had other people who wanted to discuss job positions with me, but I knew that this was God's path for me. I had to make a decision that was tough but in line with God's will. After three or four months I realized why God had put me in that place. My father behaves so differently at home compared to the office. He exhibits his true self at the office. What I saw was a very broken man. I knew that he had a hard time with his own father. My grandfather was not the most affirming father. He had a lot of expectations, and in a sense he did not give my dad the affirmation he needed as a son. I saw it playing out in my father's life. He always had a point to prove, and that caused some emotional deficiencies.

I managed to engage with my father during this time. He is not a believer, but I knew he needed his son to be with him. It was not an easy journey as I encountered this different side of my father for the first time, but I knew it was a journey that God ordained for me. When I put in my resignation letter to MCYS, I received a note from a dear brother in the Lord reminding me about the time that I had given up a good career opportunity for my children's sake, and that now I was doing the same for my own father. Even as we turn our hearts towards our children, we need as well to turn our hearts towards our fathers. For practical reasons, Singapore is a greying nation, and the needs of our fathers must be cared for by their children.

I hope that my testimony shows vividly how God's Word plays out in the hearts of our children when we as fathers turn our own hearts towards them.

THE "DADS FOR LIFE" MOVEMENT

A survey conducted by MCYS in 2008/09, "which polled 2,220 Singaporeans and Permanent Residents aged 18 and above, found widespread agreement that fathers play an important parenting role, but that fathers spend less time with their children than mothers. Ninety-five per cent of fathers surveyed also agreed that being a father and raising children was one of the most fulfilling experiences a man could ever have, but cited parenting challenges such as work responsibilities, financial pressures and a lack of parenting "resources".[1]

> *With support from MSF, Dads for Life was launched on 19 November 2009 in conjunction with the International Men's Day, with the mission to "inspire, mobilise and involve fathers to become good influencers in their children's lives for life"….*
>
> *Dads for Life is founded on fatherhood research from the 1990s onward that point to the significant benefit of fathers' involvement*

on child development in terms of improved cognitive, socio-emotional, psychological and academic outcomes. For example, children with involved and nurturing fathers are noted to:

- *Develop higher intelligence quotients (IQs), better language and reasoning skills;*
- *Be more securely attached to their caregivers;*
- *Experience less emotional distress during adolescence;*
- *Report lower levels of anxiety and depression as adults;*
- *Perform better in school.*

Active paternal involvement is also linked to benefits such as:

- *Better couple relationships among parents;*
- *Lower levels of maternal stress;*
- *Positive changes in fathers' self-identity.*[2]

A nation is built on families. A nation's basic building block and most basic fabric are its families. For every family, it is more often than not that fathers play the leadership role. Hence, even from a national strategy viewpoint, it makes eminent sense to have strong families.

▪ ▪ ▪

Questions for Reflection

1

What kind of relationship do you wish to have with your children when they are older, as teenagers or youths?

2

If you were to be a child again, what would you hope for your father to be to you? Or to do more?

3

How do you want to be remembered by your children when you pass on? What kind of father are you?

4

What are one or two things, if any, that are more precious to you than your family?

5

What is the most suitable or appropriate adjective to describe you as a father presently?

David Ang, PBM headed the Dads for Life Secretariat at MCYS in 2012 before leaving to co-manage his family's shipbuilding business with his father due to the latter's ill health. He chairs Kum Yan Methodist Church's Local Church Executive Committee and Focus on the Family's Program Committee as a board member. He is also a Councillor at Northeast CDC, chairing its Family committee, where he introduced the Fathering & Family Initiative @ North East (FINE) to the district. A chartered accountant by training, David sits on the Board of Governors of Trinity Theological College as its Honorary Treasurer. His email address is <davidang1995@yahoo.com>.

RAGS FROM THE ROYAL TREASURY

Tan Lai Yong

The book of Jeremiah, at chapter 38, is about an invading army that is putting Jerusalem under siege and fear. It is about the changing of eras, influence and empires. New kings will reign and unknown powers loom on the horizon. Perhaps we can sympathize with these issues when we read today of the rise of Asian economies and the purported decline of the West and of waning American influence. Or this changing of eras could be likened to the unknowns we face — that new societal norms like same-sex marriage and genetic modification of human embryos may sweep over us. In such tumultuous times, we read of how the Lord uses an unknown servant, Ebed-Melech, to anchor His salvation plan.

> ***Jeremiah Thrown into a Cistern (Jeremiah 38:1–13)***
> *1Shephatiah son of Mattan, Gedaliah son of Pashhur, Jehucal son of*
> *Shelemiah, and Pashhur son of Malkijah heard what Jeremiah was*
> *telling all the people, when he said, 2"This is what the LORD says:*
> *'Whoever stays in this city will die by the sword, famine or plague,*
> *but whoever goes over to the Babylonians will live. He will escape with*
> *his life; he will live.' 3And this is what the LORD says: 'This city will*
> *certainly be handed over to the army of the king of Babylon, who will*
> *capture it.'"*

4 Then the officials said to the king, "This man should be put to death. He is discouraging the soldiers who are left in this city, as well as all the people, by the things he is saying to them. This man is not seeking the good of these people, but their ruin."

5 "He is in your hands," King Zedekiah answered. "The king can do nothing to oppose you."

6 So they took Jeremiah and put him into the cistern of Malkijah, the king's son, which was in the courtyard of the guard. They lowered Jeremiah by ropes into the cistern; it has no water in it, only mud, and Jeremiah sank down into the mud.

7 But Ebed-Melech, a Cushite, an official in the royal palace, heard that they had put Jeremiah into the cistern. While the king was sitting in the Benjamin Gate, 8 Ebed-Melech went out of the palace and said to him, 9 "My lord the king, these men have acted wickedly in all they have done to Jeremiah the prophet. They have thrown him into a cistern, where he will starve to death when there is no longer any bread in the city."

10 Then the king commanded Ebed-Melech the Cushite, "Take thirty men from here with you and lift Jeremiah the prophet out of the cistern before he dies."

11 So Ebed-Melech took the men with him and went to a room under the treasury in the palace. He took some old rags and worn-out clothes from there and let them down with ropes to Jeremiah in the cistern. 12 Ebed-Melech the Cushite said to Jeremiah, "Put these old rags and worn-out clothes under your arm to pad the ropes." Jeremiah did so, 13 and they pulled him up with the ropes and lifted him out of the cistern. And Jeremiah remained in the courtyard of the guard.

If Singapore were being invaded, anyone who goes around saying, "Give up. Don't fight. Surrender!" will be arrested for treason. This is expected in affairs of the state. The court officials led by Shephatiah son of Mattan did the very same to Jeremiah. They did not want him to discourage their soldiers.

Note that while they criticized Jeremiah's message, they did not say (or could not say) anything negative about his character. They did not say that Jeremiah was proud or haughty or a coward. Their criticisms were against his message, not his character. This is an important foundation that Christian men who seek to have a "salt and light" prophetic influence in their workplace need to pray over — that our character reflects godliness, truth and love. People may disagree with our message but let's pray that they will not find our character and values dishonouring to God. We need not be perfect — Jeremiah wasn't — but we do need to reflect God's love and light in our deeds and words.

Nevertheless, Jeremiah was thrown into a cistern and left to die in silence. But in this dire straits, the Lord had a man who prior to this had served silently in Jerusalem. Ebed-Melech stepped up and became the Lord's servant in rescuing Jeremiah, the Lord's prophet.

Who is this man Ebed-Melech? He was a Cushite who was serving in the king's palace. Actually, he was a eunuch. We can imagine that he was kidnapped or sold as a slave while in Cush, which is modern day Ethiopia, and then cruelly castrated and eventually ended up in the palace of Zedekiah.

Relatively speaking, he was a nobody. He did not really have a name as "Ebed-Melech" literally means "servant of the king" — it was more a term or a job title like "chauffeur", "chef", "butler" or "*aide-de-president*". This is in marked contrast to the other court officials who had proper names and who were "sons" of someone, such as Shephatiah son of Mattan, Gedaliah son of Pashhur and Jehucal son of Shelemiah. Ebed-Melech may have had an important courtly position but had no real name. It was this nameless servant who stepped up to serve the Lord.

My wife and I had the privilege of living and serving in Yunnan in south-western China for about 14 years (1996–2010). We were part of a community development team that had the motto, "Caring for the Poor, Sharing Knowledge, Loving People". I was involved in a training programme for village health workers or "barefoot doctors". These workers were the ones responsible for primary healthcare in their villages. They were mostly farmers who had a secondary or primary school background and were appointed to the post of being healthcare workers as they were the most literate villagers in these remote settings.

It was a tough but thoroughly meaningful job assignment and I was given an honoured position as a "foreign expert", with an important looking document that I could use as my ID while in China. Later on, when the administration and regulations changed, this title of "foreign expert" was slowly being withdrawn.

There were times when I looked longingly at my special ID and was worried or felt useless if it were to be taken away. The task and the job description did not change but I was hooked on having a name, an important position. Ebed-Melech had no name and no expert ID, yet he served his God and did so brilliantly in most appropriate ways.

Ebed-Melech did three things that showed that he was wise and culturally connected. Firstly, he approached King Zedekiah when he was sitting at the gate. In the traditions of the Old Testament times, the king would meet people at the gate to hear petitions and pleas. This is like the "Meet the People" sessions that Members of Parliament in Singapore hold in HDB areas. Ebed-Melech chose an appropriate time to speak with the king.

He also chose his words carefully. He did not go out with "all guns firing" (well, guns were not invented then), accusing the king of imprisoning a man without trial or bowing to cronyism. Ebed-Melech told the king about Jeremiah being cold and hungry — playing on the common suffering that perhaps all were in because of the coming invasion. Justice and human rights are *not* outside the realm of Christian advocacy. Indeed, we should be at the forefront in championing these causes. However, at this moment, Ebed-Melech decided wisely and discerned that he needed to use words of compassion. He used appropriate words in an appropriate setting. And when the king was convinced, he told Ebed-Melech to go and rescue Jeremiah.

> "Justice and human rights are ***not*** outside the realm of Christian advocacy."

We must understand that Ebed-Melech had to get out of his comfort zone to meet the king at the gate. He was after all a eunuch in the palace. He would have some authority in the palace and would likely be commented on, if not laughed at, when he ventured out of the palace to go to the Benjamin gate. We need to follow the adage to "bloom where we are planted", but we must also be ready to step out of our comfort zone and speak the truth, and step out of our comfortable areas of control and serve in areas where we don't have control, but knowing well by faith that the Sovereign Lord is in full control.

The third and wisest decision that Ebed-Melech made was to take rags from the royal treasury. King Zedekiah gave Ebed-Melech 30 men and the authority to rescue Jeremiah. He went to the king's storeroom, where there would be all sorts of precious items — weapons, food, silver — but Ebed-Melech took some rags. Why?

He chose to use that which was appropriate in the situation. He knew that Jeremiah was starving and emaciated. He was thin and had a wasted body. He lowered the ropes with the rags and asked Jeremiah to use the rags to pad his armpits. He wanted to rescue Jeremiah in a way that would not break any bones or cause any more discomfort.

Appropriate timing.

Appropriate words.

Appropriate methods.

As Christian men, there are two important areas to think about as we ask God to help us to be "Ebed-Melech" — first in our families and then in our workplace. As men in the home, we need the wisdom of being there at the right time, with the right words (or right ears) and right methods to win the love of our spouse and children. We cannot outsource manhood. The eunuch Ebed-Melech was neither a coward nor a softie. He stepped in and spoke up. He was there when Jeremiah needed to be rescued. Think about the times when we need to get out of our comfort zones, out of our routine and control, so that we can bring God's love and light into our very own families.

I encourage fathers to go camping with their kids and teens — especially with their sons. Bring the nephews along. Children often share many things with their dads when cooking a meal over a fire beside a tent. These are fun times. But many parents tell me, "*Aiyah*, it is too hot" or "There are too many mosquitoes". We may not be naturally inclined to bring our kids outdoors. This is where we look to friends to help us along with the appropriate plans and support. I can assure fathers that it is more fun to bring our children (and grandchildren) to go camping than to bring them to tuition classes or guided tours — and they learn more, too.

The same applies to our witness in the workplace. There will be ethical and personnel issues. We are in the mix of things and times do get tough and rough. You may feel that you are in the wrong job. But think about the attitudes and methods of Ebed-Melech and pray to apply them. Share about these with other Christian men and pray for wisdom. Lean on the experience of godly brothers.

Go to the royal treasury of Jesus Christ — and we will find that the riches of the world are but rags and the "rags" from the Word, the fellowship of believers and the presence of the Holy Spirit are truly treasures for eternity.

In Jeremiah 39:15–18, we see Ebed-Melech as being very human. He has fears. But the reassuring thing is that God knows that. For He says, "I will not allow the man whom you are afraid of to harm you" (see Jeremiah 39:17). Jeremiah 39:18 (ESV) says, "I will surely save you, and you shall not fall by the sword, but you shall have your life as a prize of war, because you have put your trust in me, declares the LORD".

This is salvation by grace. And when God meets Ebed-Melech again, He will say it is not because of the good deeds Ebed-Melech has done, nor because he was clever in choosing the right forum, seizing the right time or using the right methods, but because Ebed-Melech trusted in Him. Salvation is through God's grace to sinful human beings like all of us — it is unconditional and unmerited. And the key is how we appropriate this grace in practice. We may use the best technology, the best human resource practices, the best information technology techniques and the best management system, but we would still not attain salvation. The best thing that we can and should do is to reflect our trust in the Lord. We are not to do this so as to try and "buy" more faith. It is the other way round. It is an expression of our faith that we fully trust and obey the Lord. Let all that we do therefore be an expression of our trust and obedience in God.

We will face challenging times and may have to endure injustice. As parents, we are aware of this reality. We should educate our children about the challenges ahead but we must not burden them with anxiety and worries. Instead we should be ready to be Ebed-Melechs — knowing that we are saved by grace with a super-secure eternity — and thus able to serve God even in trying times, asking Him to give us skilful words, favoured timings and the courage to use rags from the royal treasury.

▪ ▪ ▪

Questions for Reflection

1

Think about your work. Has there been a meeting or an occasion when a wrong word sparked off a misunderstanding? Or share about a time when an appropriate word or action helped to solve a problem. Read Colossians 4:2–6, then pray for each other to be gracious "salt and light" at work. It would be good to identify some colleagues to bless and pray over.

2

Share about a threat or an unwelcome or unforeseen change that you feel is encroaching into our society. Why are we uncomfortable about this encroachment? How would we respond if we were asked to be an Ebed-Melech in this situation?

3

As fathers, name three things that you would be anxious about if your children have a lower income or social standing than you. Why? Read Jeremiah 17:5–10. How can we be examples of prospering in the Lord as He promised and yet, like Ebed-Melech, serve as He has purposed? Take time to pray for each other's children and families.

Dr Tan Lai Yong is a lecturer at the National University of Singapore and Director of Outreach and Community Engagement at the College of Alice and Peter Tan. After graduating as a doctor in 1985, Lai Yong left for Yunnan, China in 1996 with his family to join a community development team working with the poor in remote villages caring for orphans, disabled children and the leprosy-affected. He returned to Singapore in 2011. His work has caught the attention of the Chinese government, who awarded him the prestigious Friendship Award for Foreign Experts in 2004. Lai Yong has written several books and has a column with Impact *magazine. He now positively impacts the lives of migrant workers in Singapore through HealthServe. His email address is <drtanlaiyong@nus.edu.sg>.*

WHAT IS YOUR LONG-TERM GOAL IN LIFE?

Hsieh Fu Hua

Let me preface what I am going to say with this guiding principle of mine, that is, we must be accountable in what we do and say. Although ultimately it is between God and us, we also need to be accountable to "real people". That is why there are a few selected people I hold myself accountable to. A key lesson I have learnt in life is that if you do not have someone to account to, like a "real" boss, things can go wrong. Indeed, in this sharing of my journey today, I am holding myself accountable to you too.

My journey as a Christian has not been a very long one — about 18 years in all since 1996. How did it happen?

I have an open mind to things. And that is why I became a Christian, eventually. For a long while, my mind and heart had been searching earnestly for the purpose and meaning in life. Being hard-headed, reasoning and "an understanding that seeks faith" were my guideposts as I sought the truth in life.

In my early years, I was inspired by Albert Schweitzer (a missionary doctor, philosopher, musician, theologian and writer), Viktor Frankl (a Nazi concentration camp survivor, psychiatrist, activist and author) and a play that centred on Sir Thomas More (Chancellor of England, a principled man who lost his life against an unprincipled king). I shall return to speak more of Thomas More later on. In later years, I sought direction and enlightenment from Buddhism, going to Myanmar to learn meditation and seeking to discover my "inner being" in the process. This and other attempts at discovery led me step by step to open my heart to follow Jesus Christ.

How did it happen? Early one morning, around four o' clock, I suddenly sat up in bed. Inexplicably, I pledged to seek and find God with all my heart and not turn back. I urgently called my friend, a church pastor then and now the principal of a theological college, to meet up. He had always been gentle in his approach and had not insensitively tried to proselytize me. We met the same day and I raised three questions and his replies assured me that he would minister well to me. I attended his church and on the first visit felt my heart strangely moved by the Holy Spirit. Thus, my journey with Christ began.

I have entitled this sharing, "What is your long-term goal in life?" This piercing question was posed to me in 1983 during an interview that could have potentially changed my life path, veering it towards a political one. It had the effect of peering into my soul. How would a self-assured aspiring banker, aged 33 years, respond to such a pointed question? I kept silent for a long while, the seconds and minutes ticking away. Then, I responded meekly after the long silence, "Honestly, I don't know." Well, as you would have guessed it, that reply brought the interview to an abrupt end.

In part, I feel I could not reply definitively because my life goals had been shifting. I had ended up doing a business degree quite unexpectedly. I did it to prepare myself to make a living. My goal for a long while since young was to be a doctor, having been a sickly child who spent much time in hospital. But somehow, when I was in pre-university at ACS, I changed my mind. I then tried enrolling as a cadet pilot, both in the Air Force and Singapore Airlines, but was rejected. Perhaps, when confronted suddenly by such a pointed question that appeared to call for a clear answer, I was speechless.

This and other setbacks such as being unceremoniously fired from a high position in the banking industry, which resulted in my relocating to Hong Kong, were humbling points in my life. In retrospect, I see them now as turning points lit by the Holy Spirit to guide me.

The "what" and the "who" are the two big questions that I want to pose to you today. In our formative years, we tend to concentrate on the "what" we want to do and be (our studies, qualifications, skills), building up our career and family, developing networks, establishing our standing, etc. We continue to be occupied in our efforts, thoughts and time with the tangible "what" in our later years and even throughout our lives. In the race of life, we may think we have done well and even arrived, but in truth, we have lost our way, waylaid by the "what" of living.

Yahweh, "I am Who I am", has made us all in His image. Do we see our image in Him? Do we do enough to relate to Him and our fellow men as people who truly know Him and know who we are? In the search for my own image, the story of Sir Thomas More left me with an indelible mark.

> "Yahweh, "I am Who I am", has made us all in His image."

The fortitude of Sir Thomas More, amply portrayed in the play *A Man for All Seasons*, is a beacon to me. As Prime Minister of England, More did not support his king's (King Henry VIII) move to divorce the queen and re-marry. England then was under the Catholic church, which refused to endorse the divorce. As a result of this episode, England split from the Catholic church and the Anglican church was founded.

Thomas More kept avoiding the numerous negotiations to find a way out for the king to divorce and re-marry. Eventually, he was cornered and he reluctantly but surely took a stand: "No, I can't agree." Thereafter, More was executed.

This story struck me that within us there is an "inviolable space" which is sacred and cannot be violated. It constitutes a line that cannot be crossed, a principle that cannot be breached. This got etched in my consciousness — "the inviolable space" that you regard as sacred and sacrosanct and guard zealously. If it is violated, your life is not worth living any longer! That was precious learning for me.

Another writer who made an impression is Viktor Frankl, who wrote *Man's Search for Meaning*.[1] The book was based on his experiences as a detainee at an Auschwitz concentration camp. Frankl tried to understand why some people survived and some did not. He realized that many who survived found a deeper meaning to life, which kept them going. Many who died had given up, their spirit broken.

Before I became a Christian, a spiritualist and author who had an impact on me was Thich Nhat Hanh, a Buddhist monk. He caught my attention with his book entitled *Living Buddha, Living Christ*.[2] This was in 1993, the year I was fired from my job. It was a time of searching and seeking for me. For much of my life before then, I was focused on the "what" of life — do this, do that, be this, be that. I had become reasonably successful in the field of finance, climbing up the ladder relatively quickly.

But then came this big fall in 1993 when I was unceremoniously dismissed. My fall became public as the press covered the story. After that, for a number of years, I was marginalized in the financial sector in Singapore. And so, I went to Hong Kong and spent some years there. During this time of exile, I was accompanied and encouraged by a team of close friends who made the switch with me, many uprooting themselves to work in Hong Kong, too. They made huge sacrifices and I am eternally grateful to them.

Thich's book was instrumental in helping to open my thinking that gradually became receptive to Christianity. At that time, I was exploring Buddhism, a faith that attracted me. What I understood Thich to be saying was that one did not have to go far to find Buddha because he was in Jesus Christ. And so suddenly the revelation came. While my mind was closed all this while, Thich opened my eyes to seek Christ.

As I have shared, the various low points in my life afforded me great learning moments. Another low point emerged when one of my children was afflicted with a mental health problem. That was the key reason why I signed up as a patient at the Institute of Mental Health (IMH)! Mental health is nothing to shy from. Indeed, research has shown that a quarter of us end up grappling with this issue at some point or other during our lifetime.

Having elected to support mental health as a cause, I decided to enrol for psychotherapy at the IMH. I had decided to do this to learn first-hand the dynamics at play when a mentally unwell person is under treatment. I had earlier consulted a psychiatrist friend on this. Being mindful of public perception, he gently directed me to a polyclinic, which would have referred me with little or no trace (as compared to an IMH record). But I insisted on going directly to IMH because I wanted to be as authentic as possible in undergoing this experience. Thus, over a period of one and a half years, I underwent about 40 sessions at IMH. Yes, my patient record is there!

As it turned out, it was a very useful exercise in self-discovery. The extended period of undergoing therapy was indeed an enriching time, which primed me for my efforts in supporting mental health. It was also a humbling experience that has taught me to empathize better with those who are mentally unwell. Above all, it was a great journey of discovery and self-realization.

A key lesson I drew from my time at IMH is that each one of us has a "mental construct". We all think we are whole, buttressed by our beliefs and experiences. We feel safe and secure in this familiar, comfortable self-construct. However, when I was undergoing therapy, the psychiatrist helped me to peel myself open bit by bit, and I discovered gaping holes in myself and the hollowness of my conscious self.

The feeling is not unlike how one feels when renovating a house. You knock down a wall here, a wall there. Things become uncomfortable. That was how I felt undergoing psychotherapy. There was self-examination and self-reflection. This led me to feeling unsettled, uncomfortable and not so confident even though I am quite self-confident. It is dispiriting when confidence seeps out from you. You lose your bearings and become disoriented or troubled. This may be how a person with mental health issues feels. In this very poignant way, I had a memorable glimpse of what mental health patients may go through.

Emerging from this journey, I began to appreciate better one's "inner core of being" which dwells in the depth of the heart, soul and spirit. This core may be sensed as we learn and try to draw nearer to God.

To cultivate this nearness, I suggest going on retreats. Elijah offers an excellent example of his experience of a retreat. We all know how Elijah fled into the desert, spending 40 days and nights in solitude and silence, and eventually hid in a cave (1 Kings 19). Was he hiding or was he immersed in a deep personal retreat, just like our Lord Jesus who retreated into the desert? Finally, Elijah came out and the wind blew, and God passed near the mouth of the cave where he stood. God encounters us not just in our cave of solitude and silence but also as we step out into life to do His work.

I go on silent retreats. Pure silence. No prayer, no speaking — just being quiet, listening in deep silence, letting God and His Word speak to me. I learnt this from the Catholic nuns who have a strong tradition of retreats.

So, this is my journey and I hope my sharing has offered some thoughts for your own reflection. Have you focused too much on the "what" of life, neglecting "who" you are? What is the "inviolable sacred space" within you? And finally, have you sought and engaged the "inner core of your being"?

■ ■ ■

Questions for Reflection

1

Have you focused too much on the "what" of life, neglecting "who" you are?

2

What is the "inviolable sacred space" within you?

3

Have you sought and engaged the "inner core of your being"?

4

Have there been "learning moments" from the low points in your life?

5

Have you experienced any silent retreats in your life? How may you go about embarking on one?

Hsieh Fu Hua is chairman of the United Overseas Bank and Tiger Airways Holdings. He is also a board member of GIC Pte Ltd, and advisor to Prime Partners Group which he had founded. Previously, he was CEO of SGX (2003–2009) and a board member of Temasek Holdings (2010–2012). Called by the Lord to be active in the community, Fu Hua serves on the boards of a few non-profit organizations and heads the National Art Gallery, National Council of Social Service and the Stewardship and Corporate Governance Centre. His email address is <hfh@prime.com.sg>.

"And we know that in all things God works for the good of those who love him, who have been called according to his purpose."

(ROMANS 8:28)

GOD IN THE MARKETPLACE

GOD IN THE MARKETPLACE: CHALLENGES FACED

Philip Ng

By God's grace, I am delighted to be here with you this morning to talk about God in the marketplace, in my life and the key challenges I face as a business person in the workplace and marketplace.

The topic of "God in the Marketplace" is not an easy one. I found this out as I went about preparing for this talk. I wanted to share something that would honour the Lord and also be meaningful to you. I could not say no when asked to share. At that time, I did not realize how difficult the topic was.

"God in the Marketplace" has many facets. Initially, I thought that I would just talk about my life and my walk as a Christian businessman, but on further reflection, I felt that would not really do justice to this important topic. There is so much written about it and so much thought out there — though I will not call it "a theology of work" — that is now being developed about God in the marketplace and how God works through all of us, His human agents.

Faith and Work: Literature References

These various thoughts can be grouped under the faith and work movement, as reflected in the literature I looked at. I think it is important that I first share with you what some of these authors say in their books and outline the ideas and notions that have been developed, as that will make my presentation more complete and rounded. I have not read all of them. But still, these are some very useful books that I hope some of you will check out in the bookshop to at least familiarize yourself more with this topic.

First, let me mention C. Peter Wagner, who tops my list of "must-read authors" on the marketplace and workplace. He is one of the leading figures in this faith and work movement. One of his books is *The Church in the Workplace*, which is an excellent book, and I recommend it to you.[1] In it are many insightful questions, with helpful answers given. Topics covered include: How do I apply biblical principles to my business? Does God really care about my business decisions? How do I honour God when I have to fire someone and make other difficult business decisions? How do I guard myself from temptation? How do I wait on the Lord when time is money? How do I know God's will for my life?

Another key figure in the faith and work movement is Darrow Miller, who writes about discipling nations — that as Jesus' disciples, we should be discipling other Christians. Discipleship in our work is something many of these leading thinkers urge us to do, for indeed, work is sacred. More than just having a ministry in the workplace and the marketplace, our work itself is sacred.

Another book is titled exactly as our topic today, *God in the Marketplace* by Henry and Richard Blackaby. This is quite an interesting book as it pans through many issues and questions posed by CEOs and others in the Fortune 100 and Fortune 500 lists which the authors attempt to answer. It is a book designed for the corporate world.

Another book by Dennis Peacock addresses the issue of winning the battle for the minds of men. In it, he talks about the need to embrace a worldview and opines that Christians have been in a way asleep for a long time! Interestingly, recently, I read *The Commonalities* by Pope Benedict, who wrote about how Christians should never fall asleep, as did five of the ten virgins in the parable of the ten virgins who failed to top up their oil! They were thus caught napping, which Pope Benedict reminds us should never happen to Christians. On his part, Dennis Peacock argues that many Christians have fallen asleep because they do not have a worldview — a participatory view as to how they can change the world.

Of course, we all know that, at the end of the day, the final outcome is that God has victory. But from now till then, what are we doing about it?

Some of these books have many interesting thoughts about Christian movements revolving around para-church or market ministries. One such movement is the Full Gospel Businessmen Fellowship (FGBF), of which I am a member. The FGBF sees its "marketplace ministry" as covering seven mountains, derived from the notion that there are seven moulders of culture. These are family, religion (where the church is situated), government, media, education, business and the arts.

The FGBF calls these seven moulders of culture the seven "mountains" or "gates". Hence, outside of the church, almost everything else can be banded under this "marketplace ministry", broadly defined.

The marketplace is outside the church domain, in the outer court or in fact beyond the outer court. C. Peter Wagner talks about the nuclear church, which is the core church, that is, the church as we are all familiar with. And church is what our entire Christian existence revolves around! For many Christians, this has affected our thinking. I know that this is not the case for all of you as you are here this Saturday morning, extending your spiritual horizons to beyond church. But many Christians are led to believe that Sunday worship is the most important thing; the rest of the week just leads up to Sunday.

Instead, our thinking should be that Sunday is the day for corporate worship and nourishment; for the rest of the week, we are out there in the world as Christians. So, my encouragement to all is to think of church, firstly, as the nuclear church beyond which there is the extended church. And that, as Christians, we can make an impact by bringing God into the marketplace.

I remember watching a video presented in the Alpha ministry. The presenter, Nicky Gumbel, said that the people who worship in the Church of England think that God has left the church. They arrive at this conclusion because the feeling they get while at church is so hollow, so much so that they feel that God has left it. Is it the case for church members then that whilst it is quite a blow, they just have to get on with it and live without God?

Perhaps we are in a similar situation. If we as Christians do not respond to the call and be obedient to God, for many people, God would be absent in the marketplace!

"God and Business"

Let me now read you an interesting extract from Wagner's book:

> *Many leaders in the extended church consider the release of the July 9, 2001 issue of the* Fortune *magazine as a watershed event. It came across as a de facto cultural stamp of approval on a movement that had started some 70 years earlier, that had moved through various stages of development and had accelerated notably in the late 1990s, but still lacked the assurance that what they were doing could actually contribute to transforming our society.*[2]

The cover story of that issue was "God and Business" with the subtitle, "The surprising quest for spiritual renewal in the American workplace". Even *Fortune* seemed a bit self-conscious with such an unusual issue. In fact, the managing editor at that time wrote:

> *Did you ever expect to see those two words on the cover of this magazine? Me neither. At* Fortune *our articles of faith are limited to belief in free trade, unfettered competition, and the proposition that capitalism works best when companies stick to creating value for shareholders. Our normal beat: mammon.*[3]

But *Fortune* did publish this article, "God and Business". This was more than ten years ago. The article goes on to show why faith in the workplace is more than just another trend of the day. The author of this piece is a somewhat religious person, describing himself as a minimally observant Jew who had rediscovered his faith in recent years. He usually covered media and not spiritual things in his professional beat. He said that once he got into it, he was "amazed at the number of business people, especially baby boomers, [who were looking] for a higher purpose in their lives, willing to talk about their faith publicly, and trying to integrate it into their work".[4]

Here are a few quotes from the *Fortune* article:

> *This is a diverse, mostly unorganized mass of believers — the counterculture popping up all over corporate America — who want to bridge the traditional divide between spirituality and work. Historically, such thoughts operated below the radar, on*

> *their own or in small workplace groups where they prayed or studied the Bible. But now they are organized and going public to agitate for change....*
>
> *When the Gallup Poll asked Americans in 1999 if they felt a need to experience spiritual growth, 78% said yes, up from 20% in 1994; nearly half said they'd had occasion to talk about their faith in the workplace in the past 24 hours....*
>
> *People who want to mix God and business are rebels on several fronts. They reject the centuries-old American conviction that spirituality is a private matter. They challenge religious thinkers who show disdain for business as an inherently impure pursuit.... They disagree with business people who say that religion is unavoidably divisive.*[5]

So this is happening in America already. And you know, America is really in need of God. It is such a great nation but has lost its way a bit as we can see from all the things that are happening there. The gay pride and emphasis on self-actualization and human rights are, to me, a deceitful cover to displace God. When we as humans argue to have purportedly more rights than God in the world, the sovereignty of God is questioned. When we talk about human rights to the nth degree, we are displacing God. God then no longer has a say; He no longer has any hold on us.

That is what is happening in America today. But at the same time, what we see in corporate America is that many Christian business people are feeling a need to respond. There is something that is agitating them to want to transform society. So, indeed, as we observe through our reading of Scripture, God does allow things to happen and in the end it will be "for the good of those who love him, who have been called according to his purpose" (Romans 8:28). And we can see that crisis can lead to positive changes.

So, there you are — a short summary or extract from the various points that I have culled from reading the literature that is out there on the faith and work movement, and on leadership in the marketplace ministry.

Our Response in the Marketplace

In the next part of my talk, I will focus on what our response should be. The above sharing sets out some of the key literature on the subject. Individually, how do we respond so as to bring the Light of Jesus to the marketplace, to make it real to those around us?

John 17:18 says, "As you sent me into the world, I have sent them into the world." So we know that we have been sent into the world, into the marketplace. What is clear is that God has put us in the marketplace for a purpose. And it all starts with the Lord Himself. As disciples, we are called by the Lord, "Come, follow me" (Mark 1:17). By following Him as disciples, we bring the Light of the Lord into the marketplace and workplace (1 John 2). Also, in 1 John 2:15–17, we are exhorted to "not love the world or anything in the world".

Now that is difficult, that is tough — to not love the world! This is indeed a challenge that we face as marketplace Christians. How do we operate in the world and not love the world or anything in the world? This is the case only when God is with us. Because whenever there are blunders and difficulties and matters that we cannot resolve, it means we need God; we need Jesus to guide us.

This is especially so for me. As a real estate developer, my "world" is about bricks and mortar; it is about land and building developments. In a way, it is about fuelling desire! And when I think about it a bit more deeply, sometimes it disturbs me. When I was not walking with the Lord, before I became a committed Christian — this was because I had been searching for God for a long, long time — fuelling desires did not appear a bad thing. My mindset then was purely that of a business person. But today, I am very much more conscious about what God's Word says. I must say that I have not fully resolved this issue yet. If I do not fuel desire, I cannot sell my products. But still, my Christian conscience informs me that there are certain constraints and restraints that I should place on myself.

Truth in Business

To begin with, we have to speak the truth in our business. Truth in business is a very important thing, a key starting point. So, for a start, truth in business is what I ask my colleagues and staff to uphold. Like many of you, when confronted with moral issues in business, I spend much time praying about it during my devotional time. I encourage you to do likewise for issues that confront you. After all, our God is a God of love and truth, one whom we should worship in spirit and in truth.

I have asked God for specific guidance on this matter — how can I conduct my business in a way that honours Him, not stepping beyond the boundaries set by Scripture? In Singapore, it is helpful that we have quite a regulated property market. I am thankful that I operate here. In other jurisdictions such as Hong Kong, there is more latitude in advertising and promoting developments for sale. For example, for a long time until the law stepped in, developers in Hong Kong were selling their properties based on gross floor area, which included the area of the lift lobbies, staircases and other areas that could not be used. For a while, they got away with that until government regulations stepped in. And we all know that governments are there by the divine appointment and pleasure of God.

So, is God in the marketplace? God's presence can actually be manifested through the work of these government agencies, to ensure that there is equity and justice. Now in Hong Kong, you cannot sell your unit based on gross floor area anymore; it has to be based on the net floor area of usable space.

Another challenge that I face in my work is when colleagues and staff ask me, "You know, so-and-so is doing this. Why can't we do it too?" They feel that we are disadvantaging ourselves. Everyone is running with two legs but here we are — tying up one leg behind us and trying to move along with the rest with just one leg! Indeed, to them, we disadvantage ourselves when we seek to uphold the Lord's name and speak the truth in business.

Jesus Christ — My Guide and Shield

In our walk as Christians in the marketplace, we have a lot of scriptural material that guides us as to how we should behave. Revelation 13:8 reminds us, "All inhabitants of the earth will worship the beast — all whose names have not been written in the book of life belonging to the Lamb". In the end times and the last days, the system of the world will become more and more corrupt and malfunctioning. Spiritual warfare will be very real. We have to be very conscious that we do not go down that path and step onto the slippery slope. To ensure this, we have to think consciously about and guard against the system of the world whilst operating in the world.

This is where Romans 12:1–2 is a fantastic exhortation. It has been very helpful to me as a Christian businessman; not only to me, but also to many of my Christian friends who are in business. The passage exhorts us not to "conform any longer to the pattern of this world, but be transformed by the renewing of your mind". We are also reminded to offer ourselves as "living sacrifices, holy and pleasing to God". 2 Corinthians 4:5 reminds us that "we do not preach ourselves, but Jesus Christ as Lord". That is, our lives reflect and "preach" or declare who our Lord is as we go about our ways in our business. This brings me to the quotation that I gave to be put in the publicity brochure for this talk, which reads as follows:

> *I cannot be a Christian on one hand and a businessman on the other. I am a Christian first and a businessman second. One cannot compartmentalize; first and foremost, one has to follow Christ. I make it a point to subtly let my prospective business partners know that I am a follower of Christ. Christ is a shield that I put in front of me, and He guides the way that I do business, of which the means is more important than the end.*

Our Lord Jesus is indeed my shield when I meet prospective business partners. At these meetings, I make it known to them that I am a Christian. This way, when they interact with me as a business person, they get to know upfront that Jesus will also be part of our business partnership. In this way, I "preach" Jesus in the difficult arena of the marketplace. I preach Jesus in order to deal with deceit as well as conceit. This is because I want to make it clear to people I do business with that I cannot do anything that is deceitful, nor would I do anything that is borne out of conceit.

"I am a Christian first and a businessman second."

This has been a real shield to me as we explore business opportunities and embark on business projects in many countries. In fact, we are quite careful in choosing the countries we do business in. We steer clear of countries where our integrity may be compromised. This is where Micah 6:8 is so relevant: "He has showed you, O man, what is good. And what does the LORD require of you? To act justly and to love mercy and to walk humbly with your God."

To "act justly and to love mercy and to walk humbly with your God". These words really resonate with me and I try to reflect them in my work. And in a real sense, the exhortation holds everything together for me as a Christian businessman. This is because in business, sometimes we do not act justly. It could be our sales and marketing staff down the line who do not act justly, not because they want to be unjust, but because they are not guided properly. They think, "My job is to protect the organization. My job is to protect the interests of my company, so if I am too just, my company loses out and whoever I deal with, gains."

This is something I have to deal with all the time. There are some loyal and faithful employees who feel that they have to do their utmost to safeguard the interests of the company. They then think like the company's owners, where the mantra is: "I win, you lose" — which is how they think owners think.

Stewards Versus Owners

Therefore, in recent years, I have told my colleagues that in the first place, I myself am not even an owner; I am just a steward of God's provision. God has given me everything, and it is by His bountiful grace that I am entrusted with all that I have. Likewise, the founding family members of the company are also stewards. Nothing really belongs to us; all that we have belongs to God. We are just passing them on to successive generations of stewards.

The last thing we want our executives and staff members to do is to act or think like owners. Instead, I ask them, "Please act and think like stewards." Somehow, in the Asian context, when you tell someone to think like an owner, the worst comes out of him, not the best. Their approach will be, "Well, if I am the owner, I am going to be very tough. If the tenant asks for this, I am going to say 'no', because, you know, I am the owner and if I say 'yes', I lose out."

This is the basic mentality I have to deal with. It's a reality. While I do not wish to judge, it is something that is very real for us in business, whether in a corporate setting or in different spheres of businesses. Regardless of the marketplace setting that we find ourselves in, it is best to think of ourselves as stewards. I suggest that the idea of stewardship — in the biblical sense of being God's stewards of all that He has given us — is the best thing that we can bring to our workplace and the marketplace that we operate in.

Even if we do not operate in the marketplace, it is still good for us to embrace the idea that we, at the end of the day, are only stewards. This is because when we think that we are the owner and God has, by His grace, given us full ownership of all that we have, we can get carried away. Our ego will become a real problem, as the enemy is always around working on our ego. And our ego then eggs us on to take unwarranted risks and make bold gambles, because at the end of the day we think — even if we lose, we lose what is after all ours!

To me, this is not a responsible approach. As stewards of a business, we must always build on it. We must always manage and measure our risks, making our enterprise better than when we found it. At the end of the day, we want to ensure that the enterprise we are steering is robust enough to feed all the people whom we are responsible for, such as our family and the people in the company who work and serve alongside us, and, hopefully, for the Lord too.

Therefore, there has to be a reciprocity and responsibility which we may not embrace by thinking of ourselves purely as owners. But by thinking as stewards, we will. The apostle Paul, when writing to Timothy in 1 Timothy 6:10, hits the nail on the head when he says that "the love of money is a root of all kinds of evil".

Guard Against Covetousness and Greed

Business people do not like to hear this. As Christian businessmen, we wrestle with certain passages of Scripture. One of these is the parable of the rich man and the camel concerning the eye of the needle: "It is easier for a camel to go through the eye of a needle than for a rich man to enter the kingdom of God" (Matthew 19:24).

But, of course, there is hope for all of us because at the end of the day, with God all things are possible. With man, some things may be impossible, but with God all things are possible. Through the passage in 1 Timothy 6:10, I believe that Paul is reminding us to guard against covetousness and greed, which may seize us when we operate a business and want to do well. Almost instinctively, for those of us in business, we are covetous and want more, as a result of our fallen nature. We are also greedy, wanting to accumulate and acquire more than what may be justifiable.

I thank God that my enterprise is very robust. I need not go for the last dollar. I accept that some people may not be in this happy situation as they operate on a different scale where every dollar counts. But to me, the basic point remains that we must guard against covetousness and greed. So when my company looks at projects today, a key consideration is to provide value for our customers as well as to make our enterprise even stronger.

One may ask where to draw the line between covetousness and being good stewards? With our calling as developers and with the resources that God has given to us, how do we position ourselves to make good use of the talents and opportunities that the Lord has given us? Where do we draw the line between this and covetousness?

Here again, I go to the Lord in prayer during my devotion time to seek His will. For many of my projects, I make it a point to pray for the Lord's guidance. Likewise, when I submit bids at land tender exercises, I seek the Lord's will to prevail. Indeed, many times, my company does not win the bid but I still feel blessed because the Lord has shown that it is not His will for us to undertake the project. All of us in the marketplace will have to prayerfully consider where to draw the line for ourselves between being covetous and being good stewards.

Over the past five years or so, developers have done well in Singapore. It is a phenomenon that has occurred all over the world, with very low interest rates and high liquidity. Yes, we all have had a bumper time, blessed by God's grace. But how we now deploy our surpluses is really a big challenge facing us, bearing in mind our testimony for God in our work. This is what my company is working on: How do we meaningfully channel our surpluses and do things in accordance with the Lord's command?

In this regard, the book of Timothy has something to say in 1 Timothy 6:11, "But you, man of God, flee from all this, and pursue righteousness, godliness, faith, love, endurance and gentleness". 1 Timothy 6:17 then commands those who are "rich in this present world not to be arrogant nor to put their hope in wealth, which is so uncertain, but to put their hope in God". And in 1 Timothy 6:18 we are commanded to "do good, to be rich in good deeds, and to be generous and willing to share".

This is the challenge that I have, as a business person and Christian, to use surpluses accumulated to the glory of God, and at the same time, to be a vessel of grace for Him. Indeed, this is yet another key challenge I face — which is how to bring grace into the workplace and marketplace. It is not an easy thing to do.

Grace in the Marketplace

I planted this thought in my colleagues when I talked about grace at one of our Annual Company Dinners — the need for grace in the workplace and marketplace. As business people operating in the work context, we tend to be rather rules bound, rigid and "cut and dry" in our approach. We say that our enterprise is guided by Christian values and we are more open about the fact that we espouse Christian principles in the way we do things, yet we are not vessels of grace.

If we do not exercise grace in our workplace and marketplace, the expression of our faith becomes stilted. Here again, I must confess that I am still struggling with it; it is not something that we have fully achieved. Being successful in business is not just about measuring efficiency and effectiveness. The key is to derive an operating framework where law and grace co-exist, sitting side by side.

The exercise of grace has two dimensions: firstly, with regard to our employees and secondly, with regard to our customers. For employees, there are times when they are not well, when they are found not suitable for a specific job or assignment, when they are passing through a difficult period in life, or when they face family issues. How does the company, as a good employer exercising grace, help and support them to overcome these difficulties and tide them through these periods?

As for customers, how can we show grace? An obvious example would be when we grant a grace period for vehicles parked in our car parks. Another example is when we extend a grace period to our customers to make payments for their home purchases, especially when there are compassionate grounds to do so. For example, when a breadwinner, whether husband or wife, passes away just after signing the contract of purchase but before making the full payment, do we enforce the contract? Here, we have to exercise compassion and good judgement, presenting yet another challenge for me as a business person in the marketplace.

Unity in the Body of Christ

The final challenge I want to share is how to contribute to the unity of the body of Christ in the workplace and marketplace.

I am a baptized Anglican. I worship in a Catholic church with my wife who is a Catholic. I also worship in a Methodist church as my mother is baptized in a Methodist church and I accompany her to the Chinese service there on Sundays.

I feel that in the marketplace, there should be no denominational divide, or at least nothing that we cannot address sincerely and openly.

This is something I take upon myself as a project — building up the unity of the body of Christ in the marketplace. This is really what the extended church, so to speak, is all about — a church where denominational differences count for less. The marketplace is a good place to manifest this unity. In this vein, I commend Mount Carmel BP Church and the Bible Church, belonging to different denominations, for being pioneers in the sharing of your church complex, Clementi Bible Centre (CBC), here in the West Coast. That CBC was built and started services in 1985, 30 years ago, is a testimony of God's goodness.

On this note, I thank you and give all glory to God.

▪ ▪ ▪

Questions for Reflection

1

Where in the Bible can we find references to God and business? Does God approve of business?

2

How do we operationalize the practice of discipleship in the business context?

3

How does one reconcile the practice of grace in the workplace and the need to deliver results and excellence in business?

4

Can judgement and grace co-exist, both in the spiritual and earthly realms?

5

Can stewardship be an attractive proposition in the competition for talent in the corporate world?

Philip Ng is the Chief Executive Officer of Far East Organization, a family-owned property development and investment group operating in Singapore, Malaysia and Australia. Far East Organization operates as a Christian enterprise which seeks to be a community of love and a workplace of grace doing business guided by the eternal truth of Jesus Christ. Philip and his wife, Vy-vyen, have six children and they worship at the Church of The Holy Cross. His email address is <philipng@fareast.com.sg>.

FORTY YEARS AND COUNTING: MY PILGRIMAGE AS A PROFESSIONAL IN THE MARKETPLACE

Lim Hua Min

The Beginnings

I was converted at a Youth for Christ meeting during my pre-university days in 1963. At that age, you try to read everything. You try to discover yourself. I was hungry to know more about God. A Christian classmate invited me to his church and that was the beginning of my spiritual journey. God led me to commit my life to Him, the first to do so within my family. Thereafter, He touched my other family members over the next 50 years. Now I am 66 years old. God has been good!

How did I end up as a securities professional? After my engineering course in England and three years in Shell, I took the opportunity of joining the Singapore Stock Exchange as a research manager. Another three years lapsed before I was invited to join Phillip Securities as a junior partner.

Looking back, I can see the Lord leading me one step at a time. There was no shortcut. I could be found short, but God was always faithful. When we reflect on our own pilgrimage in life and try to measure ourselves, it is not so much a measure of success that counts but rather a measure of our own faithfulness to His calling. The parable of talents is a parable on the measure of our faithfulness.

Living My Life in Stages

Upon graduation, I joined the Graduates Christian Fellowship (GCF) and became active as a member and later as committee member. Between 1979 and 1982, I was GCF President and we were able to initiate the Bible Centre at North Bridge Road. Till today, my wife and I still participate in "SPIREN", a GCF Bible study group started some 60 years ago! I am thankful for the fellowship and friendship so graciously shared.

Life, in essence, is very much a journey lived in stages with certain milestones. The first 25 years is the "Age of Beholding" — beholding the wondrous things that God has created. You study, you learn, you discover and you go the second mile because somebody taught you something exciting. Wow! Aha! So you pursue mathematics, science, technology, literature, etc. All these excite you.

The second 25 years is the "Age of Becoming". During this period, you complete your studies, you start work, fall in love, marry, have kids and become a father. God has blessed me with four kids. All are working and two are married. I am now a grandfather of three grandchildren. In fact, I have just come back from a holiday in Japan with my Japanese in-laws. Singapore has become very globalized. My daughter married an American and now lives in Chicago. My second son married a Japanese girl whom he met in Singapore. During this second stage of life, I became a father, and I became a professional in the marketplace. At this stage, becoming the man that God wants you to be is the hallmark of success.

Now at 66 years old, I am in the third stage, the "Age of Being" — just being myself, reconciled to my Maker as a child of God, learning to relish the relationships that God has given me, working side by side with people God has put in my path. I continue working, running my own business but spending much time with people and appreciating them. Coaching, coaxing and mentoring are my current prerogatives.

A book my wife has written describes a commonplace scene I will never forget. A grandfather was having breakfast with his three or four-year-old granddaughter at a *kopitiam* in Middle Road. The grandfather ordered a cup of hot coffee for himself and soft-boiled eggs for his granddaughter. Evidently, the granddaughter was not happy, her eyes focusing on the grandfather's coffee. Noticing it, the grandfather then poured some coffee into his plate and passed it to her. Her eyes beamed with delight and her pair of hands lifted the plate to sip her coffee.

Would her parents have allowed it? No! Coffee probably is not good for a little child. But her grandfather understood that the little girl wanted to be like him. She wanted to be an adult like grandfather. The grandfather appreciated the essence of being. Hence the Bible, in Paul's letter to Timothy, exhorts us as older men to teach younger men.

Corporate Ethos and Corporate Code

CORPORATE ETHOS

Man, being created in God's image, is endowed with distinct gifts and talents in varying measure. Our high view of man demands that our organisation prevails upon each person to develop himself to his fullest potential by availing opportunities in training, service and responsibility. In the process of achieving our corporate goals, we will put every effort towards the complementation of individual gifts and talents such that the composite whole is greater than the sum total of its individual parts.

CORPORATE CODE

1. Man is created in God's image and therefore has tremendous potential.
2. We prevail upon man to develop his gifts by providing opportunities in training, service and responsibility.
3. We uphold integrity in our conduct. Honestly is telling the truth; integrity is fulfilling the truth.
4. We believe in the process of deferred gratification that rewards comes only after performance. A work well done brings intrinsic satisfaction.
5. We prefer to build businesses rather than trade and therefore would go for the long haul.
6. We see ourselves as stewards to one another, to our families, to our community and to our environment.
7. We are our brothers' keepers.
8. We will play only positive sum games.

When I started at Phillip Securities in 1975, I was 29 years old. As a young man, you really do not know very much. So you plod along. Over time, as you try to live up to your Christian faith, God speaks to you. In the process and in moments of epiphany, our company's "Corporate Ethos" and "Corporate Code" were drawn out, as shown in the charts above.[1] These are key life principles which have stuck with us for the last 30 or 40 years.

Twice a year, I conduct a five-hour session for all our new recruits, covering our corporate history and profile, and Corporate Ethos and Code. The latter starts with the very basic premise that God has created man in His own image. He endows man with distinct gifts and talents. Our high view of man demands that our organization prevails upon each person to develop himself to his fullest potential by availing opportunities for training and service, and the taking on of responsibilities. The diversity and complementation of gifts and talents allow for the expression of teamwork over individual efficacy.

"As our brother's keeper, we also act as gatekeepers."

The Corporate Ethos and Code embrace our company's worldview and values. The first and second codes acknowledge who we are. Codes three to five cover our conduct, the way we perceive and do things. We uphold honesty and integrity in our conduct. We believe in the process of deferred gratification. Work well done brings intrinsic satisfaction. The best reward is a job well done. We prefer to build businesses than trade. The Bible talks about generational transfer in terms of values and legacies, and we would therefore go for the long haul.

Codes six to eight give expression to our roles and relationship to all stakeholders. We see ourselves as stewards to one another. As our brother's keeper, we also act as gatekeepers. In the financial world, anything can happen quickly. Millions can be lost in a few minutes. When you sit next to a colleague daily and you sense that he is not acting normally, what would you do? Do you take the path of convenience and mind your own business? You are your brother's keeper!

God's Blessings in My Business

As CEO, I started Phillip Securities as a small outfit with a few partners. One partner subsequently passed away while another was made bankrupt because of his property business. I took over the business with my three brothers joining me over the years. In the early '80s, the Lord blessed and we started expanding abroad. In 1983–1984, we ventured into Hong Kong. Then, it was never considered Singaporean to invest abroad; some perceived it as almost disloyal to do so because we needed all the capital to create jobs.

In Hong Kong, we started from ground zero, buying a small office space and recruiting staff. Today, we operate one of the largest retail outfits amongst the hundreds of stock brokering firms. Since 1985, we proceeded to replicate our business in Malaysia, Indonesia and Thailand. Our preference is to be counter-cyclical, expanding when times are difficult. This year alone (2012), with many economies still weak, we bought four businesses in far-flung places like India, Turkey and Dubai. Would you believe it? And yes, Georgia — not Georgia, USA but Georgia in Central Asia, which was formerly part of the USSR. There, it was an investment in real estate.

Ever conscious of God's providence, we have never lost money as a group since our founding. People ask, "What has been your secret?" To manage any financial institution well, you only need to manage three variables — risk, expected return and liquidity. Risk is always commensurate with expected return — high risk, high return; low risk, low return. In an efficient environment, there is no free lunch. A great deal of research and scholarship had been done on the risk-return relationships. However, liquidity, the third variable, is often ignored at our peril.

Liquidity is multidimensional. One dimension is the narrowness of the spread between the bid and offer prices. Another dimension is the volume or quantity you can transact without losing on the bid and offer prices. There is also the dimension of time, by which you can complete your transaction. In practical terms, too often, we would have to cap the maximum size per transaction or the total exposure with any counter party, no matter how creditworthy. If the counter party delayed paying Phillip for whatever valid or invalid reasons, we could be in deep trouble.

Useful Business Concepts

From Charles Handy in his book, *The Age of Unreason,* I learn that there are only two types of errors in life: Type 1, not doing the right thing, and Type 2, not getting it right.[2]

In everyday living, the great majority of our errors are Type 2 ones. Type 1 errors are not common as God has provided us with enough common sense and moral compass. If you step out of bound, break the law, steal or you know you are not doing the right thing — these are Type 1 errors. If you are appointed to run a marketing campaign and it turns out to be a failure, is it a Type 1 or Type 2 error? Having a marketing campaign is normally the right thing to do (Type 1). The campaign fails because you are not getting it right (Type 2). If the error is Type 1, it is the higher management's responsibility. If the error is Type 2, it is your problem and you need help. Too often, when things fail (Type 2), there is the temptation to blame and make it a Type 1 error. When a couple divorces, do you think it is a Type 1 or Type 2 error? "She is not the right woman for me" — we tend to categorize it as Type 1. But actually, it is Type 2 — we are not getting it right. We fail to work hard at our marriage.

Another useful concept in management comes from Jim Collins and Jerry Porras' book, *Built to Last*. They introduce two different concepts to distinguish between companies that are successful and lasting, and companies that are less successful and temporal. Successful companies tend to "build the clock", while less successful companies tend to "tell the time".[3] If you are a very good salesman and work hard on your sales, you will do very well. But you are effectively telling the time because when you are no longer around, your sales will decline completely. If you are a good salesman and spend your time training and recruiting more capable salesmen, to the extent that you build a sales force or even a whole distribution system, you are effectively building the clock. When you build the clock, it will tell the time. You can of course build many clocks.

In management, there is always a perennial confusion between causes and effects, or what we call lead and lag indicators, or motivators and hygiene factors. If the toilet is dirty, everybody is unhappy. This is a hygiene factor. A better quality or cleaner toilet does not make us more productive and effective but we need a clean toilet. We have to provide the hygiene factor to ensure that people will not complain. However, when we run an organization, it is more important to concentrate on motivational factors. What are the motivational factors? It has to do with recognition; it has to do with acknowledgement; it has to do with trust and empowerment; it has to do with giving people a sense of purpose and direction where they are going.

In our society today, we have armies of people in organizations churning outcomes and results. When we look at our monthly financial figures or annual reports, we concentrate on results, results and results. But we do not have any report on the causes or drivers that lead to the results. What are the factors that bring about the results?

In management, I have learnt to use the four 'P's to draw out the causal factors — people, products, processes and platforms. The four 'P's have to do with implementation to bring about the results. Get the right people to do the job of driving and building the right products, processes and platforms. It is the efficient combination of these four 'P's that establishes results which are effective and efficacious. Building the four 'P's is effectively building the clock rather than telling the time. In management, concentrate on the four 'P's. Where do we identify the right people? What are the products we are offering? What are our value propositions? To ensure quality and reliable customer experiences, what are our processes and platforms? How do we build rhythm into our processes? Every organization needs to focus on the four 'P's. This includes churches and para-church organizations.

A Christian Worldview of Doing Business

I have been approached many times to sell Phillip. What makes me feel that I should not sell the company? If life is all about money, I would have sold Phillip long ago. I was enchanted by the idea of community and continuity. What is a company? It is essentially a group of people who choose to commit to one another for a common purpose. Over the years, together, we have nurtured quite a few leaders. The whole idea is to create community within the company so that this organism will have a life of its own. The idea of creating an organism beyond your lifespan proves alluring. To sell Phillip will only break up the personal bonds that have been so painstakingly forged. The personal must take precedence over the material.

The conceptualization of a worldview will give us a framework by which we can organize our lives and our business. When I was a young Christian, there was always a dichotomy between the secular and the spiritual. We separate these two spheres, treating spiritual as spiritual and secular as secular. They do not mingle. Later, I discovered that the Bible also has a secular worldview. In John 15:5, Jesus says, "I am the vine; you are the branches." In 1 Corinthians 12, we are reminded that the body has many parts and if "one part suffers, every part suffers with it; if one part is honored, every part rejoices with it" (v. 26). This is evidently a biological worldview.

Since the Industrial Revolution in the mid-eighteenth century, the civilized world cultivated a mechanical worldview. The world is seen as a machine, compartmentalized into many independent parts, working together to serve a common purpose. The conceptual view is convergent and definitive. This Newtonian worldview has prevailed upon us over the last few hundred years. It has influenced how society functions and even seeped into the way we run our churches and the way we conduct our lives. We tend to compartmentalize —church is church, career is career, work is work and family is family. No wonder then that we sometimes live our lives like Dr Jekyll and Mr Hyde.

It was an epiphany to discover that God embraces a biological worldview, which is more integrative and interdependent. The highest measure of us being interdependent is that we are a community of people that thrives on relationships. I recently read a very good book, *The Empathic Civilization,* by Jeremy Rifkin.[4] It talks about how society is moving towards empathy. What Rifkin argues for is that the poor and the deprived do not need our sympathy. What they need is our empathy. What is empathy? It is the ability to understand the other person as though you are in that person's shoes. This is something I treasure deeply. It is very real to me and I try to promote it through the biological worldview of interdependence.

Darwin published his theory of evolution in 1859, in the midst of the first Industrial Revolution. Allusions were made about the survival of the fittest, strongest or biggest. These ideas appealed to the business world in the twentieth century. But actually, Darwin highlights the survival of the most adaptable! Today, in business, we are being taught that it is about the survival of the most competitive. May I suggest that survival is not caused by any of the above. Instead, you survive by being the most collaborative. This is more aligned to the biological worldview, which promotes the essence of interdependency.

Today, because of the Internet, we talk about hubs and ecosystems. Amazon is an ecosystem of suppliers collaborating together to supply consumers with every imaginable item. Through collaborations, the Internet has created a multi-lateral network. Bill Gates looks at the world of computers and servers as a "nervous system". The Bible exhorts us to embrace a biological worldview that conceives of our total interdependency. We are conscious that whatever we do is not just an isolated action, but also one that impacts others. Even a butterfly flapping its wings can create a storm somewhere else. It is a world of interrelationships.

For my own business, I see the need to build networks and ecosystems. Twenty years ago, the word "ecosystem" was probably non-existent. Today we use this term as common parlance. Look at the tropical forest. I was told that one acre of Bukit Timah Hill contains more biological species than the whole USA! This richness and diversity is drawn from the interdependency of building a living ecosystem. Change is ongoing and at a fast pace; we have to keep up to cope with the bottom line. The Lord has called each of us to our own role and place. It is a personal and communal journey.

GCF once invited Sir Fred Catherwood, who wrote *The Christian in Industrial Society*,[5] to speak at our fellowship meeting on the topic, "Influence or Affluence". As young graduates then, we wanted to change the world. We thought that "influence" must be more important than "affluence". But instead of "influence" or "affluence", Sir Catherwood chose to speak on "servanthood". He pointed to the apostle Paul and the beginnings in many of his letters where he addressed himself as an apostle or as a servant of Christ. Interdependency involves the mutuality that comes from serving one another. His message sank deeply into my heart, and I feel humbled even today.

■ ■ ■

Questions for Reflection

1

What do you think of the three stages of our life journeys — the Age of Beholding, the Age of Becoming and the Age of Being?

2

Do you think you can introduce a Corporate Ethos and Code in your organization?

3

What is your worldview? Should Christians have a secular worldview?

4

Why are we often confused of the difference between "causes" and "effects"?

5

Ideas are cheap but execution can be tough. Where do you think we can go wrong on the four 'P's — people, products, processes and platforms?

Lim Hua Min is the Executive Chairman of PhillipCapital Group of Companies, a home grown stockbroking firm that has expanded overseas strategically. He has served on a number of committees at the Stock Exchange of Singapore (SES). In 1977, Hua Min was appointed chairman of SES' Review Committee which devised a conceptual framework to make Singapore's capital markets more globalized, competitive and robust. He was previously a board member of the Inland Revenue Authority of Singapore and also chairman and elder at Covenant Evangelical Free Church. His email address is <limhuamin@phillip.com.sg>.

IMPACTING THE MARKETPLACE FOR GOD

Patrick Liew

Facing Looming Failures in Life: Psalm 32

Let me start with this statement: I was one of the worst failures in Singapore.

If you are not looking for the most successful person, you have found the right person. In fact, my partner and our business story won an award for being the worst corporate failure in Singapore. This occurred many years ago when the Economic Development Board (EDB) realized that corporate failure was just as important as success. They wanted to recognize those who had gone through the worst business failure and risen again, like the proverbial phoenix (a legendary bird in Greek mythology which attains a new life by rising from the ashes of its predecessor). So they created an award called the "Phoenix Award", which was awarded to my partner.

How many of you have problems in your life? If so, I encourage you to read Psalm 32, a beautiful psalm. Each time when we feel down or are faced with a big challenge, we should turn to this psalm. Verse 6 of the psalm says: "Therefore, let all the faithful pray to you" (NIV 2011). And that means all of us in this room. Now please turn to the people around you and tell them that this verse is for him, too.

Verse 6 says: "Therefore let all the faithful pray to you while you may be found; surely the rising of the mighty waters will not reach them" (NIV 2011). When we are in trouble, we feel like we are going through a flood. Just as the water rises gradually, we feel like all our problems — disappointments, resentment, etc.

— are rising around us. How many of you have had these kinds of feelings before? This verse is for you: "surely the rising waters will not reach you". Why? Because "You are my hiding place" (v. 7). Isn't that fantastic? God is our hiding place. I am a visual sort of person, so I imagine that in the midst of a storm, when water is rising and people are throwing darts at us, there is this beautiful scene where there is a little cave with a warm fire and that is where we are.

Verse 7 says: "You are my hiding place; you will protect me from trouble." That is what God says He will do. He says that He will always be with us to the ends of the earth — "You will protect me from trouble and surround me with songs of deliverance". The interesting thing is that not only will He protect us and be our hiding place, He will also, if I may paraphrase this verse in today's language, "put us in a karaoke lounge to sing and party together". Isn't it beautiful? It's not just about being protected while you wait around for the rain to stop. God says that while there is a storm raging on, there will be a party and He will be there to party with you.

Verse 8 says: "I will instruct you and teach you in the way you should go." Not only will He give us a party when we are in trouble, He will also speak to us. If we open our hearts and minds, He will tell us exactly what we need to do. And not just in church, but also in the office, at the workplace and in whatever organization, club or society that we are involved in. On top of all these, He will surround us with His love. So this is the complete picture: God surrounding, sheltering, guiding, speaking to, loving and watching over us, and finally, God says, we all can sing with one mighty voice.

Almost Brought to My Knees by SARS!

SARS struck Singapore in 2003. Our economy almost ground to a halt, with the property market taking a steep nosedive. I was overseas on 21 March 2003 when I received a very urgent but interesting call that changed my life forever.

"Patrick, you'd better come back to the office, quick!" the caller shouted. I asked: "Why?" Another screamed: "People are carrying things out from your office!" I thought, "How can that be? This is Singapore, an island nation ruled by law. Such unruly behaviour cannot occur!" I put down the phone, feeling uneasy.

The following day, I returned to Singapore. I remember this day very clearly because I still have my passport bearing the date stamp of 22 March 2003. I went to my office on the same day. It was probably the second time I had retired from work as I had left it to a professional management team to run the business. By then, I could take time off from business to do charity work. Every month, I would be in some remote village building houses, roads and toilets, or digging wells. The management team had moved the whole office to an entirely new area without my knowledge, from a low rental one to a posh area in the Central Business District — Shenton Way, then the most prestigious business address in Singapore. We occupied one of the most beautiful commercial buildings on the ground floor — the most expensive level in a commercial building.

So I called the Managing Director and asked him, "Is everything okay?" He replied, "Everything's okay. Here's my envelope." When I asked what was in the envelope, he said, "This is my resignation letter. I am going to join your competitor. Some of the people are leaving to join me and we are going to leave very soon."

At that point my wife and I dropped everything and returned to work. When we audited the company, we realized that our revenue was shrinking fast, and even went below the cost line. We were losing thousands of dollars every day. My wife and I were also carrying personal liabilities to the tune of millions of dollars! We were bleeding to death. Thank God we were able to pull back in time. We cut losses and ended up losing eight million dollars!

Not only was I losing money, my staff were also leaving us. I did some soul searching as to why they were leaving. Was the company at fault? The first guy who left probably complained that the company was going bankrupt and was unable to pay his salary and commission. My colleagues were leaving the company in droves. It was most disturbing.

Every night, I cried myself to sleep. I cried incessantly until I could cry no more. To me, women are the stronger gender, and men the weaker one. That is why women outlive us. When they cry, they feel relief. "Macho" men try not to cry. In fact, if we do so, we feel much better! The worst situation to be in is when you want to cry but cannot do so. A Chinese saying aptly describes my situation then — "a half death" — you want to live but you cannot live on and death is not an option. For many months, I slept curled up like a foetus in the mother's womb! Every morning, when I walked out of the door, I felt like a zombie. If you were in my position, what would you do?

And Then God Spoke to Me

I did everything possible. I consulted every person I could get in touch with, speaking to classmates, army mates, coaches, mentors, business associates, professors, neighbours, relatives, friends, etc. I sought their advice. I read almost everything I could lay my hands on — books, journals, publications, magazines, even signage — just to look for answers. One fateful night I did what I think all of us would do, and you probably would have done it, but probably not with that kind of intensity. I had come to my wit's end, knowing that I would soon fall into a dark abyss. In despair, I fell on my knees. For the first time in my life, as I looked up to heaven, I screamed at the top of my lungs: "Help me, help, please help me, Lord, I don't know what to do now!"

Right at that moment, I felt Somebody speaking to me. I thought I had gone mad and was hallucinating. I felt Somebody telling me just two very simple words — "touch lives". The message was later further expanded: "When you go in to work tomorrow, treat humans as humans, bring out the best from them, so that they can give their best to their work and life. Be their friends as they journey in life, and help them to live a meaningful and exciting life".

When I had this feeling that I have to go in to work and treat humans as humans, I almost laughed. Of course we treat humans as humans! If we don't, what do we treat them as? But as we all know, do we really treat humans rightly? Because in society, humans are oftentimes a number or a digit, and in the business world, we are just a part of the business model, just a platform, a tactical tool. We even have a department called Human Resources. So when I heard that, I said, "Okay, Lord, if that's what you want me to do, then I'll do it."

After I said that, I felt God telling me that that was only part one and there was a part two to come. So I asked, "What is part two?" And then He said something to me that we are all familiar with, though it frightened me to the core. I shuddered when I first heard it. God said, "Go back to work and tell the people around you three very simple words — 'I love you.'"

For women to say "I love you", it's very easy. But not for men. We are not wired that way. It takes a lot from us to utter the phrase. At work the next day, I said to the first colleague I met, "I want you to know that you are very important; you are not just an indicator, a number or a resource; you are a human being. I want to bring out the best in you and help you do your best in life. " It took everything in me to muster up enough courage to look at him and say "I love you". I had to tell him that as I was not the perfect leader nor the perfect person, I needed him to teach me how to love him, to show me how I could help him feel love, warmth and compassion.

It was then that I started to write a love letter to all my staff. Every month, I would write a love letter. This led to a weekly love letter. When I discovered the power of social media, I sent them a daily love letter which I called "Love Byte". So, I sent every staff a Love Byte every day. Later, some of my colleagues joked with me, "Boss, please do not send me any more Love Bytes as I have been bitten all over already!" I replied, "Love is not just a word, love is an action. Love is not a noun, love is a verb. I want to show you how I can love you with concrete action."

I Love You!

The strange thing is that when I decided to do that, my company's climate and organizational culture started to change. I could feel the "atoms" changing. As I shared earlier, my office is at the heart of the Central Business District (CBD), which is a problem. Strategically, my real estate business should not be located in the CBD. When you drive into the CBD, there are many Electronic Road Pricing (ERP) gantries. Parking charges are also high and there are insufficient parking lots. Nobody wants to go there.

The saving grace came when I discovered that people loved to stay on in the office even after office hours. People did not want to go home. I then hit on an idea and converted half of the office space into what I called a "lifestyle office", sensing that an office should not be just a workplace but an extended home to have fun, to enjoy, to have a sense of meaning and satisfaction. I had a karaoke lounge, a billiard table, coffee and tea dispensers, TV — everything to make it very comfortable and relaxing.

At that point, my business started to turn around. Some people would just walk into my office saying, "I want to give you some business." In 2003, nobody would walk into a show flat for a viewing. Amazingly, out of the ten best-selling projects that year, about six of them were undertaken by my company. Many staff had left the company thinking it was going bust. As they saw that this was not the case, many re-joined the company. Our office was so crowded that I joked that if you want to faint, you have to wait until the end of the day when everybody has gone home!

In the following years (2003–2008), we became one of the fastest growing companies in Singapore, being number one in our industry. According to the Singapore 1000 and SME 500, we were ranked number seven then. We were the seventh fastest growing company, and by 2008 we were ranked number one for productivity as measured by return on equity (ROE). Shortly after, we publicly listed the company. Throughout the whole journey, we won about 45 business awards. Then, miraculously, three years ago on a Thursday evening, my banker contacted me and said there was a guy who wanted to buy over our company. I was overseas then. I flew back to meet him on a Saturday afternoon and within half an hour, my wife and I sold most of our shares to him.

Just a week and a half before that, my wife had experienced a prompting from God. She chairs what was then known as the National Christian Women's Conference, which brings women together for fellowship and mutual encouragement. She had been lamenting, "How can I go back to ministry? I am running a listed company. I cannot announce out of the blue that I will be selling my shares. The share price will tumble!" The funny thing is that shortly after I had encashed the cheque representing the proceeds of the sale, the property market crashed! Everybody told me that we were sharp and our timing was impeccable.

Actually, I did not time the transaction. In fact, I did not want to sell my shares in the first place. I had asked the purchaser, "Why do you want to buy my company?" And he replied, "I want to transform your company and take it in a different direction altogether." A few months later, I felt bad and wanted to apologize to the new owner. I told him that I did not know that the market crash was imminent. He said he understood for he was also a business person. Fortunately, he was very wealthy. He said, "You did not foresee that, neither did I. If I had foreseen that I would not have bought over your company. Anyway, I am taking your company through a different trajectory altogether."

Heartware, Hardware, Software, Soulware

I learnt valuable lessons from this episode. Let me now share them.

God spoke to me first about **heartware**. Every computer has a "heart" that drives it. When the Lord looks at us, He looks right into our heart. Where your heart is, there will your treasure be (Matthew 6:21). Where your heart leads you will be your destination in life. So the question I ask you today is: Why are you an employee? Why are you self-employed? Why are you a business owner? Why are you an investor? Why are you a teacher, a broker, a manager, a supervisor, a director or whatever vocation you are in? Why do you do what you do? For money's sake? Many people do many things for money, power, glory, livelihood, survival or success. Why do you do what you do? That is an important question to ask yourself. Colossians 1:10–12 says that you should shine or excel and witness with the work God has put you to do. When Paul wrote to the Colossians he was speaking to the people in the workplace and marketplace, in the government and public sector.

The second thing I learnt was about **hardware**. The computer is in a large part a piece of hardware. When God calls us to do whatever we do, the best way that we can love people is to help run the best managed company. That entails putting in the best structure, system and processes to ensure that everything is effective and efficient so that we get the most desired outcome. At that point, my company participated in all kinds of business competitions, not so much for the awards (although that was important as well) but to see how we measured up against our competitors, especially the best performers in our industry. What could we learn from them? Initially we did not win, but when we learnt why the others were so good, the awards gradually came our way.

"Where your heart leads you will be your destination in life."

We also delved into benchmarking studies to understand what "the gold standards" were, and the accepted yardsticks by which to run a company. Indeed, God called each of us not to be perfect, but to be excellent. There is a world of difference between being perfect and being excellent. Perfection cannot be achieved. Excellence, however, is an attitude of the mind. How do you do your work? How do you operate in the marketplace? Ultimately, we witness for Christ not just through our lips but also through our lives, our vocations and the way we live.

The third thing I learnt was about **software**. Every computer is run by software. The software in an organization refers to people. The second greatest

Commandment in the Bible is to love other people just as we love ourselves (Matthew 22:39). And when I say that software is the people aspect, I am talking not only about other people but also about ourselves, because it is the people in your organization that makes the organization work. It is the people in the government that makes the government work. It is the people in your team, your department that makes your team or your department work.

How do you treat people? Do you love people and use things? Or do you love things and use people? How do you actualize the second greatest commandment? It begins with loving ourselves. If we cannot love ourselves, it is going to be very difficult to love others. If people know that we do not even respect ourselves, it is very hard for them to respect us. So may I suggest that today, before the day ends, stand in front of the mirror and have a good chat with yourself. Tell yourself, "I love myself." And try to do it as often as possible. At the same time, share your love with the others.

When I was involved in charity work, I discovered that a lot of people gambled, including Christians. I currently co-chair the "Responsible Gambling Forum", which tackles social issues arising from addictive gambling. Out of ten Christians, four gamble! They find it hard to stay away from this vice. So tell yourself, "I love myself." Do it every day. Sometimes we unwittingly put curses on ourselves. We say, "I wish I looked better", "I wish I had a better body" or "I wish I was more intelligent". When we think this way, we unconsciously put curses on ourselves, as we tell ourselves, "I wish I were different."

In a 2011 study conducted in many countries, the Singapore workforce ranked at the bottom one-third in terms of happiness. In another 2012 study, 91 per cent of Singaporeans said that they woke up in the morning with no excitement, no passion and no enthusiasm for work. Why is this so? Because there are a lot of *lonely people* out there with their struggles, fears and unfulfilled dreams. If we do not reach out to them, who will?

The last thing that I learnt is what I call **soulware**. Every organization has a soul, so does every business and family. What is the soul of your department, your team, your company, the work that you do, the society that you join, the clubs that you are involved in, the people that you mix with? Our Lord Jesus Christ said that His calling was to do the will of the Father, and God has a will for you too (John 6:38–40). But this calling must begin at the workplace, where we spend most of our time, other than sleeping. While God calls us to also serve in church, we must not forget to discern God's calling for us at our workplaces.

The Six 'C's to Being a Leader

So, what is God calling you to do in your workplace? In my company, we have a "six 'C's" framework to being an entrepreneur and a leader. The first 'C' is **colleagues**. God miraculously gave us a building in Toa Payoh. At our peak, you would enjoy complimentary valet service if you were driving. According to *The Straits Times,* we were the first company to have such a service. We even had a childcare centre for all our staff's children. There were also a restaurant, gymnasium, al fresco dining area, function room, a spa and a hair salon where all our staff got free haircuts. There were even masseurs who gave free back massages and foot reflexology. We held health enrichment classes, conducted free medical check-ups and organized shopping trips, movie nights and overseas trips with families.

The second 'C' is **customers**. In the early 1990s, it was said that 70 to 80 per cent of transactions in the real estate business were either illegal or unethical, with names such as "silver bullet", "cash back" and "cash down". Hence, I made my staff wear a corporate lanyard with a code of honour that says that nobody is to commit any illegal or unethical act. Many colleagues, including fellow Christians, told me that if they were not allowed to make those transactions, they would be foregoing 70 to 80 per cent of the market share. They said, "Not only will I suffer losses, you will also be affected." My reply was that if I were to die, I would rather die gloriously. My family shall be proud that I did an honest day's work for an honest day's pay. Integrity is key. Integrity is first and last in a business transaction. So look after your customer.

By God's grace, I have helped to publicly list three companies in three different countries. Over a period of a month before each listing, anyone can write in to the stock exchange and complain about the listing. Many company bosses who have taken their companies public would undergo this "blame and shame" period. In business, one has "enemies" who can exploit this process. But, praise be to God, no complaints were made against me or against the public companies that I listed. I would like to believe that it is because customers and investors know that I stand for integrity, I believe in integrity and I practise it.

The third 'C' is **community**. I discovered that there are many lonely people in our community, living alone and sitting at HDB void decks. Just look around you. When the Lord came, He saw the hungry, the blind, the deaf, the lonely and the poor, and His heart was moved — His heart went out to these underprivileged people. Today, they are all around us. What is our response to them? Like most of us, I was quite oblivious to them, regarding everything as good in Singapore. Then one day, a colleague asked me, "Boss, I saw a lot of aged poor and lonely people out there. Is it okay if I bring all these people to our office cafeteria to enjoy a meal? I'll pay you $500 and we can prepare some food and hold a party for them."

At first, I thought he was joking. Where do we see old, poor and lonely people in Singapore? But not long after, I saw many elderly, lonely people, and they were so happy when treated to a meal at our cafeteria. I told my colleague not to pay me the $500; I would instead sponsor the whole event. We eventually ended up hosting 50 elderly people and spending much more money to serve them. We also went to their homes to improve their living conditions, brought them out on excursions, organized educational classes for them, brought them to parties and did things that they cannot do on their own.

The next 'C' is **country**. Our calling is that when we are in Rome, we do what the Romans do. This means that while we are first and foremost Christians, we are also citizens of this country. What do you do for the country? My Christian friends and I started an organization many years ago to train children. We trained about 20,000 students, and our volunteers now run our charity organization as effectively as any well-run business. And we do it in a very cost-effective way. This is because we do not have any office or a large staff, so there are no major recurrent costs like salaries or rentals. Basically, we outsource to contractors all the work that needs to be done. This way, we have trained 20,000 students, imbuing in them life skills such as money management, entrepreneurship, leadership, giving presentations and managing interpersonal relationships on an annual basis.

The fifth 'C' is **church**. The Lord impressed on my heart that I should go and plant churches. I said, "Lord, my job is to be a CEO, not to start churches!" I am a businessman and an entrepreneur, and our God is also an entrepreneurial God. Not in the sense of starting a profit-making business but in helping us see challenges and find solutions to them by thinking out of the box. So He prompted me thus: "You are a businessman, there are things you can do that nobody can."

That was how God, in His mercy, opened the door for me to help start a school of missions to train pastors. In this way, my wife and I have planted more than ten churches.

There are things you and I have learnt in the marketplace that can be used not only there but also to bless pastors. So I told them that I could not teach them theology, but I could share with them what the Bible says on managing organizations. I can share with them biblical principles on money management. In fact, the Bible has more verses about money than other topics. I do not believe in the prosperity gospel — God does not want all of us to be rich and wealthy. But if we do what the Bible tells us about money, we should never be in need. You should be able to live comfortably and raise the resources you need to fulfil your dreams and aspirations.

Besides working with pastors in the region, my friends and I have also been undertaking **crisis relief work** since 2003 (the last 'C'), whether it is the Asian tsunami, the typhoon in the Philippines or the nuclear power station crisis in Japan. My wife has also started a prayer house, something God had impressed on us to do. We not only want to encourage people to pray 24/7; she has travelled around the world to link up prayer warriors who now pray 24/7 for countries that are in crisis. As we prayed, God opened doors for me to preach in the strangest places to the strangest people. I have a Facebook page that I use to reach out to non-Christians, discussing topics and using words that they will understand and can respond to. Engaging them this way, I slowly expose them to the gospel. Thank God that through this, about 60 to 80 people have been brought to the Lord each year.

Overseas Opportunities Through Business to Testify for Christ

Being a businessman has opened many doors for me to share Christ overseas. I have just returned from China where I was teaching in a Bible school. As I taught, I felt that I lacked relevant practical applications in sharing the gospel. So I sought the organizer's permission to hold an evangelistic meeting. During the break time, I asked the pastoral staff to invite all their business friends to come for a session where I would share on tested business principles. At this meeting, when it was about to end, I invited those who could stay back to hear my personal testimony. I also shared about praying to God. When I asked them how many of them wished to open their hearts to accept Jesus Christ as their Lord and Saviour, almost everyone in the room put up his or her hand! Through this way, I also had the privilege of guiding nominal Christians and people in the business world to the Lord.

On another occasion, I was preparing to visit a Muslim country to attend a conference of pastors from all across the country. As I prayed, the Lord impressed upon my heart to study the rich history of that country. Just before the week-long conference started, the organizing pastor surprised me with an urgent request for me to be a speaker at the opening session. Being unprepared for it, I ended up telling the assembly of pastors about the history of their country and the wonderful things they had done. Can you imagine the audience's reaction? If you have a foreign guest speaker at a pastors' conference telling you all about Singapore's history — from the time Sir Stamford Raffles arrived and all the wonderful things that have happened — you would not be happy with me because I did not refer to the Bible and exegete any verses!

But later, the organizing pastor took me aside and confided, "You've created a miracle for us. The secret police were waiting to nail us, but you were saying all these wonderful things about our nation! They went away happy and never came back." From the second day onwards, we held the planned training programmes for the pastors and even ran evangelistic meetings every night. So, through this and other avenues, the Lord opens doors for people like you and me to do things that otherwise, would be difficult to do. Praise the Lord!

Psalm 32 Once More

In closing, let me quote Psalm 32:6–7, 11 again.

> *Therefore let everyone who is godly pray to you [LORD] while you may be found; surely when the mighty waters rise, they will not reach him. You are my hiding place, you will protect me from trouble and surround me with songs of deliverance.... Rejoice in the LORD and be glad, you righteous; sing, all you who are upright in heart!*

I remain ever thankful to God for my company's strong rebound from the SARS year. I want to acknowledge, with humility, that all that I have done has been possible only by God's grace and enabling. I am ever grateful and this is my motivation now to give of my time, experience and resources to supporting humanitarian, philanthropic and charitable causes.

▪ ▪ ▪

Questions for Reflection

1

How can you tap onto God's wisdom to enhance your work and results?

2

How can you demonstrate the love, joy and peace of God in your workplace?

3

How can you leverage your work to share the gospel with your colleagues and others?

4

How can you help to enrich Kingdom values in your organization's operational model, structure, system and process?

Dr Patrick Liew is a founder of Success Resources, a large personal development seminar organizer. He is also CEO of HSR International Realtors and a major shareholder of a company listed on the Australian Stock Exchange. Previously, he was the Executive Chairman and CEO of a public listed company on SGX-ST. Patrick serves in the community as Chairman of Junior Achievement, which provides life skill development programmes to more than 20,000 students, and as Co-chairman of the Responsible Gambling Forum. At the Grace Assembly of God, he is a member of the church board, missions board and management committee of the REACH Community Services Society. Patrick and his wife founded the Worldwide House of Prayer to encourage believers to pray unceasingly to reclaim the world for the Kingdom of God. His email address is <patrick@srpl.net>.

SERVING GOD FULL-TIME IN THE MARKETPLACE

Timothy Liu

I am here to encourage those of you who are gainfully employed. There are two misconceptions I wish to deal with. The first is that you can only do God's ministry or be involved in the church when you have financial and time independence. The second misconception is that you have to wait till "halftime" to be meaningful in life and ministry. That means wasting half your life, since your graduation from junior college, ITE, polytechnic or university. I believe that right from the very start, even as a student, we can be fully involved in God's ministry. Do not waste half your life thinking that you cannot be involved in ministry just because you have a full-time job or do not have the same kind of flexibility as somebody who is retired or semi-retired. Our full-time job should also be our ministry. And throw away the use of the word "retirement". There is no concept of retirement in the Bible.

Let me now share a little bit of my own journey. I did not grow up in a Christian family; I became a Christian when I was 12 years old. I did not attend church regularly when I was young. I became more serious in my faith only when I was in Secondary 3. I was involved with the church for a year or so, and then at the age of 16, I decided to further my studies. That was a challenging time for me socially, if not intellectually. I went overseas to the United States for my tertiary education. And at that time I felt God calling me into what I knew then as full-time ministry. I got very involved — preached my first sermon at the age of 18, and became the Adult Sunday School superintendent of the Chinese church that I was attending. I also became a student leader at the InterVarsity Christian Fellowship. But inside, I was very, very broken. At that time, my parents were not Christians (by God's grace, they are now). I felt very much challenged.

The first thing I did when I graduated was to go and look for a good seminary to study in. From Wisconsin, where I was an undergraduate, I flew to California, as I was excited about one of the programmes at Fuller Seminary. But then, I had to return to Singapore to serve my national service. I was not happy about it because I wanted to stay on, but had no choice. Again, God does strange things in our lives. I served in the army and really enjoyed my army days. As I was a clerk, there was not much to do. So, I got involved with the student campus ministry at Ngee Ann Polytechnic. I was an associate staff worker with the Fellowship of Evangelical Students (FES) and I spent many of my evenings interacting with and helping students. It weighed quite heavily on my mind that I should get involved with the pastoral ministry. But upon my Operationally Ready Date (ORD), I started work as a sales engineer for a local company, selling science instruments and data loggers. You could do amazing things with these instruments, which rekindled my love for science, particularly physics.

I enjoyed my work very much, but there was a tension. My then-pastor told me, "Go enjoy your work, but don't spend too much time in your workplace. The real ministry is in your church." But at the workplace, I was always finding opportunities to minister, because I was constantly interacting with professors, researchers and lab technicians. There were lots of opportunities to listen to their life stories as they shared them with me over coffee, and there were many times where I was able to share Jesus with them.

After two years, I managed to clinch a big project for my company shortly before I left. It was exciting to climb the corporate ladder and work in a multinational corporation, but I ended up going into a different field, the field of semiconductors. The interview went a little like this: "What do you know about semiconductors?" to which I replied, "Zero. I'm just willing to work hard." Guess what? I got the job! I was appointed as sales accounts manager. The first day I drove to work, as I pulled into this six-storey building, I felt God telling me that this would be my mission field. I had no idea then how this six-storey building was going to be a mission field. But within two years, we had started a Bible study group in the office itself. We grew from three people to about 20 to 30. We found a small corner and had regular Bible studies. We sang quietly so that nobody would bother us.

Again, I really enjoyed my work. I got to travel to Israel and see the Holy Land even though I was only a sales accounts manager. I continued to serve in my home church. During those days, I remember sharing with my wife the "crazy things" we did at the workplace. The most ridiculous things happened, yet at the same time there were opportunities for me to share Christ, to encourage somebody who was down, to do ministry work. After two years, my first boss called me up and told me an international company was looking for a regional manager, and asked if I was interested. I was, and the first thing I had to do was to fly to New Jersey and Canada to be stationed there for a year as an international training manager, to learn their vast product lines as well as conduct product training for customers.

This was when I started reflecting on my work life. I said to God, "I enjoy my work a lot, but why do I feel like a second-class citizen in church just because I am not a pastor or called into a foreign mission field?" So I studied the Scriptures and for a while I thought I was going bonkers until I found out that the Bible does not have any separation between the sacred and secular arenas. Paul was a tentmaker; he was working and making a living, and he was sharing about God as he went about his tentmaking. More than two-thirds of the characters that God uses in the Bible were not full-time ministers. I then realized there was no part-time Christian. We are all called to be full-time disciples! So now, when people ask if I am in full-time ministry, I joke and tell them I am in "overtime ministry"!

When I returned to Singapore, I started a ministry called Marketplace Christian Network, basically to teach a theology of work, helping believers to see themselves as full-time ministers and adopt their workplaces as their mission fields.[1] A lot of us do not understand that God has called us to be where we work, which is often also our mission field. Every time we step out of the church doors, we enter the mission field. We do not have to go anywhere — our life is a mission.

My primary calling, as I understand it today, is to be a salesman. My job is to sell vocational training and laboratory equipment to universities and polytechnics. I talk to the professors and see what they need to teach in the engineering laboratory. I then configure the equipment and experiments for them as much as I can. I travel throughout Asia doing this. I am proud of my primary calling as it offers tremendous opportunities for ministry. Sometimes, we fail to connect the dots between what we do and how we become part of what is described in Genesis 1:26, where we are called to have dominion over the earth, so that we are co-creators or co-carers of God's creation, caretakers of God's creation.

There are a few things I have done for my company that I am proud of. I have helped to create a whole line of products that teaches engineers about renewable and alternative energy. These are the best trainers, the most in depth that are currently available. We make good products, and I am proud of my company for that. So what does my work entail? It entails teaching the world and engineers how to conserve God's creation, the environment. We provide skills and training to students especially from Third World countries. We help to alleviate poverty; they learn skills that enable them to develop their countries. There is an element of poverty alleviation in what we do.

I was particularly interested in one project in Malaysia where I co-wrote a diploma curriculum, which was verified by a Canadian college. The concept was to take 'O' Level dropouts and put them in a training school so that they would have some skills. Otherwise, they would probably have gone on to become drug addicts. My agent and I sat down for almost two weeks. We had paperwork the size of a small mountain just to get through the project.

It is tough work and I have no fantasies about the reality of being in the business world. Especially when working in Asia, there are a lot of challenges and issues. In and through my travel, I meet up with fellow brothers and sisters in Malaysia, Thailand, Philippines and so on, and we start talking about our professional lives, how we live out God's calling as we walk through life. Those times of encouragement become a place where I share and teach a theology of work. I do it in Singapore and throughout the region, which I believe is part of God's call. I fly to different cities for work, and in the evening when I am free, I call up friends and meet them for dinner or coffee.

Sometimes, I have to take leave and pay for my own airfare. This March, I was invited to a Christian university to speak at a missions conference for 8,000 students. I was very encouraged by one of the students who told me, "Thank you. I thought I had to become a pastor. Now I know God has called me to be a teacher. I won't go to a prestigious school. I'll go to the slums, to the poor neighbourhoods of Los Angeles, and I'll be a teacher there. Thank you for the encouragement." I cried, because this is what God has called each of us, including that young person, to do.

In our daily lives, we can do God's work in and through what we do. We do not have to wait till something happens; the key is to be intentional in how we live our lives. The Graduates' Christian Fellowship (GCF) is a natural platform for me.[2] I served as GCF's president for many years (2007–2014), encouraging professionals to see their work as a calling, and exploring how we can promote social justice, how we can care for the marginal folks in our society, and how we think Christianly about topics such as population and urban renewal.

Some of our people are involved in bioethics committees and we try to be a bridge between professionals and church leaders. We network with other organizations such as the National Council of Churches in Singapore, Love Singapore network and Evangelical Fellowship of Singapore. This past year, we have been very involved in trying to think through what it means to be a citizen of Singapore. We have held national conversations and explored how Christians should engage in the Public Square and so on. Recently, some of you would have heard of the Lesbian, Gay, Bisexual and Transsexual, or LGBT issue. There are efforts to publish a paper that is balanced. These are the various things we do at the local level.

> "In our daily lives, we can do God's work in and through what we do."

Regionally, I work with the East Asia Graduate Conference, and we link up with other Graduates' Christian Fellowships throughout the region. I am involved with some of the leadership planning. In August, I will be helping to facilitate the Leaders' Track for the East Asia Graduate Conference. I am also involved in the Lausanne Committee for World Evangelization.[3] As one of the Senior Associates for the Marketplace Ministry, I help Christians link their faith and work.

I hope what I share encourages you. I am just a simple person. I do not think I am extremely smart. I do not think that I am any better than any one of you seated here. Probably some of you are more highly educated than I am or more articulate than I am. But what I am saying is this: wherever you are, God can use you, whether you are gainfully employed or happily "time and financially independent". I would like to counter Peter Drucker about this whole world of choices. Yes, in a sense we do have a lot of choices, but more and more we will see these choices diminishing particularly if we are PMETs (professionals, managers, executives, technicians).

The world is changing very fast. The attrition rate is the highest among PMETs who are 40 years old and above. I am right at the edge of 40 years. We have groomed an entire generation of engineers who are now turning to become taxi drivers. Is it a bad thing? Not necessarily so. But how do we begin to face the challenges that are coming? I do not think Singaporeans are very well prepared for that. You do not have to wait to make a significant impact in the world. You can start where you are right now, gainfully employed or not. The only question is how we seek God intentionally to serve Him where we are today.

■ ■ ■

Questions for Reflection

1

In what ways have you lived your life separating the sacred and the secular?

2

Have your witness in both word and deed at the workplace been representative of God's Kingdom values?

3

How can you live missionally at your workplace?

4

Are there ways you can influence or change the culture at your workplace to be more aligned with God's purposes?

Timothy Liu served as President of the Graduates' Christian Fellowship for seven years before stepping down in 2014. He founded the Ministry for Marketplace Christian Network in 2001. He is also a Senior Associate for Marketplace Ministry at the Lausanne Committee for World Evangelism and Council Member of the Biblical Graduate School of Theology. In church, he is a deacon involved in the Care Group ministry. His email address is <timliu@marketplacechristian.net>.

CHALLENGES AND ISSUES BEING SALT AND LIGHT IN THE MARKETPLACE

Gregory Vijayendran

I want to share with you about "Challenges and Issues Being Salt and Light in the Marketplace". A number of the points I will be raising are familiar to you at a cognitive level. But what I want to do here is to share some anecdotes from my own life and walk in the marketplace. I share these with you in humility, knowing that the journey for each of us in the Lord is unique. The way that these find expression in our lives and the way each of us overcome these challenges that we face in the marketplace will be different. Nevertheless, I hope that what I share will encourage and inspire you in your own journey.

There are seven points I wish to cover. I'm not going to devote equal time to all of them. Some are more important than others. I will share about purpose, passion, perseverance, the pitfall of pride, pressure, passing the baton and finally, prayer.

Purpose

Every one of us, young and old — whether we have just started on our careers or we are older, more senior, mid-career, or at a stage where we are in leadership positions in our various organizations — have a powerful destiny and purpose. One of the things we need to combat, especially in difficult seasons at our workplaces, is purposelessness. Times when we cannot sense the direction and meaning of our lives. I believe that purposelessness is the reason why some men go through what is known as mid-life crisis. We need to take to heart the opening words of *The Purpose Driven Life*: "It's not about you".[1] It's not about any of us individually. Personal fulfilment, satisfaction and meaning can only be found by understanding and doing what God has placed us on earth to do. So it is not about our purpose but rather God's purpose for our lives. The biblical verse that supports this is Acts 13:36a: "For when David had served God's purpose in his own generation, he fell asleep".

This verse tells us that we are called to serve God's purpose wherever we are, whatever our work may be. I believe that each of us has a unique purpose bigger than ourselves, that is within a certain specific window of history, bound in a place that we are called to be at. Acts 17:26–27 (NIV 2011) reminds us that:

> *From one man he made all the nations, that they should inhabit the whole earth; and he marked out their appointed times in history and the boundaries of their lands. God did this so that they would seek him and perhaps reach out for him and find him, though he is not far from any one of us.*

There is a general purpose found in Matthew 5:13–16 about being "salt and light". Sometimes we may find ourselves in a setting where we as Christians are the minority. We then wonder: what good can we do? What change can we bring? Can we be used by God as instruments of righteousness?

Be encouraged to know that it does not take a lot of salt to bring out the flavour in our food. Sometimes, it just takes a little bit of salt that has not lost its flavour to make a big difference to the taste of the food. In a similar vein, we are called to let our light shine before men.

Alongside this general purpose, I believe that God has a specific purpose wherever He has placed us. I want to share from my own career journey. I started in a major law firm, as a pupil of one of Singapore's top litigators. I learned much of my early craft in litigation and dispute resolution by watching him in action. At one point, I was his key research associate. After about five to six years, I felt the Lord saying very clearly to me that my season in that firm was over. So I gave notice. When I did, my mentor came to my office and asked whether I was leaving. I said, "Yes, my season here is over." It was a bit difficult to tell him that God had spoken to me! This was without having any offers on the table but just knowing (in a deep place) that my purpose at my workplace had been accomplished and there would be something else in the pipeline.

I waited on the Lord, and He said, "Don't apply anywhere." Even then, word soon got out in the market and three offers came. I went for interviews and two of them were actually quite promising. I felt the Lord telling me to say no to two of them. And so I ended up in another major law firm, where I spent a decade.

Soon after I started in this second firm, I began to ask the Lord, "Why am I here? What's my spiritual purpose?" It wasn't apparent straightaway. I was still doing my work, preparing cases, going to court, advising clients, practising commercial litigation. It only became apparent about a year into that new firm what my spiritual purpose was. I was then starting to have opportunities to connect with other Christians. As part of the ministry to the Christian lawyer fraternity, I was encouraging Christian lawyers to set up prayer groups in the law firms they were in and to gather together as believers to build each other up. These groups did not start as big groups; some were just small Bible study or prayer groups.

As I shared with my other believing colleagues in the firm, we decided to set up a prayer group and meet every Friday for lunch, where we would share testimonies and pray for each other. It was just for that one-hour lunch slot. But we committed to be faithful and meet weekly. The Lord then impressed on me that this was my purpose — to help set up this prayer group. When I left the firm in 2007, it was with great joy, as the prayer group was still carrying on and others had stepped forward to lead it.

Our spiritual purpose at work doesn't have to be something super spectacular. It can be something as simple as being a part of a group that sets up a new work of God in your workplace. I believe that as we came together to pray and encourage each other, it made a difference. Many such groups began to spring up in other law firms. People began to see that it was important to pray — for their firms, bosses and situations in their colleagues' lives. By drawing from this example, I want to illustrate the idea of purpose. As I look back, I am persuaded that the greatest spiritual purpose I had was to set up that prayer group, which continued to meet long after my departure from the firm!

We cannot expect God to work in the same way He had worked His purposes for us in the past. When I left as a more senior lawyer ten years later, surprisingly, I was blessed with even more job offers. This time, the Lord taught me about being discerning. This involved listening to Him in prayer and finding counsellors who offered words of wisdom. This process of discernment led me to my present firm. In this new firm, my purpose was not to set up a prayer group. Instead, I stumbled onto the new spiritual purpose "accidentally" as I began to see this picture of how God was shaping my legal team.

It started off as a mix of Christians and non-Christians, and slowly there were more Christians. With these young believers, I had the privilege of mentoring them. Once, in a project team where all team members were Christians, we prayed together as a group right outside the court for the outcome of the case. Shortly after we went inside the courtroom, the plaintiff informed the court that she wanted to withdraw the case. It remains a privilege and a responsibility for me today as the younger ones look to me as a mentor and a role model. I have a golden opportunity to show them how a Christian lawyer behaves. I am not perfect and still stumble but I have the privilege of leading and showing them what it is like to practise in a godly and different way.

Let me now share how God led me to serve in the Law Society of Singapore. For the most part of the last 15 years, I have been privileged to servant-lead Christian lawyers. I have always seen myself as a pastor to Christian lawyers. Some junior lawyers would come to me, saying, "I'm at a crossroad. Can we meet for coffee? I want to share with you my struggles and have you pray for me." Praise God for the work He has done during those sessions, even though I couldn't always discern the impact immediately. I had also been asked to consider serving in the Law Society but had consistently rejected the overture as I was not interested in "politics". Indeed, I was very content for a long time with being a "pastor" to Christian lawyers.

In 2012, I got a call from a mentor asking me to consider standing for the Law Society elections, to throw my hat into the ring. I said, "Let me pray about this," and gave an equivocal response. Shortly after that, I attended a conference in Hawaii called "Transform Our World", organized by Ed Silvoso's ministry, and my mindset underwent a paradigm shift. One of the things that God impressed on me as I heard testimonies from around the world was that Christians in the marketplace are often called to be pastors of the organization, profession or place of their calling. I realized that there are many needs within the law profession. Besides Christian lawyers who need to be pastored, there are other lawyers who are hurting (in a variety of ways), facing unjustified complaints, wounded or discouraged. So I asked God to provide a sign by having my mentor call me again after I got back from the conference, if this calling were from Him.

When I got back, my mentor called me again to ask me to reconsider. I knew then that this was from the Lord. He had also given me a Kingdom attitude by that time. I stood for election, and by God's grace, received the highest votes in the Senior Category. This was not because I was great or popular but because it was God who wanted me to serve Him on the Council. It was not about power or prestige. Instead, God had given me a pastor's heart, not just for Christians, but also for the wider pool of lawyers. And there are ways this calling has begun to manifest.

Recently, there were a few lawyers who were wounded and discouraged. Some of them asked to meet up. I met up with them over lunch and they shared the wounds in their lives. This particular small group had faced complaints and felt so hurt, even though they had ultimately been vindicated and the complaints found unjustified. The Lord used that opportunity for me to speak about forgiveness to this multiracial and multi-religious group and they began to receive that. I asked them to take the opportunity to step forward and defend other lawyers too. God began to use that moment to impart purpose to the lives of others. God changed my pastoral heart — from being a pastor of Christian lawyers to being a pastor of the legal profession. This is how I want to illustrate that God can give us a sense of purpose, not just in an organization, but also in the profession we are based. We can be salt and light in the season and place we are called.

Passion

The second 'P' is for passion. Here, let me quote Steve Jobs from the famous commencement speech he gave at Stanford University on 12 June 2005:

> *I didn't see it then, but it turned out that getting fired from Apple was the best thing that could have ever happened to me. The heaviness of being successful was replaced by the lightness of being a beginner again, less sure about everything. It freed me to enter one of the most creative periods of my life.*[2]

Getting fired freed him into one of the most creative periods of his life. You've got to find what you love. The only way to do great work is to love what you do. Jobs, of course, shares from a secular perspective. But there is profound truth in loving what you do and coming to that place where you have passion for the work that God has entrusted to you. It is something that Christians can have because the Lord has given us a passion to excel in our performance, to do our work wholeheartedly as unto the Lord, and not unto man. And so, this aspect of passion is an area in which we need to continually examine ourselves.

There are some challenges to passion. The first is talent alignment. We need to ask ourselves if we are in the right job for our gifting and talents. I was with a believer who leads a company focused on matching people to jobs based on their talents. It is very interesting how they try to align people to their talents. He said, for instance, that when they looked for receptionists for one of the clients (a six-star hotel), they looked for people who smile naturally. The point is to align people to their gifts. Sometimes, we do not have passion because we are not aligned with the talents or gifts that God has given us. We need to examine that.

The second challenge is this: we tend to lose passion when we let it become dissipated by over-thinking things. Essentially, "paralysis by analysis". We do not let God's passion drive us to do something when we begin to over-analyse aspects of each decision and end up paralysed by inaction. A strong quality of masculinity is doing things. God is calling us not to sit idly on our chairs but to be actuated by His passion. It is the love of Christ and the compassion He gives you that begin to constrain you (2 Corinthians 5:14).

The Bible provides a warning to us men about failing to act. This is the Genesis account about what happened in the Garden of Eden. Eve took the fruit after being tempted by the serpent, and she gave it to her husband "*who was with her*" (Genesis 3:6; emphasis added). Adam was actually next to Eve! Adam was guilty of not intervening. So husbands, when you see a snake talking to your wife, be sure to intervene! But the point is a broader one. Sometimes we suffer for the sin of omission.

The third challenge to passion occurs when we lose our childlike quality. Jesus says that if we are to enter the Kingdom of heaven, we must humble ourselves like a little child (Matthew 18:3). Not to be childish, but to be childlike. There is something about children — their enthusiasm, innocence and curiosity — which we must continue to have if we are to stay passionate. As Steve Jobs said in that famous Stanford commencement address, we should "Stay hungry. Stay foolish".[3]

For the Christian, there is a powerful truth in Ecclesiastes 5:19. The ability to have joy in the work of our hands is a gift of God. God wants us to have that joy restored for those who have lost it. God looked at His creation, and He said that it was very good (Genesis 1:31). There is definitely that rejoicing and natural passion when we create and do something. I believe a significant part of man's sense of self-achievement is found in the workplace, just as it was for Adam who was created to tend the garden. We need to do that work in the pleasure of God, in all that we do.

Some of us have seen *Chariots of Fire*.[4] There is a scene where Eric Liddell talks to his sister, Jenny. His sister asks him why he was not involved in Christian work, preferring to run. Eric says, "God made me fast, and when I run I feel His pleasure." Now, he probably did not say those words but it makes for a great movie! Nevertheless, we know that it is true; we need to experience the pleasure of God in all that we do. If we are aligned with our talents where we are called, and as we begin to be faithful to that purpose, God will give us the passion or joy in the work of our hands, even if on the surface our jobs look like a very dry, dead place.

Let me now share a story from my own journey. In the second firm that God placed me, I was made partner in 1999. At the time, we had a Law Society directory, and the firm took out a full-page advertisement. In this advertisement, the firm advertised another partner and me as having expertise in "Wills, Probate and Administration". I looked at the partners listed under "Commercial Litigation and Appeals" and said, "Wait a minute, I'm more experienced than some of the partners listed under that!" I looked at it and thought, "I deserve to be there!"

It seemed like I had been given a second-tier practice area or sidelined. Part of me was welling up (or perhaps swelling up!) and I wanted to go to the managing partner and tell him he had made a mistake. That was my initial reaction, but I took it to God in prayer straightaway. As I did that and submitted this potential point of bitterness to the Lord, He began to deal with me. I believe He often wants to deal with us first before He deals with the situation. He showed me this is part and parcel of His hand in allowing the advertisement to go out that way. God impressed upon me that He was behind everything — a promotion comes from the

Lord, not from man (Psalm 75:6); God decides who He wants to appoint, where and when; and He is more interested in our hearts and motives.

As I began to give thanks to God, He changed my attitude and I started to see things from a new perspective. And the perspective was this. Over and above all the goodwill and good reputation I had already been blessed with at a relatively young stage of my career, with many clients approaching me directly instead of indirectly via the firm, the firm had now seen it fit to promote me as a specialist in wills, probate and administration! This was not a minus; it was a plus! So when God deals with our attitudes, we start to see things from a new perspective. And so, no, I did not end up going to my managing partner to tell him that he had made a serious mistake.

The story does not end there. About five years later a book came out which many litigators consider the "Bible" of civil litigation. The editors of that book, *The Singapore Court Practice*, sought out lawyers to write the various chapters. The commissioning editor called me and said, "We are planning a chapter on the rules relating to wills and probate, and we saw that advertisement which said you have subject matter expertise on wills. Would you be willing to contribute?"

Note that this is the leading book in Singapore on Civil Procedure! "Would I be willing to contribute?" It was a no-brainer! I knew it was the Lord's blessing for having the right attitude. I ended up contributing to the relevant chapters. And the blessings continued. I was appointed the inaugural subject coordinator for the elective of "Wills, Probate and Administration" for the Part B examinations. A third of the law students have to take this paper to be called to the Bar. It is your attitude that will determine your altitude.

The additional point here is that God can give you the passion if you align yourself to where He wants you to be. Even areas that seem dry and dead (or a dying subject like wills!) can become a place of blessing as God gives you His heart.

Perseverance

The third 'P' is perseverance. Earlier, I mentioned Eric Liddell, who was an Olympic champion runner. But what happened thereafter? After that gold-medal-winning race, he became a missionary to China where he continued to run his spiritual race well. I remember when I was in school, my Christian Union teacher told me, "Be a sticker, stick to what you do." I do not know about the rest of you, but

I am prone to giving up and moving on if I do not see results in what I do. Jesus speaks about the quality of perseverance in Luke 18:1 in the parable of the persistent widow. In Galatians 6:9, Paul tells us not to be weary in doing good.

The metaphor of a race appears many times, in verses such as 1 Corinthians 9:24 and Hebrews 12:1. The "great cloud of witnesses" is like the spectators in a great Olympic stadium. We are called to run the race and finish it as in 2 Timothy 4:7. This is not a sprint but a marathon. It calls for perseverance, especially when we do not see results. As we know from the parable of the talents in Matthew 25:14–30, it is not about the talents we do not have, but whether or not we are found faithful with the talents we have. We want to hear that commendation from the Master, "Well done, good and faithful servant".

> "Faithfulness and fruitfulness go together."

Now, let us not swing to the extreme end of the spectrum and think that "we don't need to be successful at all; let's just be faithful". If you look at the passage carefully, there was also a reward that came with the faithfulness. The ones who were faithful were given more responsibilities. We too will be appointed with more influence and responsibilities in God's appointed time if we are found faithful. Faithfulness and fruitfulness go together. So I think the challenge for us is to take to heart what Winston Churchill told his audience once: "Never give up! Never give up! Never give up!"

At times when we feel the hardest hit, we are called to persevere. Moreover, as Christians, we are called to ask ourselves whether it is God or our own heart's desires calling us out of our firms or organizations. It is so easy to be seduced by our desires for money or power, but we need to discern God's purpose. For the place He has appointed you to, have you finished there? Have you completed what He had planned for you to do in that setting?

I believe that for the Christian, when He calls you out of your place of work to somewhere else, it is because there is either an enhanced ministry or there are some other positive things He may be doing in your life, like teaching you to have a better work-life balance. For the believer, I do not believe that money per se, or the trappings of a glamorous title or position are sufficient reasons to move. It may be part of the package or part of the incidental benefits. For the believer, the Word of God tells us in Acts 17:28 that "in Him we live and move and have our being". That means that sometimes we are called to persevere where we are. It is funny how at those times when I feel the most discouraged at the workplace, I get a call from a headhunter or hear about an opening elsewhere! The devil knows exactly when we are most vulnerable to being tempted. That is precisely when we are called to persevere and be faithful wherever God has appointed us.

Pitfall of Pride

The fourth 'P' is the pitfall of pride. Many of us know about this. The pride of life is referred to as one of the trilogy of sins in 1 John 2:16 — "the lust of the flesh, the lust of the eyes, and the pride of life". We know from the Bible that Eve fell into the trap because she wanted to be as wise as God (Genesis 3:6). The devil's incarnation is because of Lucifer's pride. Another example comes from Nebuchadnezzar, who thought that he was God (Daniel 4). We need to guard our hearts, just as the Word of God says in 1 Peter 5:5–6. It is my belief that this is a major battlefield for many of us men. We have an ego. This morning, for many of us who struggle with this, we need to say, "Ego be gone!" and ask God to remove that pride from us and let Him instil the humility we need in our lives.

The question is, what is humility? We often mistake true humility from false humility.[5] C. S. Lewis says, "True humility is not thinking less of yourself; it is thinking of yourself less". That is a profound insight. When I came back to God from a season in the wilderness in 1995, He was dealing with me in a series of revival meetings by showing me layers of pride in my life. I believe that God wants to deal with us even in subtle areas of pride, such as not wanting somebody's help, or false humility (where we secretly yearn for the praise of others). This is a constant war zone and we need to guard our hearts. I believe there are three things God wants us to understand to overcome this pitfall of pride.

The first is to come to a proper understanding of submission and authority. If you study the way David responded to Saul, it is a classic picture of godly submission to authority, even to an ungodly figure. What if you are the person in authority and you have an Absalom under you — how do you respond? Again, look at David's example. There is an excellent book which really guided my thinking as a young believer called *A Tale of Three Kings* by Gene Edwards.[6] It is a deep reflection which shows you true brokenness and submission to authority as well as how to respond when there is somebody under your leadership who is not submitting. I believe that, as men, we need to understand issues of submission and authority to avoid being a Saul when in leadership and an Absalom when God has placed you under leadership.

The second is to receive rebuke. My wife and I have a marriage altar. For a season, we went through the book of Proverbs as we prayed for our marriage. With 31 chapters, it is one chapter a day for each day of the month. It is interesting how Proverbs say so many things about rebukes. I feel that, as a body of Christ, there should be more space for loving rebukes. We need to speak the truth in love to one another. I do not think the depth of love that God wants us to have is namby-pambyism. I have thanked God many times for the people in my life who have rebuked or corrected me. Of course, we do so in love!

Recently, I was ministering to a young Christian lawyer. I was praying with him as he was struggling in the workplace, unsure about aspects of his ministry. As we prayed, I thought it was a one-directional ministry. Then before we ended and I left, he said, "I'm going to share something with you in love." He told me he had received feedback from a lawyer who worked with me that since I had gotten married, I had been edgy! The natural instinct for me then was to think, "Wait a minute, this is a young Christian! He shouldn't be the one giving me feedback; I should be the one ministering to him!"

But then I realized that God can speak through anyone; He can even use a donkey to rebuke a prophet (Numbers 22:28–30)! As I began to reflect, I realized that since returning from my honeymoon, I had been on overdrive in the workplace and may have pushed some of my juniors more than I needed to. I realized that I had not done right. So, I called the junior lawyer who worked with me and apologized for possibly pushing him too hard. It would have been a very different outcome if I had rejected that rebuke! God can use anyone to speak to us and He can do so at anytime. We must keep our hearts open.

The third is to have a multitude of counsellors, for Scripture says that in a multitude of counsellors is a safety net (Proverbs 11:14). This is self-explanatory.

Pressure

The fifth challenge is pressure. I believe men are designed to cope with a high degree of pressure whereas women are designed to cope with a high degree of pain. Some even say men work best under pressure. I will not go into that, but there is a role for pressure in our lives. Some situations in our workplace that put us under tremendous pressure include assignments that are beyond our capability or instructions that are ambiguous. Sometimes the Lord allows us to undergo pressure in our lives so that we have the opportunity to display perseverance and be stretched. Through pressure, He refines us, creating a jewel from our lives and making us a vessel for Him. Pressure is another challenge we need to overcome in the workplace. We should not run away from it but face it relying on the Lord's grace and strength. Can we experience the pleasure of God even while we are facing the pressure from man?

Passing the Baton

Passing the baton is the next 'P'. I believe every man needs to have a Paul, Barnabas and Timothy in his life. A Paul to mentor us, a Barnabas to encourage us, and a Timothy for us to mentor. All three are valuable relationships involving different roles both by us and the other brother. In the Law Christian Fellowship that I have been privileged to lead, we started a mentorship framework where senior lawyers mentor junior lawyers. I meet a few junior lawyers regularly, and we pray with each other and share our lives. The great joy I have is that God has turned the hearts of the senior lawyers to the junior lawyers.

God is also stirring something in the hearts of the younger lawyers to rise up and become "parents" themselves. I was very encouraged when I heard from the younger lawyers who now have a vision to mentor undergraduates and even teenagers. Some of them recently shared how they felt the call to minister to children of prisoners, divorcees, etc., aged from 12 to 14 years old. This is what the Lord does through this mentorship framework, so that the mentored can rise up and in turn become spiritual parents of their own. I am excited to see what God will do with this cascading mentorship that is starting to arise. I encourage all of you to respond in obedience as the Lord shows you whom He wants you to mentor.

We need to have a father's heart or the heart of God in us. I think it starts from the heavenly Father healing us from hurts caused by our own fathers. Not just biological fathers, but authority figures God has placed over us in the workplace. Some of us have experienced wounds. For me, God previously allowed me to have a father figure who was accusing and abusive in the workplace. What was the purpose? God showed me that part of it was to be able to understand and minister to others who have to endure an authority figure who is accusing or abusive. So we should not evade the "suffering" and bolt at the first opportunity. Sometimes God allows it so that we will experience the ministry of consolation from Him (2 Corinthians 1:4), so that we will have the comfort to comfort others. He may put us under apathetic, abusive, absent, authoritarian or accusing work-fathers because He wants to see our heart's response — how we respond to them. I believe that every one of us, single or married, is called to be a father in the workplace or ministry.

We also need to have a legacy mindset. We need to look beyond our lifetime and see what spiritual legacy we will leave behind. What are we going to leave for our children? What is the mark we are going to make?

Prayer

A final 'P' — prayer. Of all the challenges I have shared, this is the most foundational or fundamental area of my life. We must rise up as men of prayer, even in the workplace. We know that the great Mount Carmel victory and the many other miracles in Elijah's life were punctuated by prayer. An Australian intercessor once shared with me that in a church in Australia, the fathers came together to pray, and during that season, there was no divorce in the church. But when the men stopped gathering, the number of divorces rose. This is an outstanding anecdote. I believe that we are called to rise up like Elijah and pray the effectual fervent prayer of the righteous that avails much as in James 5:16. It is illustrated in the life of Elijah, who prayed for rain. The story of my career is still being written, yet as I look back, I see so many areas of my life transformed by the power of prayer.

One story I would like to share is that of a client referred to me by my previous big boss who was not a believer. I met the client and it was, frankly, a hopeless case. He had a default judgement entered against him for a sizable sum (over $200,000) because he had failed to appear in court to defend himself against the suit. In essence, his opponent got a technical knockout. The creditors wanted to apply to court to adjudge him a bankrupt. As I was sitting across the table from him in the 58th storey of UOB Plaza, this man said, "If I could jump out of the window here, I would do it." And straightaway the Holy Spirit told me, "I want you to pray for him after this meeting."

I thought, "Oh my goodness, if word gets back to my senior partners, I will soon be praying for something else ... a new job!" But I knew I had to be obedient. So when the consultation was over, I asked if I could pray for him. He agreed, and we prayed together. I believe it was a turning point because I sensed that God gave that man peace. Even though we were out of time to appeal when he came to us, we filed an application for an extension of time to appeal. That application was allowed and amazingly, in the subsequent appeal, the earlier judgement was set aside, based on a technical legal point, which we found by God's wisdom. But the greatest thing I remember from that case was not the wisdom to set aside a default judgement and avoid the bankruptcy proceedings. It was that special moment in that room when I prayed for someone in need and the Lord's presence and peace were palpable.

Another example was the AWARE (Association of Women for Action and Research) saga. I was then the legal advisor for AWARE. The Lord had opened up an avenue for me to serve as a lawyer during the meeting. I was independently appointed to give advice to the Exco and to the House on the conduct of the meeting, as well as on the legal effect of a motion of no confidence. My advice was that although legally the Exco was not compelled to step down, as a matter of convention, custom and common sense, they should indeed step down. That was God-given wisdom. I also want to share with you that the whole experience for me was saturated in prayer. Many believers were praying for me. At that point in time, this case was the most controversial matter with which I had ever been involved.

Looking back, I can see that my involvement was orchestrated by God. I was sitting there in the hall during the EGM. If I said anything wrong, I knew that I would be heckled. Potentially, hundreds of high heels could be hurled in my direction! Yet somehow, whenever a question came to me during the meeting, I seemed to receive a download of wisdom from the Lord to deal with it. The whole experience was surreal. As each lady took to the microphone to present their question, the Lord impressed on me to pray for different ones. And I said, "Lord, this is amazing. You didn't appoint me here just to be a legal advisor. You have a strategic role for me here in terms of intercession for all these women!" This is just another example of how God positions us for prayer and also to fulfil His purpose.

A final example of prayer that I would like to share is from my time at my second law firm. There I was, on my first day as partner in 1999, feeling all self-important. It is quite impressive to be a partner. You get your name on the letterhead, name cards reflecting your new status, and all the associated prestige. On the very first day at lunchtime, my secretary knocked on my office door. She told me she has an operation coming up, and asked me if I could pray for her. I thought, "Oh my goodness, it's my first day as a partner at a secular law firm and my secretary wants me to pray for her. If word gets back to my partnership, they might wonder about their choice to make me partner."

Again, I decided I had to be obedient to the Holy Spirit's prompting. So we went to the meeting room and I prayed a short prayer with her. As it turned out, she was healed very quickly during and after the operation. Indeed, I experienced one of the greatest joys at my workplace almost a decade later, when I had the privilege of leading her through the sinner's prayer to accept Jesus Christ as her personal Lord and Saviour. She remains my secretary till today. I believe that the pivotal point came when I prayed for her at her point of need. A simple prayer can sow seeds to win another soul for Christ. It does not need to be a prayer for some grand purpose or a prayer for deep needs.

▪ ▪ ▪

Questions for Reflection

1

What do you discern to be God's specific purpose for you in your place of work?

2

How have you taken prayerful and intentional steps of obedience to align yourself with that specific purpose?

3

Are your gifts and talents aligned with your job? If so, do you have joy in the work of your hands (Ecclesiastes 5:19)? Why or why not?

4

Are there aspects of your work or your work itself that you need to persevere on?

5

What are the specific areas of discouragement or pressure points that you need to take to the Lord Jesus in prayer?

6

Are there areas or forms of pride that could become a pitfall for you? Prayerfully repent of those secret sins and ask God to give you true humility.

7

Do you have a Paul, Barnabas or Timothy in your life? Are there persons whom you could prayerfully consider approaching to be a mentor, encourager or mentee? Prayerfully draw up an intentional plan to approach these individuals.

Gregory Vijayendran is a litigation and dispute resolution partner in the law firm, Messrs Rajah & Tann LLP. He is Chairman of the Law Christian Fellowship and a serving Vice President of the Law Society of Singapore. His involvement in community service includes being a longstanding former President of Club Rainbow and currently, Honorary Secretary of the Prison Fellowship Singapore. Gregory also helps churches and other voluntary welfare organizations improve their charities governance. His email address is <greg68sg@yahoo.com.sg>.

“Jesus replied, “Very truly I tell you, no one can see the kingdom of God unless they are born again.”

(JOHN 3:3)

GOD IN THE WORLD AROUND US

THE BIBLE AS HISTORY: MY CALLING AS A HISTORIAN

THE BIBLE IN HISTORY: MY CALLING AS A HISTORIAN

Ernest Chew

Let me begin by sharing my own spiritual journey. I was a Christian before I became a historian. How did I become a Christian? How did I become a historian?

The English historian E. H. Carr in his book *What is History?* pointed out that in order to understand the history a person is writing about, we should first know the historian.[1] In order that you may know the history I am going to share with you, let me share something of my own journey. It is important to know where a person is coming from. History is fact plus interpretation. You must know something about the interpreter who is interpreting all these facts.

I came from a wonderful Christian home, and I am always thankful for that. But one problem of coming from a Christian home is that you might assume certain things. So I assumed that I was a Christian just because I went to church and to Sunday school. My father, Dr Benjamin Chew, was a church elder.

As I dutifully attended church service and Sunday school, I began to have a different idea of who a Christian is, not just someone born into a Christian home. It is amazing how this happened. I still vividly recall the very first Sunday school class I attended, which my older brother brought me to. Mr Lauw Kim Guan was the teacher; the lesson was on John 3, on Nicodemus and about being born again. So I was introduced to the concept that you are not merely born or raised as a Christian, you need to be born again!

It was rather amusing because I was wondering why Jesus was talking to this girl called Valerie: "Valerie, Valerie I say to you". Of course you know how a child mixes up things; maybe I was a bit dyslexic. Jesus had said, "Verily, verily ..." which means, "Truly, truly ...". It is from Latin, "*veritas*", which means truth. "Truly, truly, I say to you, unless one is born again he cannot see the kingdom of God" (John 3:3, NASB). That was my experience in my first Sunday School class.

Later I learnt that God does not have grandchildren, only children. And how do we become children of God? It is through our personal relationship and faith in God. But it only really sunk in — strangely enough it was not at an evangelistic meeting when I made a decision of some sort — when I heard Mr J. Oswald Sanders from the Overseas Missionary Fellowship speak on Romans 6:1–2, "What shall we say then? Shall we go on sinning so that grace may increase? By no means! We died to sin; how can we live in it any longer?" Can we go on sinning so that God may give us more and more grace?

I was supposedly a Christian, raised in a Christian home, but I knew then that my life was not right with God. I was assuming and presuming on God's grace. Those verses turned me around. I then knew that I needed Christ, I needed God's grace and I wanted to be a "true" Christian.

This was the turning point in my whole spiritual life, not unlike John Wesley's conversion. Wesley, who also came from a Christian home, was so sincere in his spiritual endeavour that he started a "holy club" in Oxford with his brother Charles. He even became a missionary in America, but confessed later that although he tried to convert the Indians, he himself needed to be converted. When he returned to London, he was still very troubled. He went to Aldersgate Chapel, where someone was reading Luther's comment on Romans 1:16–17.

As Wesley heard this passage being read, "For in the gospel a righteousness from God is revealed, a righteousness that is by faith from first to last, just as it is written: 'The righteous will live by faith'" (Romans 1:17), he suddenly realized how God justifies and changes a sinner and gives him the assurance of salvation. On 24 May 1738, Wesley wrote that his heart was "strangely warmed" as he received the assurance of salvation.

After my own "conversion", I became very enthusiastic for the Lord and was led to witness and start a Bible study group in the pre-university class at ACS. When I was finishing my 'A' Level exams, I asked the Lord whether I should go to

Bible college. I sought God's will through godly counsel, praying earnestly over it and discussing it with Mr David Adeney and my father. Doors opened and closed as well. I entered the University of Singapore and studied in the Arts faculty. I did three subjects — English Literature, Economics and History — and the Lord stirred my interest in History.

A key reason for this was the large historical component in the Bible, supplemented by dinner table conversations we had at home on topics such as what had happened in Singapore during the Japanese occupation. That sensitized me to the need to know more about history, as part of the process of shaping our identity.

I thank God I did well enough to secure a first-class honours degree in History, which further opened doors. Never for a moment did I think that I was not practising my Christian vocation. As secretary of the Varsity Christian Fellowship (VCF), I helped to organize a John Stott mission to the University.

Upon completing my studies, doors that led to a scholarship opened when I became a research assistant and tutor, and then again to allow me to go to Cambridge University to pursue a PhD. Step by step, the Lord opened doors, closing other options in the process. As the psalmist reminds us, "Your word is a lamp to my feet and a light for my path" (Psalm 119:105).

Speaking of opened or closed doors, I almost never made it back to Singapore! There was no opening at first in the History department. To paraphrase a very senior University administrator, "If you want to come back, you must show that you can get a job elsewhere first. As a historian, why should we take you back into Singapore?"

That sounded very strange. I had received my first degree and my master's degree in Singapore, and I was about to get a PhD from Cambridge University. So I applied to several British universities. Hull University offered me a research fellowship at its new Centre for Southeast Asian Studies. With that job offer, I secured an appointment at Singapore University's History department! I am sharing this with you to show you that often "God moves in a mysterious way".

Having gained a foothold, God helped me step by step in my academic career. To me, these promotions were incidental because the important thing was that I was the Lord's servant on campus. I became an agent for ministry on campus, both as a student and later as faculty. As a faculty member, I spearheaded the formation of the University Staff Christian Fellowship, for academic as well as administrative staff in the university. The USCF is still going strong after 30 years. Through these years, my home base was my church, where I served actively as a deacon and then an elder. God used me in the Missions Board to encourage younger brothers in the Lord, one of whom, Tan Lai Yong (a fellow contributor to this book), God used mightily in China.

God uses us in different ways. Some He calls into full-time ministry. Others, he calls to be equippers of those who do full-time ministry. For me, my calling is to be a Christian historian and Bible teacher. This morning I want to share a little on why history is so important for our Christian faith, our walk with our Lord, our worship and our witness.

As a Christian historian, what have I learnt? How does my vocational calling connect with my faith? Remember, I was a Christian before I became a historian. People often ask, "Can we see the hand of God in history?" They do not mean just biblical history. "Can we see the hand of God in historical events?" This may be a rhetorical question, and the Christian historian is going to say yes.

However, let me quote how Professor Herbert Butterfield, a Cambridge historian, responded. Professor Butterfield was the doyen of British historians, a distinguished white-haired gentleman, and a humble man. He once led a group of research students to the Public Record Office in London and bought us lunch! Yet he was Master of Peterhouse (the oldest Cambridge College), as well as Regius Professor of Modern History, and later knighted by the Queen. In his book, *Christianity and History,* he writes, "I am unable to see how a man can find the hand of God in secular history unless he first finds that he has an assurance of it in his personal experience."[2]

If you ask, "Does being a historian mean that he is able to see whether God is at work in history?" Butterfield's reply is that the first thing to ascertain is, who is the historian we are talking about? Does he have a faith or belief? Or is he an atheist or agnostic? That is the crux of the matter. In the case of Professor Butterfield, he was able to see certain trends and make moral judgements as a Christian.

Similarly, for me, I was a Christian before I became a historian. So I try to see history through a Christian lens, through my understanding of the Scriptures. I can see God at work in the history of Israel and the surrounding nations until the advent of Jesus Christ, as narrated in the gospels and the book of Acts. There is a saying, "*Credo ut intelligam*", which means, "I believe in order that I might understand". First comes the faith, then the understanding and then the application.

I suggested earlier that our Christian faith affects our work, our witness as Christians and our worship. In my case, being a Christian was the starting point. After that came my vocational calling as a historian — learning history, studying history, teaching history and sharing reflections on it. As an undergraduate, I wrote an article in VCF's *Logos* magazine where I drew the links between the Christian faith and God's revelation, as well as the Christian faith and history. What part does history play in helping us to understand better who our God is?

Here, I refer you to a very helpful book I read some years ago (now into its third edition) by Gordon Fee and Douglas Stuart, *How to Read the Bible for All Its Worth.*[3] The authors show us that as we study the Bible, we come across different genres of literature. The amazing thing is that almost every genre is there, and all kinds of history. There is secular history, sacred history, Old Testament chronicles and New Testament narratives. There is wisdom literature and philosophy, poetry and songs — found in Job, Psalms, Proverbs, Ecclesiastes, Song of Songs — and many books of prophecy. There are war stories, war strategies and military history.

Military history is very close to my heart because I taught it at the University, when I was also preaching at church services. One day, my children were interviewed for an article and they were asked, "What does your father do?" They replied, "Dad teaches war during the week and he preaches peace on Sundays!"

Let me share a story relating to my preparation to teach the course on "The American Way of War", which showed me clearly how God was at work. In 1988, I was in America preparing course material on American military history. I had lined up some key people I wanted to meet and some departments I wanted to visit. During an earlier visit in 1974–75, I had visited key institutions like the US Air Force academy in Colorado, the US Military Academy in New York and the US Naval Academy in Maryland. In 1988, I had only about a month to complete other visits and interviews — a very tight schedule indeed. This is where God worked in marvellous ways to link me up with two crucial appointments which I would otherwise have had great difficulty arranging.

Here, I am reminded of what Lorne Sanny, the former president of The Navigators said when he visited our home in Singapore. Lorne was giving examples of how God works quietly behind the scenes to make things happen. Sceptical friends would say, "Ah, coincidence, coincidence, coincidence," to which Lorne's reply was, "Who makes the incidences 'co'?" Indeed, who makes them come together? Romans 8:28 says, "And we know that in all things God works for the good of those who love him, who have been called according to his purpose".

This is what happened during my short 1988 visit. I went to Philadelphia, hoping to meet the leading historian in US military history, Professor Russell Weigley, who had written a book entitled *The American Way of War*. The amazing thing is I was able, through a friend in Boston, to stay with a Mennonite brother-in-Christ in Philadelphia. While there, I contacted Professor Weigley, who told me that I had contacted him at the right time; he was heading to Philadelphia the following day to give a lecture! So, the following day, I attended his lecture on the battle of Britain where he talked about World War II, after which I had precious moments with him on a one-to-one basis. Coincidence?

My next stop was Washington, DC, to try to fix a meeting with a Dr Richard Kohn, the then Chief of Air Force History. While there, I paid a courtesy call on Ambassador Tommy Koh who asked, "Ernest, what brings you to Washington, DC?" I said, "I am here to visit a couple of institutions and I hope to make contact with a man called Dr Richard Kohn." Tommy replied, "Ernest, I just met Dick for dinner." He picked up the phone, "Dick, this is Tommy. I have a person here who wants to see you. Are you free tomorrow? Morning? Bolling Air Force Base? You will send a car? Okay."

Coincidence? How did it happen? I don't know. After our meeting, I received, per Dr Kohn's courtesy, boxes and boxes of material on the US air force and its involvement in Korea and Vietnam, etc. All free of charge. When you really need something and your life is in God's hands, the Father delights to surprise you. He does not just give your daily bread. He gives you eggs as well. This is how God works. How would I know the hand of God in history if I had not experienced the hand of God in my own life? "We walk by faith, not by sight" (2 Corinthians 5:7, NASB).

As a Christian historian, I hold certain views on world events as they unfold. I have written a paper on the Gulf War, which was waged in 1991, its connection to 9/11 (the attacks on the World Trade Center in New York and the Pentagon in 2001), and on post-9/11 developments and their implications for the church and missions. My students asked me in 1991, "Sir, what's going to happen next? What's going to happen in Iraq?"

I told them, "I am a historian, not a prophet." Having said that, of course, I gave them my two cents' worth. This is because, as a historian, you may not know the future, but history does provide you some instincts, especially as to what to anticipate. I presented the paper in 2004 at a Lausanne Consultation in Thailand. Basically, I felt that the war waged by America and the "coalition of the willing" against Iraq was a wrong move.

In this last part of my talk, I want to address the question: How much of biblical history can you trust? Let me share with you not just what I have learnt, but also what some other Christian scholars and historians have said about God and history as He reveals Himself in the Old and New Testaments. On the Old Testament, let me mention an excellent book written by Professor Walter Kaiser Jr., *The Old Testament Documents: Are They Reliable and Relevant?*[4]

We mentioned earlier the different genres of literature in the Old Testament. Embedded in them would be narratives. For example, in the book of Genesis, we have narratives of people. Definite names are mentioned there, with genealogies set out. Now the question is, are all the historical accounts set out in the Old Testament reliable? Did the events actually take place?

Professor Kaiser was formerly Professor of Old Testament and President of Gordon-Conwell Theological Seminary. His book is the Old Testament equivalent of Professor F. F. Bruce's book, *The New Testament Documents: Are They Reliable?*[5] He has devoted many years to studying, researching and writing about the Old Testament.

> "How much of biblical history can you trust?"

In his book, Professor Kaiser discusses the Bible in relation to secular history to show its reliability. Another useful reference is John Oswalt's *The Bible Among the Myths.*[6] Do not be misled by the title. The author is not saying that what we have in the Bible are myths. What he does is to compare the Bible account in Genesis and so on with contemporary accounts in the Middle East — accounts about creation, the flood and so on. He shows how historical and realistic — rather than being fanciful and fantastic — these events described in the Bible are.

Now, let us get into the core of our faith, which is Jesus Christ Himself, as found in the gospels. How do we read the gospels? What kind of history do you find there? Is it something we can demonstrate, that Jesus really existed? And that He spoke the things that are recorded in the gospel accounts? As regards His death, was He really crucified? Let me just say it would be different from the kind of history we study in, say, the National University of Singapore (NUS). In NUS, what we teach is common, secular history, while the Bible talks about salvation history. And remember, all history has a purpose. Whatever history course we run, there is a purpose for doing it.

Take military history, for example. Why was the course introduced? Because of national service (NS). With the boys coming to university upon completing two and half years of NS, it would be good to teach them some military history. So whatever God has put in the Bible, there is a purpose too. Let me cite Luke, a medical doctor and also a historian, who wrote the Gospel of Luke and the Book of Acts for a person called Theophilus. This is what Luke wrote in chapter 1:

> *Many have undertaken to draw up an account of the things that have been fulfilled among us, just as they were handed down to us by those who from the first were eyewitnesses and servants of the word. With this in mind, since I myself have carefully investigated everything from the beginning, I too decided to write an orderly account for you, most excellent Theophilus, so that you may know the certainty of the things you have been taught.* (Luke 1:1–4, NIV 2011)

Pretty amazing, isn't it? Writing as a historian, Luke's purpose was to assure a person, the "most excellent Theophilus", who had obviously been exposed to some Christian teaching. One of the best books I have read in recent times has given me an insight of what kind of history you find in the gospels. What kind of history do we find there? In *Jesus and the Eyewitnesses: The Gospels as an Eyewitness Testimony*, Professor Richard Bauckham of the University of St Andrews, now attached to Ridley Hall, Cambridge, shows at great length and in great detail the reliability of the gospel accounts.[7] He makes a powerful analysis and argument of the kind of writings we find in the gospels, comparing, for example, the synoptic gospels with the Gospel of John. He is so convincing that some non-Christian historians appreciate his approach as well.

History is all about sources: no sources, no history. How do we know about any events happening without evidence or sources? Through primary sources, that is, eyewitness accounts of people who saw things as they happened; and secondary sources such as later accounts. For example, Luke's gospel would be a secondary source. In the Gospel of Luke, there are primary sources, as Luke investigated and his account reads like an interview. Take, for example, the history of this woman called Mary, the mother of Jesus. How else would he have known that Mary "pondered [these things] in her heart" (Luke 2:19)? Luke was also the apostle Paul's companion on his travels, hence his accounts in the book of Acts.

Let me also say that every historical event has different interpretations. So you must go for the one that is based on evidence. Just as in the court of law, you get different witnesses who say different things, so one must weigh the evidence. Do this also in relation to what the Bible says. Indeed, neither rule out nor accept blindly what the Bible says just because it is from the Bible. Examine carefully what is recorded. Is it plausible? Is it probable? And I can tell you, like Luke says, that you will know the certainty of these gospel events (Luke 1:4).

There are many things in this world that we cannot be certain about. We look at all the evidence, the different versions of events, different things, different perspectives and different accounts. And then we shake our heads, asking, "What is the truth?" Pilate asked Jesus, "What is truth?" Actually, Pilate was looking at Truth itself, but he did not know it. As Jesus said, "I am the way and the truth and the life. No one comes to the Father except through me" (John 14:6).

How History and "Christory" Became My Story

"Life can only be understood backwards; but it must be lived forwards."
— Søren Kierkegaard

In this final segment, I will show you a simple chart that links the historical segments and the Christian equivalent of it. On the Christian side, there is some alliteration, which I learnt from my father. So on one side, you will see all the

'E's. On the other, you see the 'C's. This is a pattern to help me remember things. Historians love to see patterns.

1. Events
2. Evidence (Eyewitness Testimony & Transmission)
3. Explanation
4. Encounter
5. Experience
6. Evangelism & Education
7. Endings (Eschaton & Epiphaneia)

1. "Christory" (Creation-Cause-Consequence-Coherence-Coming-Cross-Conquest-Church)
2. Communication
3. Connection-Calling
4. Conversion
5. Character
6. Commission
7. Coming Again & Consummation

Now let me explain this quotation from the Danish Christian philosopher, Søren Kierkegaard: "Life can only be understood backwards; but it must be lived forwards." I often ask my students, "Why study history?" My suggestion is that "all we have is history". The present is only a fleeting moment which recedes into the past whilst the future has not come. Hence, all you really have is history. There are two ways to interpret this saying by Søren Kierkegaard. Firstly, it is forward looking. As a Christian existentialist, Kierkegaard believed in the importance of living life fully. It must be lived! But secondly, the statement can also mean that you cannot live your life fully unless you look backwards and learn from the past.

Kierkegaard has guided me all these years through his writings. I still remember one of his books I came across years ago: *Purity of Heart is to Will One Thing.*[8] What an amazing thought! Think about what our Lord Jesus said, "Blessed are the pure in heart, for they shall see God" (Matthew 5:8, NASB). Indeed, purity of heart is to will one thing, and that one thing is to seek and see God.

1. Let us now look at **events**. Remember, we can only know of things having happened, through what is left behind.
2. **Evidence**. These are the remains of the past. These can be artefacts (things) or writings. Writings are often the sources of history; there is no history without sources. And for any kind of history, whether secular history or Bible history, there must be evidence. And for the gospel, as I have said, for Christianity, the hard core events of Christ, the life of Christ, the death of Christ, the resurrection of Christ would be based on eyewitness testimonies and the transmission of that history. We can apply this to any kind of history. Who are the witnesses? What are the primary sources? What kind of transmission? How is it done?
3. **Explanation**. The transmission is in accounts. This is how we learn history. And history is also a subject to study. This is also where we talk about accounts. Accounts try to interpret and explain what happened.
4. **Encounter**. When you study history, you ask, "What happened?" There might also be an encounter, as you read something and begin to understand it. How does it affect you?
5. An encounter produces **experience**. From the experience, you learn. Not just from one event, or set of events, but a whole series of events.
6. **Evangelism** and **education**. How did I become a Christian? — that's evangelism. And my education as a historian — how did I become a historian? For you, how did you end up in your vocation?
7. **Endings**. Remember what Rev David Wong has written about "finishing well" — to not only begin well but also to finish well. And beyond finishing well, to pass it on to the next generation. In talking about "endings", I use a couple of Greek words. One is "*eschaton*", which refers to "the last things" ("eschatology" is the doctrine of the last things), and the other is "*epiphaneia*", meaning "appearance", that is, the first appearance or advent of Jesus Christ and His second coming (Titus 2:11, 13). Endings are important. Please consider your ending.

Now, before I go to the 'C's, let me read from the last book of the Bible, Revelation, the "unveiling" or apocalypse of Jesus Christ.

> *He who was seated on the throne said, "I am making everything new!" Then he said, "Write this down, for these words are trustworthy and true." He said to me: "It is done. I am the Alpha and the Omega, the Beginning and the End."* (Revelation 21:5–6, NIV 2011)

The "end" here is "*telos*", a different word. This end has a purpose and a product. Christ is "the end of the law", the purpose of the law and the fulfilment of the law. And then in Revelation 22:12–13, 17 (NIV 2011):

> *"Look, I am coming soon! My reward is with me, and I will give to each person according to what they have done. I am the Alpha and the Omega, the First and the Last [Greek:* eschatos*], the Beginning and the End [Greek:* telos*].... The Spirit and the bride say, "Come!" And let the one who hears say, "Come!" Let the one who is thirsty come; and let the one who wishes take the free gift of the water of life."*

And of course you know how that book ends with, "Come, Lord Jesus. The grace of the Lord Jesus be with you all."

So, endings are very important! Here, let me mention Bishop Robert Solomon's *Reflections on Time & Eternity*.[9] It is well worth reading carefully as this is what history gives us — a sense of perspective. We serve a Lord who is constant — "Jesus Christ is the same yesterday and today and forever" (Hebrews 13:8). Likewise in Revelation, the first statement I read to you is about God the Father — He who was seated on the throne, who said, "I make everything new. I am the Alpha and the Omega, the Beginning and the End" (see Revelation 21:5–6).

Let me also read to you the statements of Jesus Christ the Son, "I am coming soon! My reward is with me" (Revelation 22:12a). And He says, "I am the Alpha and the Omega, the First and the Last, the Beginning and the End" (v. 13). The eternal Son, the Father and then you have the Holy Spirit: "The Spirit and the bride say 'Come!'" (v. 17).

So you have here a sense of wrapping things up, the apocalypse, the unveiling of God's revelation. You start with Genesis, the beginning, and you go to Revelation, the end.

Now let me just go through the second column very quickly.

I have invented a word just for you and that word is "Christory". You will not find it in the dictionary. But to me, that really embodies the core of my faith, my hope and my love too. Christory starts with creation but predates creation; read Colossians 1. Christ is "the image (*eikon*) of the invisible God, the firstborn over all creation" (v. 15), not in the sense that He was created, because Colossians 1:16–17 says, "by Him all things were created" and "in Him all things hold together". He holds all things together, which is why I put there: "creation, cause and effect, consequences, coherence".

He makes sense, He "connects" all the dots in our lives, in our journeys, in our journaling — the Lord helps us connect the dots in our lives. In our family life, our personal life, our work life, our church life, in society, in the world, the Lord connects the dots. And why? Because of His coming — His first coming, His incarnation. And the core events, as you see in so many chapters of the gospels and if you read on till the last segment — the "cross", the resurrection and the "conquest", and the "church".

1. **Church**. One of the greatest proofs that Christ has risen is the existence of the Christian church. By themselves, the disciples would have disbanded, discouraged and no church would have been formed. But because they met the risen Christ and because of the emptiness of the tomb, the church was born.
2. **Communication**, "The Word became flesh" (John 1:14). Please remember, it is communication all the time. The written Word, the Living Word.
3. **Connection-calling**. The connection is the calling, which all of us have heard in our lives at one point or another. The calling, the vocation, to salvation first. We all have handphones and when we turn it on, we have a connection. And then we can receive phone calls. It's a good illustration, isn't it? At one time, we heard the voice of the Lord calling us. He told us to come and we came. Don't forget it is a double calling, because He called us and we called on the Lord, the name of the Lord, for salvation. There is a double calling (1 Corinthians 1:2).
4. **Conversion**. Because of that you are saved; you are converted. There is a change; there is a transformation in our lives. What is our conversion for?

5. **Character**, the fruit of the Spirit. How do you know you are a Christian? Good news! We are Christians because of grace, not because of the works of righteousness we have done, but by His mercy He saved us (see Titus 3:5). He transforms us — "character produces hope" (Romans 5:4, ESV). We are saved not by good works but for good works (Ephesians 2:8–10, ESV). We are God's "workmanship".
6. **Commission**. Because the love of God has been showered on us, it is not just for ourselves but also for the Commission. "If anyone would come after me, let him deny himself and take up his cross daily and follow me" (Luke 9:23, ESV). Jesus said in the Great Commission, which involves both evangelism and education, "All authority in heaven and on earth has been given to me. Go therefore and make disciples of all nations, baptizing them in the name of the Father and of the Son and of the Holy Spirit, teaching them to observe all that I have commanded you. And behold, I am with you always, to the end of the age" (Matthew 28:18–20, ESV). The end of the age, the Great Commission, evangelism and education bring us to the last point.
7. **Coming**. "Lo," Jesus says, "I am coming soon" (see Revelation 22). Every true Christian will always have that blessed hope, looking to the glorious appearance and epiphany of the Lord Jesus. He is coming again; He is coming soon. You must be ready for the consummation. New heaven, new earth. This is what we are looking forward to.

So, there you have it, brothers. I am here this morning to share with you how history has affected me and my faith, my walk, my worship and my witness. And I know that each of us has a calling too. The Lord calls us in different ways and endows us with different giftings, but always with the same goal, that He might be glorified. Will we really be, by His grace, wholeheartedly for Him until He comes again, until He returns?

■ ■ ■

Questions for Reflection

1

"God has no grandchildren". How do we become "children of God" (John 1:12–13, 3:1–16; 1 John 3:1–2)? How has "Christory" become your story?

2

What should we forget about our past, and what should we remember, in order to have an eternal and yet timely perspective? Consider Paul's experience and exhortation in Philippians 3:1–16.

3

What is the difference between "salvation history" and secular history? How reliable and relevant is biblical history?

4

How does Kierkegaard's statement show the importance of both the past and the future in shaping our present attitudes? How then should we live?

Dr Ernest Chew taught history at NUS for nearly 40 years where he was the Head of the History Department, Dean of the Arts and Social Sciences Faculty as well as founding chairman of the University Staff Christian Fellowship. An elder at Bethesda (Frankel Estate) Church, Ernest remains active in retirement, serving on the Board of the Evangelical Fellowship of Singapore (EFOS), St Luke's Hospital, the Bible Society and Singapore Bible College. He is also a History Consultant at Findings Education and Honorary Chairman of the Singapore History Museum (now incorporated into the National Museum of Singapore). His email address is <uspchewe@gmail.com>.

THE ORIGIN OF MAN

Aw Swee Eng

The study of man and his origin is foundational to our Christian witness.[1] It is important for us to know where we came from. We know that one of the biggest theories these days is that there is no God. Humans came about through a process of slow development over millions of years of ape-like ancestors until we reached the stage we are today.

Some Homely Truths

Most scientists assume that the material world is all there is. Evolution is accepted as an indisputable fact. They know where humans came from. These assumptions determine how they view the world. The quotations below illustrate this, with emphases added.

This is what Richard Lewontin, a geneticist and renowned champion of Neo-Darwinism says (my emphasis in bold):

> *We take the side of science* in spite *of the patent absurdity of some of its constructs,* in spite *of its failure to fulfill many of its extravagant promises of health and life,* in spite *of the tolerance of the scientific community for unsubstantiated just-so stories,* ***because we have a prior commitment, a commitment to materialism.*** *It is not that the methods and institutions of science somehow compel us to accept a material*

> *explanation of the phenomenal world, but,* ***on the contrary, that we are forced by our*** **a priori** ***adherence to material causes to create an apparatus of investigation and a set of concepts that produce material explanations, no matter how counter-intuitive, no matter how mystifying to the uninitiated. Moreover, that materialism is an absolute, for we cannot allow a Divine Foot in the door.***[2]

Lewontin is, in effect, telling us that they do not know what they are talking about, but will not let anyone else tell them otherwise, because they are committed to the notion that there is no God. Anything to do with God, they must exclude.

The second truth is this: Christians tend to misunderstand the meaning of evolution. Let us be clear about what evolutionists are trying to tell us. Evolution was *not* put forward as a theory to explain how God made the world and all living things. Evolution was put forward as a theory to explain how the world and all living things came about *without God*. With evolution, you do not need God. Man is either created by God or evolved all the way from a single cell through an ape-like ancestor. Evolutionists maintain you cannot have it both ways. You do not win their respect nor bring anybody to Christ by sitting on such a fence.

Beliefs of Evolution

Standard evolutionary teaching states that the tenets of evolution are death of the unfit, and the natural selection of the fittest over long periods of time. According to astronomer Carl Sagan in his 1980 *Cosmos* series, evolution requires the deaths of enormous numbers of life forms that were imperfectly adapted for their environment. A slow change in an organism from a long succession of small mutations was needed. These tiny changes were by accident, adaptive and thus requiring vast periods of time for the accumulation of these lucky mutations. Time, it would seem, is the hero of evolution.

The following quote is from the 1995 official statement American National Association of Biology Teachers:

> *The diversity of life on earth is the outcome of evolution: an unpredictable and natural process of temporal descent with genetic modification*

> *that is affected by natural selection, chance, historical contingencies and changing environments.*[3]

George Gaylord Simpson, the famous biologist and anthropologist, also said, "Man is the result of a purposeless and natural process that did not have him in mind."

The official view is driven by the belief there is no God, although holding to this belief is against intuition and against reason. They do not want His divine foot in the door because, once allowed, we would have to admit that we owe our existence to a Creator. Admitting that, what should be our response as to how we should live our lives? So they shut Him out.

The Origin of Man

There is a famous diagram of the Tree of Life. This diagram is meant to show how starting from a single cell plant life, animal life and then dinosaurs, apes and finally man emerged. All this is purely hypothetical. The tree should not have solid lines connecting various biological groups but rather dotted lines. This would be more factual because the connections between these groups, if any, are hypothetical.

To begin with, why should a collection of atoms like us have the ability to think, enabling us to contemplate where we came from? No one, and certainly not the evolutionist, is able to explain this. How does mind emerge from mindless matter? It goes against common sense and intuition.

It is not a sensible argument to say it just occurred and that's that.

When God made man and placed him to look after the garden in Eden, He also commanded the man saying, "You may surely eat of every tree of the garden, but of the tree of knowledge of good and evil you shall not eat, for in the day that you eat of it you shall surely die" (Genesis 2:16–17). The first man was created with a name, Adam. He did not evolve from a hairless ape. His wife, Eve, was made from a bone of his side.

Death came after man's disobedience to the command. The Bible teaches that there was no death before the Fall. Creation then became subject to decay and man to the hardship of living off the land. The Bible puts it this way: creation has been subjected to futility, not willingly, but because of Him who subjected it in the hope that Creation itself would be set free from its bondage to decay and obtain the freedom of the glory of the children of God (see Romans 8:20–21). This is the Christian's hope when Christ returns to restore and renew God's creation. We cannot even imagine what it will be like; it will be so glorious!

There are scientists who see through the utter impossibility of producing even a living cell through evolution by chance mutation and natural selection from simple chemicals even over long periods of time. Jacques Monod, a French Nobel Laureate biochemist, puts it this way:

> *He who is God has the liberty to choose other mechanisms. Why would He have to start with simple molecules? Why not create man right away, as the Bible teaches? If God is God, why does He have to start with simple molecules?*[4]

Some Christians assert, "Why don't we combine evolution and creation? God could have used evolution." If God had used evolution, He would have recorded it *unequivocally* in Genesis. We want to defend the Bible teaching of creation but do not want to offend anyone. That is our problem. If God is indeed all-powerful and all-knowing, He does not have to "start with simple molecules" as Monod says. God does not need to wait for a collection of cells to become fish, amphibian, mammal, then ape, struggling through millions of years to finally become man.

That is not what the Bible tells us about our loving, great and glorious God, Father of our Lord Jesus Christ. If you have such false ideas, please get them out of your head. You are not listening to what Scripture teaches.

"Ancestors" from Studying Bones

You must read widely to compare what the Scripture says with what is taught by standard textbooks. Otherwise you will not understand where evolutionists are coming from. For a general survey, see *The Cambridge Encyclopedia of Human Evolution.*[5] Its cover has an image digitally altered to reflect the assumed connection between apes and humans. Then there is the book by Roger Lewin, *Bones of Contention: Controversies in the Search for Human Origins.*[6] The periodicals *Science, Nature* and *New Scientist* also give good coverage to these topics.

For Christian viewpoints, there are Marvin Lubenow's *Bones of Contention* and Phillip Johnson's trilogy, *Darwin on Trial, Reason in the Balance* and *De-*

feating Darwinism.[7] Websites such as <icr.org> and <answersingenesis.com> are also very helpful with topical details.

The basic assumption is that we need ancestors. Apes are a natural choice as there are the obvious physical similarities. Keep in mind though that physical similarities do not prove descent by evolution. It could be used to support the theory of a Creator using a common plan for His creatures.

If man is the product of a gradual process of change, the question is, where are these ancestors? If millions of years are required for the physical changes, there should be thousands of fossils of such intermediate ape-to-human forms. The fact is that there are very few such fossils that could be considered as candidates. It is sometimes argued that such fossils have been destroyed by geological changes. Why, on the other hand, are there are lots of fossils of animals said to be geologically older and younger than man?

A point of logic — there is the very basic problem of calling something an "ancestor".

Assuming that we are descended from the apes and must therefore have ape-like ancestors is no proof that the theory is true. Not any more logical than demanding a Spanish birth certificate from a stranger because you have already assumed that he was born in Spain.

In his book *Darwin on Trial,* Professor of Law, Phillip Johnson raises the question:

> *What is the basis for calling something an ancestor? By calling it an ancestor in the first place, you are coloring your interpretation of what may be called an 'ancestor'. You have to prove it first! Not assume it.*[8]

Findings from Fossil-hunting Expeditions

One famous fossil discovery is that of *Australopithecus africanus* in 1924 by Professor Raymond Dart of University of Witwatersrand, South Africa. He made this pursuit into a fashionable discipline called "paleoanthropology", that is, the finding and studying of human remains from the past. The Olduvai Gorge and Ethiopia in East Africa became hotbeds for this sort of research. It is assumed that our ancestors must have lived near water, and so fossil hunters go to a riverbed or a lake that has dried up and dig around it for fossils bones. There are many other sites in Europe, Israel and Southeast Asia, but the best known are in Africa. Many famous names such as Louis and Mary Leakey and their son Richard are associated with such explorations. Donald Johanson also discovered *Australopithecus afarensis* (nicknamed Lucy) in the Afar region of Ethiopia in 1974.

Note how these specimens are named. Evolutionists recognize them as apes, because that is the name they use to refer to their specimens. "*Australopithecus*" means "southern ape". Claiming apes to be our ancestors is a leap of faith based on the doctrines of evolutionism.

Interpreting the Fossil Evidence

How does one deduce the history of human evolution using fossil bones? Let us see how they interpret their finds.

Richard Leakey examined the fossil skull labelled "1470". Roger Lewin, a science writer, notes: "One point of uncertainty was the angle at which the face attached to the cranium. Alan Walker [another paleoanthropologist] remembers an occasion when he, Michael Day, and Richard Leakey were studying the two sections of the skull".[9] These were experts, mind you, with pieces of bones in front of them.

Alan had commented, "You could move the maxilla [upper jaw] forward, and give it a long face, or you could tuck it in, making the face short ... *How you held it really depended on your preconceptions.* It was interesting watching what people did with it" (emphasis added).[10]

Do you know what Alan is saying? If you hold the jawbone one way, it looks like an animal, and if you hold it another way, it looks like something else. You have pieces of bone, and depending on how you join or articulate them, you reach different conclusions. This expert confesses that interpretation of fossil evidence is an uncertain exercise. Students of fossil primates have not been very cautious in the conclusions they draw. The record of conclusions drawn is so astonishing that it is legitimate to ask how much science there is at all.

So, is what we are told of human evolution a fact or an interpretation of the purported evidence? Having examined several *Australopithecine* skulls mentioned above, Lord Solly Zuckerman, Professor of Anatomy and an expert in primate behaviour, commented that he found no link between these skulls and human skulls. His opinion was that it is only an interpretation. People just ignored him. If you ignore something, it does not get into the textbooks. It is so embarrassing to the establishment to be shown that they are playing around with bones, sticking these fragments in various places and making up stories.

Indeed, they say so themselves. "If you were to spend your whole life picking up small bone fragments of a jaw or a cranium, there is a very strong desire to exaggerate the importance of these fragments," says Greg Kirby, Senior Lecturer in Population Biology. So they see ape-men everywhere. They discover hominids and every discovery is mooted as a potential ancestor in the New Scientist or Nature.

A Summary of Ape-man "History"

We talk about ape-like ancestors, but this is confusing when we consider modern apes. They seem to have sprung out of nowhere! No ancestors, no fossil records. The true origin of man — naked, bipedal, big-brained man — is a mystery, if we are honest with ourselves. So we say, we come from apes. Well, where do the apes come from? We must then postulate that apes have ancestors, which, in the grand tradition of evolutionary thinking, *must* have existed.

To summarize, let us travel back in time. The skeletal remains of "modern man" *Homo sapiens* are plenty and found all over the world. Then there are the Neanderthals whose bones are human-like, so they are considered *Homo neanderthalensis.* Neanderthals with their craggy features seem to be good candidates among our possible "ancestors". However we are finding that they are not primitive at all. In the 1870s, they were depicted as ape-like. Over the years, they have been depicted as more human-like. In a German museum, they put a Neanderthal in a modern suit, and the similarity to an ordinary man is striking.

In fact, the Neanderthals seem to be far more intelligent and capable than many anthropologists have suspected. In other words, they were just like us. Strikingly, they buried their dead with flowers. If we look at examples of Neanderthal art, we discover reports in the scientific journals that *Homo neanderthalensis* could fashion and play musical instruments. Before them, we have *Homo erectus* and *Homo habilis,* and then we come to the *Australopithecines,* namely *A bosei, A africanus* and *A afarensis.* There are other subgroups which I have not listed.

Tracing the hypothetical lineage even further back, we eventually come to an ape-like ancestor who is supposed to have lived in the trees. The reason was that there were more forests than grasslands. We are supposed to have evolved from this animal that lived in the trees and decided to hop onto the ground. It is called the "terminal ape-like ancestor", because from this point it becomes more and more human-like, from *Australopithecus* to *Homo*. The textbooks say that the creatures swinging from tree to tree descended to the grasslands because of a change in the climate. Somebody has made the point that an animal just learning to walk on the savannahs would have been very vulnerable to predators. There would be lions waiting for these ape-like animals to come down!

A Biblical View

In truth, the available facts fit so much better with what the Bible says about mankind being made in the image of God. God said, "Let us make man in ... our likeness, and let them rule over the fish of the sea and the birds of the air, over the livestock ... and over all the creatures that move along the ground" (Genesis 1:26).

> "Humans and apes are different creatures designed by God."

Man was made fully man in the beginning. If we compare ape skeletons and human skeletons, we notice that the ape's centre of gravity is at the front of its body. This is why an ape ambles, its arms hanging in front, touching the ground (a posture called knuckle-walking), or it will fall over. Humans walk upright, the head and the centre of gravity in line with the rest of the body. This accounts for our upright, arms free-swinging, bipedal gait. Hip structures between the two also show wide differences.

How can an ape-like creature become like us? Going from a shuffling to our upright gait requires major skeletal and soft tissue changes. These changes must be well coordinated so that while they are going on, the creature must be fully functional. Otherwise a functionally compromised animal (such as not being able to run properly to escape predators) will not be expected to last long, being unfit to survive.

The position where the spinal cord emerges from the base of the skull is so starkly different in man and ape. You cannot transform an ape's skull into a human's without major genetic changes occurring simultaneously by chance, and evolutionists must be aware of this.

Humans and apes are different creatures designed by God to live and flourish in different environments.

Intelligence and the Human Genome

Human physiology and the associated genetic information are extremely sophisticated creations. Molecular biologists have acknowledged the amazing design in the individual cells that make up our body. A design requires an intelligent designer. This is a self-evident truth. That goes for all life forms — man, apes and every living thing. And, not surprisingly, for non-living objects as well. Bill Gates declared:

> *The understanding of life is a great subject. Biological information is the most important information you can discover, because over the next several decades we will revolutionize medicine.... DNA is like a computer program, but* far, far more advanced than any software ever created *(emphasis added).*[11]

Computer programs are composed of information and creating information requires the intelligence of software specialists. Information cannot arise from chance. Mutations, however, are chance events. In fact almost all chance changes in the gene are harmful. That is why we have metabolic diseases due to such gene changes. That is also the reason computer programmes have to be debugged!

For one part of an animal to change to another requires many "lucky" events to happen at the same time so that the organism can continue to function while these changes are taking place. That is too much to ask from chance. For instance, the human eye could not have arisen from chance mutations and natural selection as some imagine. You must have all the anatomical structures that make up the eye, plus the connections to the brain, plus the requisite neural connections to interpret what you see. Darwin himself was amazed at the thought of how the human eye could have evolved.

Computer-generated models which show how a light-sensitive patch of skin could "evolve" into an eye are available on the Internet. These animated videos, intelligently written and entertaining, serve only to prove the point they are meant to demolish. The evolution of the brain is supposed to have occurred over three million years from our ape-like ancestors. It is strange that the functions of our evolving brain should far exceed the needs for *mere survival.* For instance, humans are able to memorize the entire musical score of a symphony, or exhibit the remarkably fine control of the hand seen in the visual and musical arts.

A further curiosity is that once the brain was fully formed, the enormous differentiation of culture occurred over only a few thousand years. A mere twinkling of the eye in geological time separates us from the earliest records of any civilization. Simply put, it means that we have more capabilities than we really need. You do not need all that skill merely to survive. You do not need a brain that is capable of playing blindfolded chess against 50 opponents simultaneously.

All this only makes sense if you and I are made in God's image. When God created mankind He imbued us from the beginning with intelligence, language, creativity, manual skills and moral values.

The Origin of Language

The hard thing to explain is how we came to possess the complexities of vocabulary, syntax, grammar, culture and so on. Adam and Eve could converse with God in the beginning. When they sinned, they hid from God until He asked, "Where are you?" (see Genesis 3:9). If they had no language, Adam and Eve would not have understood what God was saying to them. This is the way we are made, to talk with God and each other. Even infants have the ability to recognize simple rules of grammar without being taught. I once asked a language expert how language came about, and he replied, "Which theory would you like me to quote?"

Emperor Frederick who ruled the Roman Empire in 13th century AD thought he would conduct an experiment to discover what the original language of mankind was, whether Hebrew, Greek, Latin or whatever else. So he isolated a few infants from the sound of human voices to observe what language they spoke when they began to speak. They were fed, but kept in complete silence. He reasoned that if they were isolated from anything prejudicial, whatever language they spoke would be the original language.

Nurses caring for these infants were also sworn to absolute silence. They were not to engage in any vocalization in any way. From the moment they were born, these infants never heard even a whisper by any human being. Sad, is it not? No mothers' voice, nothing. Absolute silence.

Do you know what happened to them? Within a year, they all died.

This is how God designed us in His image. God made our children to hear their mothers' voices. Their five senses have to be stimulated or their neurons start to atrophy. The moment babies hear, the neurons start working and making interconnections. A ten-month old baby can identify several hundred characters. Language is hardwired in us because God made us that way.

How "Old" Is Man?

The evidence is overwhelming that humans have always been humans. For instance, images of so-called Stone Age tools, a two-million-year-old chopper and a heavy-duty scraper used by *Homo habilis* were found in a gorge in Ethiopia and in Tanzania. A hand axe was also found, purportedly made *a million years later*. Does it take a million years for man to progress from a chopper to an axe? Moreover, as reported in the scientific journals, Stone Age musical instruments look very much like the instruments we have today.

The Bible records that "Cain lay with his wife, and she became pregnant and gave birth to Enoch. Cain was then building a city" (Genesis 4:17). A city would have buildings and streets!

> *[He] named it after his son Enoch. To Enoch was born Irad, and Irad was the father of Mehujael, and Mehujael was the father of Methushael, and Methushael was the father of Lamech. Lamech married two women, one named Adah and the other Zillah. Adah gave birth to Jabal; he was the father of those who live in tents and raise livestock.* (Genesis 4:17–20)

How many generations were there between Adam and Lamech? Yet they were already living in tents and raising livestock! What evolving hunter-gatherer society are we talking about? Genesis 4:21 says, "His brother's name was Jubal; he was the father of all who play stringed instruments and pipes" (NIV 2011). They already had stringed and woodwind instruments! No surprise, if man is made in God's image, manifesting His creativity. "Zillah also had a son, Tubal-Cain, who forged all kinds of tools out of bronze and iron" (Genesis 4:22). The Iron Age, Bronze Age came very early indeed. Civilization arrived very early indeed!

The Human Genome

We are told that our genetic makeup is very similar to that of apes. This similarity is found in only four per cent of the total genome. The remaining 96 per cent of the total genome we dismissively call "junk DNA" because its functions are not yet properly understood. The difference between apes or zebras and us may very well lie in the "junk DNA" because it contains essential controls on how the four-per-cent portion of the genome is expressed.

What about our physical similarities? Apes, all air-breathing animals and we need lungs. The genetic blueprint for making lungs where there is an exchange of carbon dioxide for oxygen cannot be that different. We have blood; apes have blood too. Our pancreas secretes insulin and so do theirs, except that our proteins are somewhat different in the finer details. Also, the quantity of DNA (how big the genome) is not the most important among living things. Some plants have *more* DNA than we human beings. It is what controls the expression of the DNA that determines how we look — our physical form and function. To be sure, there are more exciting discoveries to be made of the genome.

The Biblical Account of Creation and the Fall

What the Bible tells us is true. All of creation was made over a six-day period. God made the flower-kind, fern-kind, frog-kind and man-kind, everything after its own kind. He made everything to reproduce after its own kind.

So God created man in His own image, male and female He created them. He gave them names. In the beginning, we had an ideal world. Evil came into the world through the fall of man, tempted by Satan.

There was no reason for the temptation to succeed. The tree of the knowledge of good and evil with its forbidden fruit was in the middle of the Eden. You would really have to make an effort to go to the middle of the garden to look for it. Were Adam and Eve hungry, searching for food? No, they were not. All the fruit in the garden was good for eating. Our first parents simply chose to disobey.

Several thousand years later, there was a man who fasted 40 days and 40 nights. That man was Jesus. He was tempted to make bread out of stones by the same tempter, but He resisted. Adam and Eve had not fasted for 40 days and nights. There was no reason for them to disobey God, just as you and I have no reason to disobey God. But we disobey nevertheless as a matter of free choice, and that is why we need forgiveness and cleansing: "If we confess our sins, He is faithful and just and will forgive us our sins and purify us from all unrighteousness" (1 John 1:9).

Out of touch with His Creator, man has become a cosmic orphan by believing his own evolutionary stories about the origin of life. We seem to be living out Jeremiah 2:27: "They say to wood, 'You are my father', and to stone, 'You gave me birth'. They have turned their backs to me."

I like this quote from John S. Mbiti, an African Christian:

> *By nature, Africans are neither angels nor demons. They can be as kind as the Germans, but they can be as murderous as the Germans. Africans can be as generous as the Americans, but they can be as greedy as the Americans; they can be as friendly as the Russians, but they can be as cruel as the Russians; they can be as honest as the English, but they can be equally hypocritical. In their human nature Africans are Germans, Swiss, Chinese, Indians or English — they are men.* [12]

We are men and women made in the image of God, but we decide to be wilful and that is why we must be redeemed.

Ancient History

What we really know about earth's history is that it does not span billions of years. The oldest *human civilization* we know of is that of the Sumerians, about 5,000 to 7,000 years old. The cradle of civilization is located in Iraq. Wheat and grain cultivation originated there. So did writing. This is consistent with what the Bible teaches, and we can trace our ancestry all the way back to Ham, Shem and Japheth. The history of mankind — how and why we are here — is more consistent with what the Bible tells us than what evolution teaches.

There is a story about the Chinese character for ship, 船. The left side radical is another pictogram for ship, while the right side radical depicts eight mouths. As we know, the Ark had Noah, Shem, Ham and Japheth with their four wives, and that makes eight persons. Perhaps the Chinese descended from one of the families who had migrated east. There is a saying in Chinese that when we die, we go back to the west — where we had originated.

The well-known paleoanthropologist Richard Leakey said this in a 1990 Public Broadcasting Service (PBS) documentary:

> *If pressed about man's ancestry, I would have to unequivocally say that all we have is a huge question mark. To date, there has been nothing found to truthfully purport as a transitional species to man. If further pressed, I would have to state that there is more evidence to suggest* an abrupt arrival of man rather than a gradual process of evolving (emphasis added).

These statements should be put up somewhere in a museum of natural history.

Miao Accounts Reveal the Ancient Roots of Their Religion

In Myanmar, the Miao people had never come into contact with missionaries before, but they have written records. When missionaries came, they looked at those records and found this creation myth. Bear in mind that they had never met any missionaries before. Edgar A. Truax translated their creation myth. Reading it, I hope it deepens your belief in God's Word about the origin of mankind.

The Creation

On the day, God created the heavens and earth.
On that day, He opened the gateway of light.
In the earth He made heaps of earth and of stone.
In the sky He made bodies, the sun and the moon.
In the earth He created the hawk and the kite.
In the water created the lobster and fish.
In the wilderness made He the tiger and bear,
Made verdure to cover the mountains,
Made forest extend with the ranges,
Made the light green cane,
Made the rank bamboo.[13]

According to the Miao, creation by the one God followed a certain order, with light first. On the earth, God then created man from dirt, referring to Adam

(Genesis 2:7). Remarkably, the story states that woman was created out of man (Genesis 2:21–22).

The next part emphasizes the intelligence of the man made in God's image:

Man

On the earth He created a man from the dirt.
Of the man thus created, a woman He formed.
Then the Patriarch Dirt made a balance of stones.
Estimated the weight of the earth to the bottom.
Calculated the bulk of the heavenly bodies.
And pondered the ways of the Deity, God.
The Patriarch Dirt begat Patriarch Se-teh.
The Patriarch Se-Teh begat a son Lusu.
And Lusu had Gehlo and he begat Lama.
The Patriarch Lama begat the man Nuah.
His wife was the Matriarch Gaw Bo-lu-en.
Their sons were Lo Han, Lo Shen and Jah-hu.
So the earth began filling with tribes and with families.
Creation was shared by the clans and the peoples.[14]

Do we not hear echoes of Biblical characters in Nuah, Lo Han, Lo Shen and Jah-hu? The next part of their myth explains the origin of sin:

The World Wicked

These did not God's will nor returned His affection.
But fought with each other defying the Godhead.
Their leaders shook fists in the face of the Mighty
Then the earth was convulsed to the depth of three strata.
Rending the air to the uttermost heaven.
God's anger arose till His Being was changed;
His wrath flaring up filled His eyes and His face.
Until He must come and demolish humanity.
Come and destroy a whole world full of people.[15]

The Flood

So it poured forty days in sheets and in torrents.
Then fifty-five days of misting and drizzle.[16]

It goes on to talk about the tower of Babel (Genesis 11):

Babel

Lo-han then begat Cusah and Mesay.
Lo-shan begat Elan and Nga-shur.
Their offspring begotten became tribes and peoples;
Their descendants established encampments and cities.
Their singing was all with the same tunes and music;
Their speaking was all with the same words and language.
Then they said let us build us a very big city;
Let us raise unto heaven a very high tower.
This was wrong, but they reached this decision;
Not right, but they rashly persisted.
God struck at them then, changed their language and accent.[17]

Summing Up

God is our Creator, and "we are his people, the sheep of his pasture" (Psalm 100:3). Churches that have compromised or deserted God's Word in favour of a materialistic interpretation of man's miraculous origin have tragically lost their spiritual power to draw men to Christ.

If the Bible has told man the truth about the world and myself, what should I do now? I would acknowledge it with thanksgiving, knowing that I am not the result of blind forces but the creation of a loving God. The extent of that love is seen in His sending His Son to save us from the consequences of our sin.

To be a Christian is to have a personal relationship with the Lord Jesus. Not just coming to a church, or being in a church committee or donating your wealth. These will not bring you forgiveness or to heaven.

Whom have I in heaven but you?
And earth has nothing I desire besides you.

My flesh and my heart may fail,
but God is the strength of my heart
and my portion forever.
(Psalm 73:25–26)

Such a personal relationship with Jesus has been made possible by our Creator God: "For God so loved the world that He gave His one and only Son, so that whoever believes in Him shall not perish but have eternal life" (John 3:16).

For those who have committed themselves to Jesus as Lord and Master, I would like to close with words from the heroine of *Memoirs of a Geisha*: "Every step I have taken ... has been to bring myself closer to you."[18] This geisha loved the man deeply, and made it the aim of her whole life to be near him. If human love could be like that, how does our love for the Lord compare? How do we pursue our relationship with God?

▪ ▪ ▪

Questions for Reflection

1

How would you answer someone who says that the basic unit of life is a "simple" cell?

2

What would you list as the main differences between the biblical account of creation of man and the evolutionary story of his origin?

3

Would you like to comment on this statement by Francis Collins, former director of the National Human Genome Research Institute?
"If God, who is all powerful and who is not limited by space and time, chose to use the mechanism of evolution to create you and me, who are we to say that wasn't an absolutely elegant plan?"[19]

4

How would you explain to someone what Paul was saying to the intellectual audience in Athens, as recorded in Acts 17?

"The God who made the world and all things in it, since He is Lord of heaven and earth, does not dwell in temples made with hands... and he made from one man every nation of mankind to live on all the face of the earth.... Being then children of God, we ought not to think that the Divine Nature is like gold or silver or stone, an image formed by the art and thought of man."
(Acts 17:24, 26, 29; NASB)

5

In what ways do you think a man who denies the existence of God will find it a problem to live with the conclusions of his own system of unbelief?

Dr Aw Swee Eng is an Adjunct Associate Professor with Duke-NUS Medical School. He was previously an Associate Professor in the Department of Biochemistry, National University of Singapore, and also Senior Consultant and Head of Department of Nuclear Medicine/PET at the Singapore General Hospital. Swee Eng has been teaching Sunday School and Bible Class since 1958. His email address is <aandasg@yahoo.com.sg>.

TOWARDS A BETTER UNDERSTANDING OF MANDARIN-SPEAKING CHURCHES IN SINGAPORE

John Chew

My intention is to share a little bit on the Mandarin-speaking churches in Singapore. What do we mean when we say "Mandarin-speaking churches"? The large majority of churches in Singapore are English-speaking. And there are probably more dialect-speaking than Mandarin-speaking congregations in Singapore!

My passion for this sharing is because I have been worshipping in a Mandarin-speaking church all along. Indeed, I was educated in the Chinese stream from kindergarten right up to university. I must confess that functioning in an English-speaking dominant church environment all these years has not been easy for me. It was not by choice but one gets by. It is good that churches in Singapore, now and then, take a step back to re-look at church developments, and ask whether we have an adequately broad perspective. With greater inter-connectivity in life, we are seeing unprecedented peoples and ideas movements on all fronts, crossing and blurring hitherto clear boundaries.

Here in Singapore, when one speaks of church and church matters, it is almost by default that English-speaking churches and organizations are being referred to. In all these, it is hardly felt that Mandarin-speaking (and even more so dialect and for that matter Tamil-speaking) Christians or churches will not naturally feel at home. Singapore being Singapore, one has no choice but to speak English if only to be acknowledged! It is not so much a negative sentiment but almost a given part of church life in Singapore.

To have some perspective to better grasp my sharing, which is also in light of the run up to SG50, we need to go back in time. This year, through historic footages shown on TV, Singaporeans were starkly reminded of the MacDonald House explosion episode that occurred in the 1960s during the *Konfrontasi*. But what else is significant about the '50s and '60s to the Chinese educated? To be able to reach out and minister effectively to Mandarin speakers, it is good to understand some of these pivotal moments of their background. Then maybe we can share the gospel with them in more understanding terms.

I was all along Chinese educated, from primary school to Nanyang University in the mid-'60s. There were several student riots amongst the Chinese educated in the '50s and '60s. Rightly or wrongly, whatever the forces behind the scene were, they very much felt that they were underdogs and marginalized. The '80s was a critical period of transition for the Mandarin-speaking community. In 1984, the total student registration for Primary One classes could muster only one class of 40 students in the whole of Singapore. This meant the natural eventual cessation of traditional Chinese education and culture. This was no doubt a fundamental crisis to the Chinese-educated community at large.

So much so that at that time, a number of us relatively young Mandarin-speaking pastors were psychologically prepared that we were serving in a "sunset industry", so to speak. There was a drastic drop in the number of local Mandarin-speaking candidates entering seminary for training as pastors-teachers. The situation was even worse than in the '50s and '60s, after 1949, when the doors of China were closed to the outside world and we could no longer look to "mother" churches in China for a regular supply of faithful pastors from Xiamen, Fuzhou, Swatow, Guangzhou, etc. Then, when these churches needed a pastor, they could still turn to Taiwan and Hong Kong for Mandarin or dialect-speaking pastors. But with the tightening of the inflow of foreign workers into Singapore, this had become more difficult.

Pausing for a moment, on hindsight, a serious question could be posed to the Chinese-educated parents in the '70s and '80s: why did they choose not to send their children to Chinese-medium schools for education? There was bound to be knock-down negative effects 10, 20 or 30 years down the road for our local

Mandarin-speaking churches. The question is whether this was a concern for the churches in Singapore at large. If not, why not?

Against the above brief backdrop, the question to pose about the church in Singapore is this: "What is the Church in Singapore?" Because of the historic past of Singapore, English being the global connective language and the fact that most churches are English-speaking, it is natural that the focal point of church matters are more English and western. Just look at the resource persons, speakers, books and seminars, worship songs and styles, etc. It is not difficult to conclude what sort of church identity will emerge from all these.

Let me share a poignant experience to illustrate. I did my post-graduate theological studies at the University of Sheffield from 1979 to 1982. I have a fairly emotive feeling towards it, both joyful and sad. I enjoyed my studies there tremendously. But Sheffield University also caused me much anguish! This is because in 1979, the Chancellor of Sheffield University was invited and appointed by our government to review the future viability of Nantah. The review concluded that it was not viable for Nantah to continue on its own, as it was then. It recommended the closure of Nantah and its merger with the then University of Singapore to form the National University of Singapore. The recommendation was accepted by our government.

One must understand that Nantah was very close to the hearts of the Chinese community at large. It was built through the painstaking and sacrificial efforts of many common people, including trishaw pullers and barbers, who believed in giving their children a good education in Chinese. The sentiments expressed against its closing were strong from the Chinese-speaking communities inside and outside of Singapore. I share this heartbreaking event in order for English-speaking churches to better appreciate the evolution of Chinese churches in Singapore.

"Nantah was very close to the hearts of the Chinese community at large."

I remember that when I first graduated from Nantah in 1969, there was a group of Nantah Christian graduates who met regularly for fellowship even after graduating. Identifying with one's culture and alma mater is simply natural and goes without question. Even with the challenges and real possibility of the

Mandarin-speaking churches shrinking to a point of non-effective existence, they continued to persevere in meeting. They were not asking for a better future — in the 1980s, no one knew what to expect. China was still in the early aftermath of the Cultural Revolution, and whether it would self-destruct was still an open question. But these Nantah Christian graduates continued to meet.

During this period when the future of Mandarin-speaking churches was uncertain, one must register a profound appreciation to God that some local English-speaking churches felt the gospel call to reach out to the Chinese community, primarily through Chinese dialects. In the 1980s, Chinese dialect fellowships and services sprung up within English-speaking churches. However, whilst this was a most laudable effort, it also unwittingly gave rise to a debilitating structural problem for the quality re-development and growth of Mandarin-speaking churches in their own right.

The specific motivation to start especially dialect services was also practical or pragmatic; the primary concern being for non-English-educated parents or grandparents of English-speaking church members who strongly desired such family members to embrace the Christian faith. I know of some English-speaking brothers, moved by a strong sense of calling, who helped to start new dialect services, even using broken Hokkien in the process. They visited one-room and two-room flats in our HDB heartlands to reach out to the residents living there.

But all these efforts were rather ad-hoc and functional. I do not think the English-speaking churches at that time were missional enough to invest and plough resources into the Mandarin-speaking work. They also failed to understand that underneath all these, there was a structural issue, which if not recognized, could create or aggravate non-English "underclass" congregations.

Later, construction workers from China poured into Singapore. Many had not heard of the gospel of Jesus Christ. Even the few who were Christians could not just walk into an English-speaking congregation to worship. Mandarin-speaking churches, with all their own challenges, harnessed resources and started new ministries to reach out to them. These workers, being short-termers, produced hardly any substantive and accumulated quality growth for Mandarin-speaking churches, which were under pressure. Furthermore, the Mandarin-speaking congregations (reflective of a lack of catholic ecclesiology) did not have a common mind and heart or a sense of urgency to harness energy and resources in concerted ways to address this structural challenge threatening its very future.

I have felt this all the more because for a good period of my ministry, I had to cross over from a domain of regular Mandarin-speaking churches to English-speaking ones. The Anglican churches in Singapore (or for that matter most other church groups here), especially the larger congregations with more resources, are all English speaking. Understandably in Singapore's multi-language context, English is the common language of communication in our churches. Yet it could well be an uncritical mission mindset that led to the conduct of church business only in English, which was not the most helpful to the development of the Mandarin-speaking congregations.

I thank God that in the '80s, as mentioned earlier, there was a group of die-hard, utterly committed and unquestioning local Chinese-educated Christians who were strongly committed to the Chinese culture and education. They also believed in the future of Mandarin-speaking churches in Singapore, even though it was hard to foresee a future for these churches then! I would like to share below some of the important contributions this group made to our Mandarin-speaking churches, which have passed without much notice.

In the late '60s when I completed my studies at Nantah, some of us were associated with the Chinese ministry of the Fellowship of Evangelical Students (officially constituted only in 1969/70). We were strongly struck by the fact — albeit a phenomenon hardly noticed by others, let alone spoken about — that there were not more than five local Chinese-educated graduate Christians who could be counted in the ranks of full-time Christian workers or pastors. And with many Mandarin or dialect-speaking local pastors aging, it was a most critical issue for Chinese churches.

We somehow felt this situation could not be the norm. Some concerned members then came together to fellowship and pray about the situation. Out of this, the 前线小组 or Frontier Group was initiated in the early '70s. This fellowship was formed with the sole purpose of encouraging and challenging more to vocational full-time service as pastors in local churches and not para-church groups. Eventually, more than 30 of us responded to the call. We are now serving in different churches and capacities. Also, within the group, those who did not sense the call to full-time church ministry persevered and became committed lay leaders in their own churches.

In the early '80s, Mandarin-speaking churches faced an uncertain future. It was at this critical juncture that Trinity Theological College (TTC) played a most crucial role. This came about, however, not by design, as the general impression was that it was predominantly set up by and for English-speaking churches. It was the official college of the four mainline denominations, the Anglicans, Lutherans, Methodists and Presbyterians, and had trained the vast majority of their Mandarin-speaking pastors and lay leaders, many of whom had been acquainted with each other during their secondary and tertiary school days.

The leaders of these Mandarin-speaking churches spontaneously came together to form themselves into the 四宗华文教会理事会, Chinese Church Council of the Four Denominations or "4D" in short, which has become a very endearing term. After the critical year of 1984 when traditional Chinese schools ceased, the Chinese churches in 1987 organized a timely seminar to critically take stock of the situation and reflect on the future of the Mandarin-speaking churches in Singapore. The impact of the closure of Nantah was already being felt. The seminar proved to be a critical rallying call to not give up. It is with great thanksgiving and encouragement that on 4 April 2015, after 30 years, we met again to take stock and reflect on the challenges and opportunities in our totally unexpected new global and especially Asian environment. There was a markedly different mood and new-found confidence. The depressing mood of being in a "sunset industry" has been lifted, especially with China opening up. But of course, the Mandarin-speaking churches cannot take on all the new challenges and opportunities on their own, and we discussed how we could work better together.

I have painted in broad strokes the background to the survival of Mandarin-speaking churches in Singapore and the new phase they are now entering. Going forward, we will need to constantly adjust as no one has had the experience of this new journey. Deng Xiaoping made famous the saying, "摸着石头过河", which translates to feeling one stone at a time while crossing the river.

I know that for English-speaking churches, all this is off their radar and of not much relevance as living out their Christian faith in an English-speaking context is the norm. However, in light of the demise and loosening of ties with Christian values in western and English-speaking nations, it behoves our English-speaking churches and Christians to carefully reflect on this and consider seriously their faith implications.

Over these three decades, the 4D has played an unheralded but crucial role in keeping and growing the Mandarin-speaking churches together. It has continued to organize seminars and inspirational devotional meetings regularly, with different churches taking turns to lead and the others supporting, leveraging on each other and helping the smaller and independent Mandarin-speaking churches. The 4D group organizes and mobilizes all churches for a regular city-wide outreach, the biennial 新春祝福晚会 (Lunar New Year Evening Concert), with a budget of S$200,000 to 250,000 each time. This is definitely not a small sum for the under-resourced Mandarin-speaking churches and members. The concert is now into its tenth edition, with a very impressive track record over the past 20 years. Another important initiative is the regular quarterly and weekly teaching programme and activities in different church locations, organized by the 乐邻学院 or Seniors' Institute and its committee. It was also started some 20 years ago.

In May 2013, the 4D helped to stage an original play at the School of the Arts (SOTA), preceded by a public seminar at the National Library. The play, "问天" (Asking Heaven) features the Old Testament prophet Jeremiah and the Chinese patriot high official Qu Yuan, 屈原. It is essentially a dialogue between two ancient civilizations with common cultural values and concerns. The play ends with a voiceover declaring, through the lives of these two highly respected personalities in their own cultural context, "国家 (nation), 责任 (responsibility), 使命 (mission), 传承 (tradition)". It is an original script of great depth and quality which exceeded all expectations in its impact far and wide, both in Singapore and in China. The dialogue was set against prevalent societal concerns, not least in China, involving the breakdown and collapse of ritual propriety and rules of proper behaviour and consequentially the loss of social capital and trust — 礼崩乐坏. It turned out to be a totally new angle of missional engagement that is both biblical and cultural!

Locally, it caught the attention of a major Chinese newspaper, *Lian He Zao Bao*, 联合早报. They specially sent a journalist to interview the key people involved and an extensive report (two-thirds of a page) on the value and significance of the play was featured in the paper. The scope and extent of coverage was truly unprecedented. Because of the play, we also had the opportunity to meet

Mr Heng Swee Keat, Minister for Education and Chairman of the National Conversation movement, and shared with him the commitment and contribution of the churches and Christians (including Mandarin-speaking ones) to our nation-building process.

Of greater value, the play became a conversational topic in China, and was discussed at the Schools of Philosophy of the Universities of Beijing and Fudan. It has put a new focus on biblical faith — a faith that has succeeded in withstanding the extreme constraints and challenges of its exile, emerging as a major ancient civilization with deep life wisdom, is now in the academic curriculum and conversations in China. Official academic exchanges have also been drawn up with Trinity Theological College — surely a first in many senses — which has taken many by surprise. Interestingly, the play's director and cast were mainly professionals, with some 80 per cent being non-believers. Many of them were deeply drawn to the life and personality of Jeremiah, whom they had never known nor heard of before.

From the educational and cultural developments of the '80s in Singapore and their impact on the future of Mandarin-speaking churches here, God continues to move alongside us, every step of the way. The heightened and vibrant quantity and quality of Chinese social, educational, arts and cultural activities and presence in recent years is unprecedented. This poses new challenges and opportunities for Mandarin-speaking churches. I believe our churches, both the dominant English-speaking as well as Mandarin-speaking ones, ought to be aware of and, indeed, understand the opportunities and challenges posed, even though we may be more comfortable (naturally) with traditional and familiar models of evangelism.

To understand the Chinese and Chinese community, it is important to come round to the key concept of China and the Chinese as a civilization or nation and people, and not as sovereign state in western geopolitical terms. This is expounded persuasively by Zhang Weiwei in his book *The China Wave: Rise of a Civilizational State.*[1] Recently, *Lian He Zao Bao* devoted a full page to the 华社, the Chinese civic community, highlighting how in major Chinese holding companies, one generation passes on to the next (代代相传), signalling the importance of continuity and longevity, something we all pray for in our Mandarin-speaking congregations. Momentum is building up on this front. In January this year, a local Chinese businessman donated a cool S$10 million to set up a Confucius Thinking Foundation. Also in February, the Chinese Chamber of Commerce announced that they would finance the NUS Chinese Department's research on the lives of key community leaders of the past to recognize the important contributions of the Chinese communities in our nation building. This year too, the Singapore Hokkien Association is going to have a full-fledged Cultural Academy out of a renovated secondary school in Siglap, whilst the Federation of Chinese Clan Associations will be starting its flagship Chinese Cultural Centre. The recent formation of the Singapore Chinese Music Federation will bring all the Chinese musical groups in Singapore together. And these are very high quality groups! The now annual 河畔新春 or River Hong Bao event has also grown from strength to strength. Although the anchor performers each year come from different Chinese provinces, it will be hard to mount a programme year in, year out without any repeat items.

I trust that you too sense and appreciate the scale and scope of the opening up of China and its implications for Singapore and our Mandarin-speaking churches. My earnest prayer is that more leaders and members of English-speaking churches in Singapore will pause long enough to appreciate the new lease of life, confidence and vibrancy of the Chinese community at large, and better appreciate what it may mean for churches in Singapore to be holistic witnesses of the gospel. I encourage us to pay some attention.

■ ■ ■

Questions for Reflection

1

As Asian countries continue to rise geopolitically and economically, how should Singapore churches, which are mainly western Christendom weighted, re-orientate their thinking on their existence, mission and purpose?

2

What are some challenges churches may face in persuading English-speaking leaders and members to shift their ecclesiological and missional paradigms?

Rev Dr John Chew retired as Bishop of the Anglican Church of Singapore in 2012. Ordained as a priest in 1978, John has devoted a lifetime of service to the church, both inside and outside of Singapore. Effectively bilingual, he has drawn on his deep involvement with the Trinity Theological College since 1982 as a lecturer, Principal and Chairman of the Board of Governors to reach out to the church in China as well as the authorities overseeing religion there. Currently, he serves as Advisor to the Chinese Church Committee of the National Council of Christian Churches of Singapore and was recently elected to the United Bible Societies Global Council. He now spends much time reaching out to the work of churches in China. His email address is <johnchew@anglican.org.sg>.

RUNNING THE RACE MARKED OUT FOR US: MY SEASON IN POLITICS

Ho Peng Kee

Embracing a Christian Worldview

Let us start by taking a look at Charles Colson and Nancy Pearcey's book, *How Now Shall We Live?*[1] Colson was a key aide to President Richard Nixon, who had a hard fall when "Watergate" erupted. But when he fell, God used him to start a fellowship that is now ministering to prisoners worldwide. Since then, Colson has written many books on his political journey and how his views have changed. In *How Now Shall We Live?* he quotes Abraham Kuyper, a renowned Dutch theologian and one-time Prime Minister of Holland who argues that the dominating principle of Christian truth is not only soteriological (justification by faith) but also cosmological (the sovereignty of God over the whole cosmos, in all its spheres and kingdoms). In other words, God is involved in all of human affairs.

This is the cultural commission or cultural mandate arising from God's command to Adam and Eve: "Be fruitful and multiply; fill the earth and subdue it" (Genesis 1:28, ESV). The emphasis is that Christ's lordship is over all of life. In other words, whilst as Christians, our personal salvation is indeed important, we should stop not there. We must press on to be salt and light and an aroma for Christ wherever He puts us. After all, "faith without works is dead" (James 2:26, KJV). Individually, we express our belief in God and our love for God through actions. Collectively, Christians have a role to play in the world where we are. Originally, when God made the world, it was a perfect world. God gave us the mandate to rule over it. But because of sin, Adam and Eve were driven from Eden and they had to till the ground; not leave it or run away from it, but to work it. We are to redeem God's creation for "The earth is the LORD's" (Psalm 24:1–2). This is the first key point.

The second point I want to make is about embracing a Christian worldview. Why are Christians different from non-believers? This is something we need to affirm in us all the time, as we have accepted the Lord Jesus Christ as our personal Lord and Saviour, and the Holy Spirit lives in us now. Our future destination is heaven, home with God. That is a fundamental Christian reality. The question is, we know it but how many of us live it? How much of it is just head knowledge? There should not be dualism in that we live our church life and our work life differently. So, what should make us different from non-believers is that our daily actions are premised on a different worldview from that of a non-believer. As Christians, we recognize that God is interested in the world, and God has a plan for redeemed men — to be saved, to be salt and light, to restore His order in the world. And it begins with understanding and embracing a Christian worldview.

Norman Geisler and William Watkins define worldview as "a way of viewing or interpreting all of reality. It is an interpretive framework through which or by which one makes sense out of the data of life and the world".[2] The point is this — the Christian reality is quite different from the non-believer's view of the world. Colson and Pearsey argue that one's worldview covers all aspects of the world in terms of structure, character and norm. The underlying principles are God's law, His design and purpose for Creation. These include laws of nature, like gravity. If you pierce somebody with a knife, blood is drawn. These are observable to us. At the same time, the norms for human life are not quite visible. How is society meant to be ordered? For this, God has set out rules in the Scriptures. These have to be interpreted for our modern society, but they are there. So what is visible is seen and we readily accept it, but these unseen rules are there too. And as we espouse a Christian worldview, embrace it and work it in our lives, we have to do our part to restore God's norms in society.

Some of us have *The Complete Book of Everyday Christianity* in our libraries. If so, I commend you for that. It is a very good book. It is both Scriptural and practical. I quote from Brian Walsh who says:

> *[A worldview] connotes a global perspective, an overarching view of the world that directs our life in the world. Worldviews are communally held frameworks of interpretation that provide the normative orientation of a community.... Worldviews are both visions* of *life and visions* for *life.*[3]

A worldview is descriptive in telling us what the world is as well as prescriptive, providing us with "foundational values and norms".[4]

A person's worldview provides us with answers to four basic questions: 1) Where are we? 2) Who are we? 3) What's wrong with the world? 4) What's the remedy?[5] James Sire in *The Universe Next Door* argues that one's worldview is framed by one's answers to questions such as: "Is there a God and what is He like?", "How was the world made?", "What is a human being?", "What happens to a person at death?", "Why is it possible to know anything at all?", "How do we know what is right and wrong?" and "What is the meaning of human history?"[6] All these contribute to what forms a worldview.

We want to raise up in our Singapore churches a band of brothers infused with a solid Christian worldview, just like the men of Issachar, who "understood the times and knew what Israel (they) should do" (1 Chronicles 12:32) — when King David ascended the throne, he assembled all the tribes so they could pledge their allegiance to him. Hopefully, we will be like the men of Issachar. We will understand the times and context we live in as things happen around us — our families, our work, Singapore, the world — and then, we will know what to do.

The Roles of Men in the Bible

The Bible has much to say about the roles of men in various settings.

- Titus 2:2 — "Teach the older men to be temperate, worthy of respect, self-controlled, and sound in faith, in love and in endurance."
- 1 Peter 3:7 — "Husbands, in the same way be considerate as you live with your wives, and treat them with respect as the weaker partner and as heirs with you of the gracious gift of life, so that nothing will hinder your prayers."
- Colossians 3:21 — "Fathers, do not embitter your children, or they will become discouraged."

What about work? Some of these will be very familiar to us.

- Colossians 3:23 — "Whatever you do, work at it with all your heart, as working for the Lord, not for men."
- Matthew 10:16 — "Therefore be as shrewd as snakes (the King James says "wise as serpents") and as innocent as doves."
- John 10:7–10 introduces the concept of us as gatekeepers. In the Old Testament, there were several gates in the city. They were key points where the elders sat, where people met and where commerce was conducted and disputes settled. So we are like gatekeepers, right there in the marketplace, to ensure that things are done properly.

As citizens, we are to seek the welfare of the city and pray to the Lord on its behalf, for in its welfare, we will have welfare. The NIV says, "seek the peace and prosperity of the city .... Pray to the LORD for it, because if it prospers, you too will prosper" (Jeremiah 29:7). Heeding this passage, we should pray for Singapore and its leaders.

Ezekiel 22:30 tells us: "I looked for a man among them who would build up the wall and stand before me in the gap on behalf of the land so I would not have to destroy it". Are we, as Christian men, ready to stand in the gap as gatekeepers in the marketplace and workplace, and wherever God puts us, to infuse all around us with Christian values?

For those of us who are older, we might remember the Keswick Convention in the 1970s and 1980s. One year, for four to five days, there was powerful preaching from 2 Chronicles 7:14,

> ... *if my people, who are called by my name, will humble themselves and pray and seek my face and turn from their wicked ways, then will I hear from heaven and will forgive their sin and will heal their land.*

This intercessory prayer is for Singapore. Especially in this Jubilee year, SG50, we must not forget to pray for Singapore. How can Singapore become a society more aligned to biblical values? Is there a negative creeping effect on family and social values? Can policies that impact the poor be softened? How can we be a softer-edged, more compassionate and more inclusive society? We know the Bible has a special place for the widows, the fatherless, the poor and the broken-hearted. We are to comfort all who mourn and provide for those who grieve. So we should get involved with the underprivileged.

To sum up, there are many different roles for men in God's eyes. Each of us is an integral part of the Cultural Mandate and the Great Commission. If each of us can reach out wherever God has put us, that would be doing the Great Commission. Preaching and sharing the Word is important, as is conversion. But we are such a compact society that in reality, lifestyle evangelism or living the message is as important. Our actions should infuse society with biblical values. That is the Cultural Mandate.

So, in a sense, there is convergence. 1 Peter 3:15 reminds us to always be prepared to give an answer to everyone who asks us to give the reason for the hope we have. Prepare to give an answer to those who ask us why you are so helpful, joyful and hopeful. They should notice this by your actions every day, wherever you are. That is how we start conversations. That is how we influence others around us. Thus, 1 Peter 2:12 exhorts us to conduct ourselves honourably amongst the pagans so that they may see our good deeds and glorify God on the day He comes to judge. 2 Corinthians 2:14-15 exhorts us to "spread everywhere the fragrance of the knowledge of him. For we are to God the aroma of Christ". Even without us speaking, people can smell the fragrance that comes from what we do, how we treat people, the way we act and our response to situations.

Running Our Race and Finishing Well

Now, let me talk about fighting the fight and finishing the race. Each of us is running a race, a customized race that is "marked out for us" (Hebrews 12:1–2). This race is not a sprint; it is a marathon. It is for the long haul, unless God, in His sovereign will, decides that we stop running the race and return home to Him in heaven. In fact, Paul says it is better to be home with the Lord Jesus, but if God says that we are to run the race for now, let us run it well. Let us fight the good fight; not only run but also finish the race well, and not only keep but also strengthen our faith in Almighty God (2 Timothy 4:7). Like a marathon, we run our life's race in phases, or over seasons in life. This is something very real to many of us, including myself.

In any race, there will be stretches that go uphill and downhill, not only physically but emotionally and mentally as well. Sometimes we struggle and sometimes we cruise along. There is ever-changing scenery to inspire us, if only we pause long enough to look. We do not run well all the time. Sometimes we feel down. But during those times, there are resources to energize us. Hebrews reminds us that we do not run the race alone (Hebrews 12:1–3). There are saints who have gone before us, cheering us on. Sometimes, other runners come alongside us and they energize us as they pace us. There are also other people cheering us on. That is why we have this series of talks. As fellow runners, we are egging each other to press on!

Ultimately, even as we run, we look to the finishing line, fixing our eyes on Jesus. So, please keep running and do not give up. It is about overcoming the struggles in life, the obstacles and the temptations along the way, and running without stopping, no matter how tired we may feel. Resist those temptations! Let us finish our races not only well but also strongly.

Finally, all of us will stand before God one day at the judgement seat of Christ (2 Corinthians 5:10). What will God say to us? Is it "Well done, good and faithful servant, here is your crown of righteousness" (see Matthew 25:21)? Will we be able to say to ourselves, "We have brought glory to God on earth by completing the work God gave us to do"? (See Jesus' words in John 17:4, before He went back to heaven, having completed the work God gave Him to do.) So, the question for us is, what kind of legacy will we leave behind? How will our children turn out? Have we impacted our colleagues and clients; did we help or turn them away? What about people we have missed opportunities to witness to? Or missed doing good works that would have uplifted lives? Think for a moment what kind of legacy you will leave behind.

My Race: Time in Politics

Let me now share briefly about my own race, giving all glory to God. Everybody has a story to tell, as God deals with all of us in different ways. It just so happens that my life is a bit more public. My motivation is to glorify God and encourage brothers and sisters in Christ. I am still running my race — the race that God has marked out for me (Hebrews 12:1–2). I should be about three quarters of the way through, but nobody knows. My father passed away when he was only 50 years old from colorectal cancer, which has a strong hereditary element amongst Chinese men. That was in 1973, and I was 19 years old then. I thank God for every day I live beyond 50 years, which is 12 years ago!

I have lived my life in phases (some call these "seasons in life"). At each phase, I do my best, trusting in God to do the rest. My life thus far has followed this pattern: my experiences in earlier phases have prepared me for challenges in later phases. Take for example my involvement with the House of Hope (a drug rehabilitation halfway house) in the '70s. When I joined the Ministry of Home Affairs (MHA) in 1993 as Parliamentary Secretary, my first major assignment was to fight drugs. I was tasked by then Minister for Home Affairs, Professor Jayakumar, to form a multi-agency committee to devise a master plan to arrest the deteriorating drug abuse situation during that time.

This was where my involvement at the board level at the House of Hope came in useful. I also knew of the good work done by other religious bodies. Hence, my report made a recommendation — quite novel at that time — that religion could play a part in countering drug abuse and that the government should support these bodies, including providing financial support. A scheme was then devised to incentivize halfway houses across different religions — we even started a non-religious halfway house to cover all bases — to take in recovering drug addicts.

Another example is when I headed another multi-agency committee to counter juvenile delinquency and youth crime. Here, my earlier experiences as a Resident Fellow and Hall Master of Kent Ridge Hall (a student hostel) and Sub-Dean and Vice-Dean of NUS' Law Faculty stood me in good stead. Likewise, my days as an active all-round sportsman from my schooldays helped me tremendously in my work as Vice Chairman of the Committee for Sporting Singapore, when we devised a groundbreaking blueprint to raise the standard and impact of sports in Singapore.

Even the most mundane of things, such as enjoying my Mandarin lessons during my ACS days (unusual in those days for ACS boys!) was something God had engineered. Together with my two years of pre-school education at Kum Yan Kindergarten (which was then a Mandarin-focused kindergarten), that I took learning Mandarin seriously in school helped me to get my Mandarin up to speed quickly when I entered politics 20 to 25 years later! It is amazing how through these and other episodes the pieces came together!

Here is a general point that I would like to make: whatever vocation we are in, we should study God's Word and draw inspiration from it. In many vocations, there are either general principles or specific ones that are applicable. Verses that come quickly to mind include, "Whatever you do, work at it with all your heart, as working for the Lord, not for men" (Colossians 3:23). When I spent 14 years as a university law lecturer, I could draw inspiration from what Jesus said and did as a teacher. The different ways our Lord communicated His messages were fantastic! He used the Socratic method, posing questions rather than giving answers all the time. So, when the religious ruler asked Him, "What must I do to inherit eternal life?", Jesus' reply was in the form of a question, "What is written in the law? How do you read it?" (Luke 10:25-26).

Another example of how Jesus was a master teacher is in how He captured and aroused the attention of His listeners by opening the conversation with a provocative statement. Consider Jesus' encounter with Nicodemus, a Pharisee, who had come to Jesus in the dark of the night. Earlier on, Jesus had said this, "I tell you the truth, no one can see the Kingdom unless he is born again." Nicodemus got a real shock! How could he be born again? That provocative question was to get him engaged in conversation (John 3:1–21). Another technique Jesus used was in guiding His disciples in their thought process from the general to the specific. The Lord asked, "Who do people say I am?" After they had replied, He zoomed in pointedly, "But what about you? Who do you say I am?" He got them to open up first before probing them in a focused manner (Mark 8:27–30).

"The different ways our Lord communicated His messages were fantastic!"

Then in John 8:1–11, He taught non-verbally as well as He bent down and wrote on the ground with His finger, drawing the attention of His listeners. A final example comes from John 17, when He prayed to God with His disciples all listening. This approach is analogous to having two or three experts in a class holding a discussion while the students listen and learn. I encourage all of you to undertake a similar exercise to see which verses can guide and strengthen you in your vocation.

Making an Impact in Our Workplaces

God's Word should inspire us to make an impact where He puts us in our workplaces and marketplace.

In this regard, verses that have motivated me include Matthew 10:16, "be as shrewd as snakes and as innocent as doves". We live in a fallen world. We cannot be guileless, as there are people who mean us harm. We must be shrewd and wise. 2 Timothy 1:7 is also very meaningful to me: "For God did not give us a spirit of timidity, but a spirit of power, of love and of self-discipline". What a wonderfully poised balance to take as we tackle the challenges of the workplace and marketplace! Colossians 3:23 tells us to work heartily in all things as working for the Lord, not for men while Matthew 5:13–16 is the familiar exhortation to be salt and light. In politics, one verse in particular has been a consistent daily reminder, Micah 6:8, "He has showed you, O man, what is good. And what does the LORD require of you? To act justly and to love mercy and to walk humbly with your God".

Act justly. Thankfully, in my 18 years as an office-holder, there were many opportunities to promote justice. Take for example land acquisition laws where landowners will never be happy with the way they are compensated. I headed a committee that awarded ex-gratia payments to try to alleviate any financial hardship caused by the acquisition. Also, for over 18 years in politics, I handled a lot of appeals, especially in MHA — traffic fines, immigration cases, police cases, etc. I took pains to consider all these appeals carefully. My position in dealing with appeals was that whatever I decided had to be defensible, if raised in Parliament. I felt that, if justified, based on the facts and prevailing policies, discretion should be exercised wisely and fairly.

To **love mercy** is very much about showing compassion. As in "acting justly", here too, I had many opportunities to "love mercy". This is where my public persona came to the fore. People knew that I was a softer kind of politician, looking to exercise compassion wherever possible. To me, reaching out to everybody, regardless of race, language or religion, was important. I had the opportunity to be involved with many "second chance" initiatives. For example, a good number of prisoners are now released early under the Home Detention Scheme which was introduced in 2000.

I oversaw the formulation and implementation of community-based sentences such as the Mandatory Treatment Order (where a mentally-handicapped offender, if certified as such, can be treated at IMH instead of being sent to prison) and the Short Detention Order (where an accused person, if found guilty, can be sent to prison for a short while, for example, two weeks, which will not attract the odium of a prison record). Over at the Ministry of Law (MinLaw), God also gave me many opportunities "to love mercy" such as through the formulation and implementation of the Debt Release Scheme (where a person who could have been made a bankrupt previously may be saved from the bankruptcy regime provided certain conditions are satisfied).

To **walk humbly with God** is also important. Our Prime Minister said before the 2011 General Elections that "every PAP politician should be humble". Wow, I thought — a very Christian exhortation indeed! For a Christian politician, that must be the starting point.

The interesting thing is that the media introduced me back in 1991 as a committed Christian, a church elder, something I had mentioned in my curriculum vitae but did not publicize. Some of my close friends, including my mother, were concerned that it was not a good thing for me. In 1991, it was advantageous for anyone entering politics to be seen as being hard-headed; possessing a softer touch could be perceived as weakness! But for me, it was a fantastic thing! Once I was identified as a Christian, I could be a living testimony of Christ in me, not explicitly or "in your face" but through everything that I did or said. If I did well and touched lives, people would know that, as a committed Christian, I was motivated by Christ's love. That was my "witnessing and evangelizing", which in the context of politics in multi-racial and multi-religious Singapore, was appropriate, and probably more effective. In that way, I hope I reflected the presence of God in me every day.

God's Perfect Timing

God's timing in politics for me was wonderful. I entered politics in 1991, and retired from politics in May 2011. I attended a tea session with the party leaders before the 1988 General Election but was not fielded then. If I had been fielded in 1988, I would have been only 34 years old, quite unprepared to enter the political arena. More importantly, between 1988 and 1991, I was able to serve and grow in church as an elected elder in our church Session for three years (May 1987–May 1990). I also became Hall Master of Kent Ridge Hall (December 1988–June 1993), which was a great training ground for politics. The timing of my season in politics was perfect, both the entry and exit points. They were key turning points in my life.

I had spent two years as a backbench Member of Parliament (MP) between August 1991 and June 1993. During that time, I was promoted to the position of Associate Professor at the NUS Law Faculty. If I had crossed over to the front bench immediately upon my election in August 1991, I would have taken leave from the university as a Senior Lecturer, not Associate Professor. Whilst we should not be overly enamoured with titles and status, it is nice to have crossed this key professional milestone. Now, post-politics, I have returned to NUS part-time as an associate professorial fellow, retaining my title as Associate Professor. Hence, I remain "Prof Ho" to those who knew me in politics, which I hope is a term of endearment to those who use it!

In early 1992, I was asked to join NTUC full-time by then NTUC Secretary-General Ong Teng Cheong. This was before I took my six-month sabbatical when I had published enough to be promoted to Associate Professor. As an academic, the government felt it was good for me to go to the ground, roll up my sleeves and interact with the workers. I told Mr Ong that whilst I welcomed the opportunity to do this, the timing was not ideal as I wanted to take my sabbatical leave and work towards my Associate Professorship. I would gladly join NTUC after that. Thank God, Mr Ong agreed. In the interim period, another MP took up the NTUC position and I was no longer required there.

Then, in early 1993, a brother in the Lord who was an office-holder at MHA stepped down from office to return to the private sector and be a backbencher. This was the turning point that paved the way for me to take leave from NUS to assume full-time political office at both MHA and MinLaw, a stint that lasted a full 18 years, until I stepped down in May 2011! Indeed, God's leading and guidance came a step at a time. As it says in Psalm 119:105, "Your word is a lamp to my feet and a light for my path".

Another matter that I am thankful for is that I was not promoted to the position of full Minister in the Cabinet. Close friends, especially non-believing ones, felt sorry for me. They thought I had done enough to deserve such a promotion. But it did not happen. Looking back, it is clear that God had designed it such in His plan for me. For one thing, as a Cabinet Minister, I would not have been able to choose the timing of my retirement from politics. Quite rightly, that would have been the Prime Minister's prerogative. This means I would very likely still be in politics now, not being able to do the many things I enjoy doing, including God's Kingdom work.

Moreover, as a Cabinet Minister, life would have been very different. I would have been totally absorbed in my work, with less time and energy for anything else, including church and family. I would not have been able to attend the weekly church prayer meeting regularly or go for the annual church camp (both of which, by God's grace, I did throughout my 18 years in full-time politics). As it turned out, being deputy to two very senior ministers (both of whom later became Deputy Prime Ministers), I was not in the frontline, yet enjoyed the latitude to do many things that I felt were important for Singapore, especially in helping to make it a softer, more compassionate society. And most importantly, I had a meaningful life outside politics. When I stepped down from politics, MHA gave me a "Thank You" reception where I sang "My Way". Of course, it was not really my way; it was God's way!

"Esther Moments"

Finally, brothers, I encourage all of you to look out for "Esther moments" or turning points in your lives. God had prepared Esther to be in the royal palace as a replacement Queen, "[to] come to royal position for such a time as this" (Esther 4:14) when King Xerxes was about to decimate the Jewish people. Mordecai had asked her to go, uninvited and without an audience being granted, to see the king and plead with him — an act which attracted grave danger to herself. But she went, and that was a turning point.

How does this apply to us? I have shared my story and how God has worked in my life, including the turning points or "Esther moments". God had used me in politics to help shape Singapore's society. In turn, Singapore stands out in the region and the world for its good governance. This includes espousing godly values such as uplifting the weaker segments in society, honesty and incorruptibility, family as society's building block and recognizing religion as a force for good.

It is a matter of seeing where God leads, a step at a time. He has led me through different phases or seasons in life to where I am today. Post-politics, I try to add value wherever He puts me. This includes sharing at diverse forums on spiritual matters, especially leadership development, prayer, and men's ministry in church, both in and outside Singapore. He is working in your life too. There are certainly "Esther moments" in your life, as there were mine. How do we recognize these "Esther moments" and seize them, as Esther did? At such times, how do we respond as God would want us to, with fortitude and total trust in Him? That is the question all of us need to ask. Ultimately in your life, it boils down to your relationship with God — God the Father, the Son and the Holy Spirit.

A Concluding Prayer

As men for Christ, may this be our prayer:

O Lord, by Your grace and strength, may we live our lives for You. Make us the best man that each of us can be — as husbands and fathers in the family; as workers in the workplace; as citizens of Singapore and as soldiers for Christ in the spiritual battles being waged here on earth. Onward, as Christian soldiers, we march together. Help us, O Lord, to sense Your presence daily; tap Your power fully and live out Your purpose for our lives wholly. To God be the glory! Amen.

▪ ▪ ▪

Questions for Reflection

1

Have you formed a worldview for yourself? How does this worldview impact your thinking, words and actions?

2

What Bible verses motivate you in your work and walk with God? Why?

3

So far, what have been the turning points or "Esther moments" in your life? How did you respond? On further reflection, if given the opportunity, would you have responded differently, and why?

4

What are the areas in your life that you sense God wants you to work on to be a more effective man for Christ?

5

Are you happy thus far, running the race that has been marked out for you? If so, why? If not, why?

Associate Professor Ho Peng Kee stepped down as Senior Minister of State for Law and Home Affairs in May 2011 and returned to the Law Faculty, NUS as an Associate Professorial Fellow. An elder at Mount Carmel Bible-Presbyterian Church, he remains active in community service as a volunteer. Peng Kee chairs the Home Team Volunteer Network Steering Committee at MHA and the Community Mediation Advisory Committee at MinLaw. He is also Advisor and Patron to several not-for-profit organizations that promote mediation and sports, support children with cancer, foster youth entrepreneurship and voluntarism, and care for the elderly. He was recently appointed a Justice of the Peace.

"Now to him
who is able to do
immeasurably more
than all we ask or
imagine, according
to his power that is
at work within us"

(EPHESIANS 3:20)

FINISHING WELL

NAVIGATING LIFE'S TRANSITIONS

Andrew Goh

Each day, as we grow older, we are also drawing nearer. Nearer to our final home, heaven. Losing sight of this can be one of life's great tragedies. But we are cheered by someone like C. S. Lewis who once observed, "If I find in myself a desire which no experience in this world can satisfy, the most probable explanation is that I was made for another world."

This year, some of us may be thinking or talking about retiring. Others prefer the word "re-tyring", which means getting new treads like for the wheels of our car. Some others are enthralled by the "re-firing", as in getting all whooped up for the next (final?) stage of life.

The Caleb Spirit

In that context, I got an impression from the Lord that this year, as I get older and hopefully wiser, I can claim the spirit of Caleb. And so can you. Simply put, it is to find in him a practical and inspiring role model. In my reckoning, Caleb was God's "reserve" guy. He was the back up for Joshua. Any time Joshua had a meal that didn't agree with him or if he had fallen over a cliff, or got hit by a big rock, Caleb would step up to the plate.

But once Israel entered into the Promised Land, that role as "Mister Standby" was over. What did he desire? He asked for the hill country (mountainous territory). He did not ask for the easy parts. In fact, he wanted to get out of Joshua's way. I pray that the spirit of Caleb will come upon you and, in your latter years, you will opt for tougher assignments. Because He who is in you is infinitely great and will accomplish in your life "more than all [you] ask or imagine, according to his power that is at work within [you]" (Ephesians 3:20). In fact, "as thy days, so shall thy strength be" (Deuteronomy 33:25, KJV). You can only get stronger as the days flit by.

"Breakfast with Jesus"

Who would have thought there's a wider platform ahead? It all started with a little spare time in the final week of 2012. I wrote 31 daily devotionals on "Discipleship" and passed it to my church for them to use in any way they find useful. Since I am a "print" person, I thought they would publish a little booklet of 31 daily devotionals or put it on the church website for our members to access and read.

But God opened a different door. The younger staff members saw an opportunity to turn it into a format suitable for social media! They videotaped me in short daily segments (lasting about three minutes each) and "pushed" it to the original target of 1,600 church members' smartphones. In turn, we hoped some of the recipients would "push" it to their friends, family members or colleagues, resulting in a multiplier effect. Somebody gave it the name "Breakfast with Jesus", and it caught on and subsequently became the series' title.[1] The response was good and we produced a second series on "Hope". A little thing has gotten underway.

Once something is uploaded to YouTube, it goes round the world and reaches people from all over — Australia, New Zealand, Portugal. An American military chaplain based in Germany saw our videos. Later, he visited our church and we were introduced to each other. I welcomed him and said, "I'm Andrew Goh". He said, "I already know you." He had watched both series! How wonderful — a simple thing like that, meant for 1,600 persons in our church, went on to 8,000, then 10,000 and I am told it now has 100,000 hits.

And you know the old refrain: what He has done for me, He can do for (and through) you. Just when you think you are at the tail end of your life, God has big plans and you fit right in. I stand as testimony that God is not done with us yet!

A Life Verse

Do you have a "life verse"? It was common for people of our cohort to claim a life verse — for guidance, as a point of reference and a constant reminder of God's good hand on our lives. Mine is Proverbs 11:24–25 (KJV):

> *There is that scattereth, and yet increaseth; and there is that withholdest more than is meet, but it tendeth to poverty. The liberal soul shall be made fat: and he that watereth shall be watered also himself.*

There is a mystery in life, verily, a paradox. Contrary to general understanding, "there is that scattereth, and yet increaseth". One would have thought that dispersal means loss. But no, in the divine economy, what you give away finds its way back to you. Mainly because God owes no one anything and in His special way, as we continue to depend on Him for life and life provisions, He is always more than able. God's conduits are always in good repair. There is something special about receiving it from His hand.

On the contrary, hoarding more than is meet tips over to poverty. "My cup runs over" (Psalm 23:5, NKJV) is so apt and descriptive — that not only would my needs be met, but through generosity and sensitivity to the needs of others we get to be more like our Heavenly Father. God uses us as His channels of blessings. Recall the widow of Zarephath whose jar of flour and jug of oil never ran out because God used her to feed His prophet Elijah (1 Kings 17:14). Ultimate lesson? "The word of the LORD ... is truth" (1 Kings 17:24, KJV).

Importance of Reading

Allow me to share a little about myself. I am a "print" man. I'm still into books. I love the smell of newly printed literature. It sort of intoxicates me. More than 40 years ago, we started the *Youth* magazine, which eventually became the *Impact* magazine. Besides locals, many Third World pastors and church leaders appreciate getting the magazine. Some walk five miles to the store or library to read them. One from the Caribbean had an odd request — could we ensure that none in his congregation gets to read our magazine, because he builds quite a few of his sermons from *Impact*? To each his own and from each his best. In turn, we get Singapore Christians to sponsor their subscriptions, so those who have no time to read supply those who enjoy this resource. This makes sense and completes the loop.

Currently, we have a second platform, which is the electronic version of *Impact*. Now, for minimal incremental costs, we are able to send out hundreds of copies to email addresses anywhere in the world, to anyone with handy access to a computer. We save on storage, stamps and manpower.

It is possible to read and not reflect, but it is difficult to reflect without reading. Reading slows the mind down to grasp, comprehend, unpack and re-pack thoughts into meaningful inputs that can deeply change lives.

Heaven: Our Final Destination

As we navigate life's transitions, we are ever so mindful that sooner or later, we end up at our destination. We should all become experts on heaven. When was the last time someone asked you about heaven? If we're going to spend all eternity there, it behoves us to know much about it. The very thought of heaven should bring us cheer and a spring to our step.

> "The very thought of heaven should bring us cheer and a spring to our step."

My favourite question about heaven came from an earnest lady who shook my hand on the way out of church (where I was a guest preacher) and asked, "How big is heaven?" I tried my best to impress her that heaven is much bigger than anything she can possibly imagine. "Ginormous" was one of the descriptions. She didn't look fully convinced. So, I asked her why she raised that question. She shot back: "Because there are people I want to avoid in heaven."

Cool. Here is someone sure of getting to heaven. And she is also sure that there would be people there whom she wouldn't like! Looks like being saved by grace does have this drawback. I took a quick minute to share with her that we would all be so gloriously transformed, she may even be attracted to this person who seems to have turned her off on earth! And with that I raced to catch up with the pastor for a comforting cup of coffee.

Just after the Iron Curtain rusted and came crumbling down, a young American tourist visited a Czechoslovakian philosopher, whose house was rather bare. The young man, innocently albeit unwisely asked, "Where is your furniture?"

The philosopher asked in return, "How about you, where is yours?" To which the young man replied, "I am just passing through." The philosopher responded, "So am I."

This and similar stories may equip us to be always ready to talk about heaven. 1 Peter 3:15 (KJV) exhorts us to be ready for "every man that asketh you a *reason* of the *hope* that is in you" (emphasis added). Surely that hope is the certainty of an eternity to be spent with our dear Heavenly Father, our Lord Jesus and the Holy Spirit. We are not to be brash or boastful in sharing but meek and respectful.

Once I was invited to speak at a convention full of realtors. Halfway through my talk, I paused and shared with them that I was also a property agent. Eyebrows were raised as that was not mentioned in my résumé or introduction. I told them, I represented a Principal. I do not deal with flats or apartments. In fact, I don't even deal with terrace houses or bungalows. I only deal in "mansions" which are fully paid for. My Principal has assured me, "In my Father's house are many mansions ... I go to prepare a place for you" (John 14:2, KJV). I explained that I am duly authorized and credentialled to handle all relevant transactions, and invited anyone who had any interest to have a quick word with me after the formalities were over.

Transitions

We are not lemmings rushing in step over a cliff. My favourite story for this centres on a friend who at Primary Five (age of eleven) was already the champion athlete on Sports Day. He took home a replica of the big trophy as his prize. In Primary Six, he was the obvious champion again. He had won it for two years running. The rule, I was told, was that if someone won three times in a row, he or she would get to keep the actual trophy. I asked him to consider repeating that year in school so that he could win for the third time. He gave me an unusual look and asked in good Singaporean English, "For what?" Indeed.

It's a good life in Singapore. Despite our culture to complain — a warped expression of happiness — life is good here. And we need not make any apologies for it. But are we just marching on the spot or pursuing God's great purposes? Who are we taking our reference points from? Advertising is so powerful yet subtle — we are sucked into conformity instead of obeying Romans 12:1–2, to be transformed and take our bearings from God's Word and Spirit. We are not likely to achieve anything great while staying in our comfort zones. However, "the people that do know their God shall be strong, and do exploits" (Daniel 11:32, KJV) — they break out of their cocoons and march to the beat of a different drum. Leonard Ravenhill, though dead, continues to speak. He asked simply, "Are the things you are living for, the things Christ died for?"

Last Monday, I met a young man whose name is also Andrew. He informed me that he has just celebrated his fortieth birthday and that he had retired five years earlier! Do you envy him? I asked, "How's your cash flow?" His exact words: "God gave me eight businesses." He doesn't interfere with their daily running. His name card showed the eight businesses. I enquired further, "Any commonality among the businesses?" Nope. The only thing common to all eight? "They all make money." He spends well over two-thirds of his time doing mission work in places like Cambodia and Myanmar.

How much is "enough"? How much before we dare to live out our lives as C. T. Studd described — "only one life, 'twill soon be past; only what's done for Christ shall last"? I think each person must find that level for himself.

Till the Lord Returns

Last year, I went on four mission trips, including for the first time, a trip to Moscow, Russia. What struck me was how open Russia is to the gospel. At a public meeting that I attended, there were 2,000 pastors present! In addition, I was told that there are many young Russians who are devoting one year of their life to do evangelistic work such as distributing Bible portions, which are warmly received in the countryside. How is that possible? While I had the impression that Russians were "very" Communist, they explained that for a thousand years before that, they were called the Holy Russian Empire; the word "holy" as in "righteous". At the core, they are still very Christian, though Orthodox.

This is transition. Things change. Finally, we go to heaven. We still have time to witness and evangelize. For the first time in my life, I recognize that it is possible for the gospel to be preached to every person. When I was growing up, I was figuring out how Christ's Second Coming might have to be delayed, so that more people can hear the gospel. But today, we have the technology to ensure that people get to hear the gospel. They may not be able to read, but they can hear and understand. It may take too long to teach them to be literate and numerate, but however illiterate they are, whenever they have the gospel preached in their dialect or language, they get to hear.

As a young Christian, I always wondered how many generations would pass before Jesus comes again. Do we believe this is the last generation? Every generation thinks they are the last generation. That's the intent of the Bible. The Bible wants every generation to think they are the last generation. What would happen if you do not consider yourselves the last generation? You can play around. You can fool around. Hence, the Bible makes it clear that every generation is the last generation, even the early church. Every generation feels that they are the last generation. I see signs that this may indeed be so! Darkness is going to be so great. What is wrong will eventually become regarded as right — topsy-turvy.

In June, we went for a holiday in San Francisco. While there, we saw a brand new tourist attraction — nudists on bicycles! This happened when we were sitting at a waterside eatery. Forty of them cycled past. The waiter said to us, "It can only happen in San Francisco." This is only the tip of the proverbial iceberg. Therefore a light has to shine, especially in America. There has to be a clearer definition of what is right and wrong. But then, it depends on who or what you take as your reference point!

Applying this to ourselves, if we compare ourselves with others, we could say, "I am only 60 years old and I still have not bought my second condominium. Better work harder by giving tuition at night." Be careful who you take as your reference point. One good point of reference are godly people. These are people who have the Word of God in them and live it out in their lives. The Bible says there is no end to hoarding. Somewhere you and I will have to draw a line and say, "Enough is enough." I am not asking you to take to poverty. This would be the last thing I will ask because the riches of Christ are yours.

Never Too Late!

We all know that God is called the "Rock of Ages" and "Ancient of Days", meaning He transcends time! To the seniors amongst you, feel encouraged that some of the greatest men and women in the world became hugely successful only after they turned 65. They were "nobodies" before 65. Look at Colonel Sanders of Kentucky Fried Chicken fame. Do you know what upset him when he retired? His social security cheque was too little. Insufficient. He said something like this, "I worked all my life. Now I am ancient and forgotten! And this is the amount I have. I cannot live on this." Guess what? He then opened a restaurant. The restaurant did very well because cars were passing by. But not long after that, more highways were built and they bypassed his restaurant. He was in debt again when he was 67 years old! But did he stay defeated? He started the KFC franchise and the rest, as they say, is history.

In the End, It Will Be Okay

Let me conclude by giving you a phrase that has been associated with me. This phrase did not originate with me. But somehow, I got stuck with it: "In the end, it will be okay." Let's say it together, "In the end, it will be okay." I have confidence that it will be okay. Great men like Billy Graham and Tony Campolo have said that they had gone to the last chapter of the Bible and checked it out. And they conclude: "In the end, it will be okay."

Whether to a pregnant lady carrying her load of love, a married couple working through some troublesome spots or a child with loads of books to study, the message remains: "In the end, it will be okay". Because the second part says: "If it's not okay, it's not the end". So, stick it out to the end! He will carry you through.

In the end, it is okay.
If it's not okay, it's not the end.

▪ ▪ ▪

Questions for Reflection

Over the triple doorway of the Cathedral of Milan, there are three inscriptions spanning the splendid arches. A beautiful wreath of roses is carved over one of the arches, and underneath are the words: "All that pleases is but for a moment". Over a second arch is chiselled a cross, accompanied by the statement, "All that troubles is but for a moment". But over the central entrance to the main portal one reads, "That only is important that is eternal".

1

"Forever is real; today is temporary." How does this make sense when we are constantly bombarded to think of the present and immediate only?

2

By its very definition, "transitions" means a passage. It can be likened to "change management". What skill sets or competencies are needed to handle transitions well?

3

In mountain climbing jargon, there are supposedly three types of people:

a) Climbers, who aim to reach the top;
b) Settlers, who are satisfied with being half-way up; and
c) Tourists, who take photographs of the mountain and regale their friends with the different brands of beer they had tasted at the foothills.

Is there a parallel for Christians as sojourners in this world?

4

Will our Lord Jesus Christ return in our lifetime? Does it matter to you which way it pans out?

Dr Andrew Goh is honorary editor of Impact *magazine and has been involved in Christian publishing for more than 40 years. He earned his PhD from Nanyang Technological University (NTU). A motivational speaker and management consultant, he has worked with top Singapore and multinational companies. A founding elder of RiverLife Church, Andrew shares both in and outside Singapore, and many remember his "free-flowing" messages interspersed with quick humour and interesting stories. He was previously Chair of the Singapore Advisory Council of World Vision International and Halogen Foundation. His email address is <editor@impact.com.sg>.*

GROWING IN RIGHTEOUSNESS

Lee Soo Ann

Psalm 92

[1]It is good to praise the LORD
and make music to your name, O Most High,
[2]to proclaim your love in the morning
and your faithfulness at night,
[3]to the music of the ten-stringed lyre
and the melody of the harp.

[4]For you make me glad by your deeds, O LORD;
I sing for joy at the works of your hands.
[5]How great are your works, O LORD,
how profound your thoughts!
[6]The senseless man does not know,
fools do not understand,
[7]that though the wicked spring up like grass
and all evildoers flourish,
they will be forever destroyed.

[8]But you, O LORD, are exalted forever.

[9]For surely your enemies, O Lord;
surely your enemies will perish;
all evildoers will be scattered.
[10]You have exalted my horn like that of a wild ox;
fine oils have been poured upon me.
[11]My eyes have seen the defeat of my adversaries;
my ears have heard the rout of my wicked foes.

[12]The righteous will flourish like a palm tree,
they will grow like a cedar of Lebanon;
[13]planted in the house of the Lord,
they will flourish in the courts of our God.
[14]They will still bear fruit in old age,
they will stay fresh and green,
[15]proclaiming, "The Lord is upright;
he is my Rock, and there is no wickedness in him."

I chose this psalm because I expected that most of you today would be above 50 years old! Verse 14 correctly depicts the state of older people, that is, "they will still bear fruit in their old age". My mind focused on this psalm when I met a group of cheerful senior citizens who call themselves "9214". I asked them what "9214" meant and they referred me to Psalm 92:14!

I have come to like the verse so much that I have made it my motto in old age. I am now 75 years old. At this age, I can "still bear fruit". Wow, how wonderful! So, let me share an exposition on Psalm 92.

All of us start ageing the moment we are born, some faster than others. I was told that when we are born we have about 70 billion cells in our bodies. They start to die the moment we are born! That is why by the time I reach my present age, I'm already half-dead! A lot of cells have died. So, an older person's memory is not that good, not so sharp.

The mental picture is that of "diminishing circles" as we grow older. Some of us suffer reduced incomes. Some of us feel threatened because younger people want to replace us. Others suffer the loss of friends and family. I think I have more friends who have passed away than those who are still alive! But the good thing is that even though our friends have departed physically, they live on in us; our good friends become part of us. They manifest themselves in our personality and never really disappear.

Then there is diminution of respect for older persons when we take the MRT; few give up their seat for you. Younger people just sit there, close their eyes and pretend not to see you. A friend who is about my age deliberately stands in front of these ungracious people and glare at them until they give up their seats for him!

Technology impacts life, especially the aged. Every now and then there are new software programmes coming into the market. For today's talk, I had put the slides in my iPad and emailed them out. But Pastor Kheng Hai could not open them because they were in "pptx", not "ppt" format. Thank God that a young lady could convert the slides into a suitable format as otherwise you would not see them this morning.

Technology makes us old! As you age, if you don't keep reading, you will not be able to understand the latest iPad or iPhone models and how they work. So how do we counter that? We need to have "expanding circles".

How do we experience "expanding circles"? My circles appear to diminish, but in aggregate, they expand in these areas: time, senses, reflections, roots and fruits. If you develop all these five, which sum up as an aggregate, you actually find yourself growing. And growing can offset the diminishing.

Part of us stops growing and starts to die. But another part of us keeps growing. This is the thrust of the Christian faith, that overall, we never stop growing. To do so requires effort. But the one who gives the effort is God. And it is by the grace of God that we can expand our circles.

So let's take "time" first, before we move into "senses", "reflections", "roots" and "fruits", and then review all of them together. The first thing is "time". Time enables us to expand our circles in praise:

1*It is good to praise the* L*ORD*
and make music to your name, O Most High,
2*to proclaim your love in the morning*
and your faithfulness at night,
3*to the music of the ten-stringed lyre*
and the melody of the harp.

One of the hardest things to do is to praise, especially when one is going through difficult times. Now, praise is different from gratitude. Gratitude means saying thank you to God for what He has given you. What if God hasn't given you anything? If God gives you illness and old age and loss of income, how can you say thank you to God?

The answer from the Bible is that we must praise. Praise is different because the key note in praise is what we call appreciation. Appreciation is not gratitude. Appreciation means that when you see something good or lovely, when you recognize "whatever is true, whatever is honorable, ... whatever is pure, whatever is lovely" (Philippians 4:8, ESV), you appreciate it. Although you yourself may not be aesthetically inclined, you applaud when you appreciate something beautiful. In music, you clap your hands when you appreciate it although you yourself are not musically inclined. When it is a good performance, you show appreciation.

So appreciation starts not from looking at what God has done for you but looking at who God is. Start by asking who God is. This is called the stage of "love of God". C. S. Lewis says that there are many stages in our love of God. First of all, we tend to love God because of what God does for us. Hence, we thank God for sending Jesus to die for us on the cross. But you must move to the stage that regardless of what He has done for you, you appreciate simply who God is. So you must begin appreciating the little things around you. Then we can have an appreciative heart. You can go through life never finding anything to be grateful for and yet you are full of praise to God. So it is good to praise the Lord. Many grateful Christians say "PTL" or "Praise the Lord" all the time. No matter how small a matter may be, they say, "Praise the Lord".

I think it is a good thing to always praise the Lord, regardless of what He has done for you. We started with time, and Sunday is the time we ought to start praising God. Sunday is quite unique. It is not the Sabbath of Psalm 92. Psalm 92 as an Old Testament hymn refers to the Sabbath on a Saturday. So why are we worshipping on Sunday? The reason is that Jesus rose from the dead on Sunday — a sign of new life. And so we choose to celebrate Sunday, when new life starts.

It is very interesting when you read the Sabbath account. The origin of the Sabbath is found in Genesis 1: the first day God did this, the second day God did that, the third day He did this and that and so on. And at the end of each day, there is a statement that there was evening and there was morning. And so it was on the first day; the second day the same phrase is repeated. You find this phrase repeated in all the six days but on the seventh day something disappears. There is no statement that there was morning and there was evening and it was the seventh day. Why? The seventh day is the day when God rested. When God made the earth, the water, the animals, the plants, there is a "start" and "finish", and it is true that the physical world now is sort of "finished" by God.

But the rest of God's work has not ended yet. God is still resting, so the seventh day is actually still continuing. We Christians celebrate the first day of the week, Sunday, as Sabbath. It is a complete day of rest, which we should spend in reflection, for on this day God looked back at what He did on the earlier six days. On Sundays, you and I should not just look forward to a new life but look back on the past and to say thank you to God, to appreciate God for who He is. It is very difficult to find a Sunday that never ends. To imagine that in heaven, Sunday never ends! The praise of God never ends. It is continuous. This is the glory of how wonderful our life will be in heaven. So praise is to be accompanied with gladness and joy.

Psalm 92:4 says, "For you make me glad by your deeds, O Lord; I sing for joy at the works of your hands". Verse 5 reminds us, "How great are your works, O Lord, how profound your thoughts!" The word "joy" is a three-letter word: 'J', 'O', 'Y'. It can be taken to mean **J**esus first, **O**thers second, and **Y**ourself last — that's how I remember the word. When you think of what God has created we cannot help but exclaim as in verse 5, "How great are your works, O Lord, how profound your thoughts!" The more you understand God, the better the insights you will have in your work.

> "The praise of God never ends. It is continuous."

One of the early church fathers is Augustine. He has said there is double knowledge: you must first of all know yourself and then God. However, if you continue to know God more, you get to know yourself more. This double knowledge is very important. If you know God, you actually end up knowing yourself better. So this praise never ends. Sabbath never ends. Continuity in praise does not say, "Today I finished my Sunday Service. I'll go home and rest and do other things."

The praise should continue. Praising God will help the Church to press on, into the afternoon and night, and then the next day and so on. It may be difficult, but this is very important. If we stop praising God, we end up praising ourselves or other people. Although you and I do praise other people and ourselves, behind that there should always be the praise for God. God sustains your praise for others and for yourselves. Whenever you find it difficult to love somebody — your spouse, children or colleagues — you should praise God. It would then be easier for you to praise and love that person next to you.

The first thing you should pray about is how to continuously praise God. You say, "I cannot pray that long with eyes closed." It is all right to pray with your eyes opened. In the Jewish tradition, when Jews pray, they open their eyes. It is astonishing to discover this but it is true. They say that when they open their eyes, they actually find more to praise God. So you need not close your eyes when you praise God. I know it is very difficult to open your eyes as you may be distracted by things around you. But please remember: you can see God even though there is activity around you. You see all that is going on and you can see that God is behind it.

God gives us five senses: hearing, taste, touch, smell and sight. When you use your senses, you experience more than what appears on the surface. Take sight as an example. Helen Keller, whom we all know is blind and deaf, said that "the only thing worse than being blind is having sight but no vision". You and I have sight but we may have no vision. We don't see beyond our eyes. So, our eyes actually put limitations on us. I have a blind friend who has more vision than me. Since he is blind, all that he can see is vision. Vision means his imagination, his thinking power that is far greater than what I have with my eyes.

I would still look forward should I go blind one day. Do not be afraid of losing your senses one by one. Of our five senses, which do you think is the earliest sense we get? When the baby is born, the baby hears. Hearing is the first sense we have. If the baby cannot hear, the baby will not survive. And the moment you die, the last thing to go is hearing. That is why Paul said, "consequently, faith comes from hearing the message, and the message is heard through the word of Christ" (Romans 10:17). The Word of God penetrates into our hearts and souls because our hearing is connected to our brain. The stimulus is quite direct. Use our senses fully. Go beyond the surface — this is the first step to understanding God.

The Psalm continues thus: "The senseless man does not know, fools do not understand, that though the wicked spring up like grass and all evildoers flourish, they will be forever destroyed" (vv. 6–7). For me, this is a very important statement because all Christians are plagued with the problem of evil. Why are there so many bad things happening? Every now and then, our newspapers report bad things such as floods in China and the typhoon in Hong Kong. The whole appears to be gripped in evil. The answer lies in these words, "the wicked spring up like grass".

What is more common than grass? Everywhere we find grass. And evil is like grass. What makes grass small in comparison to the tree? Although the grass is all around, the tree still stands tall and the grass disappears. Although evil is around us, it has no roots. The roots have been destroyed. When Christ died on the cross, He hit Satan on the head. Satan was defeated, but Satan is still wriggling, still moving, that's why there is so much evil in the world. But evil is like grass; it cannot be sustained. Overturn the grass and never be afraid of evil for evil is like grass.

Let me ask you, why then are you and I often afraid of grass? Grass is grass and is meant to be walked on. You and I can walk on grass. We can triumph by digging it up and throwing it into a fire. This is how we should treat evil. Evil is not an independent force. It is perverted goodness. Evil is an angel who has fallen. So Satan is an angel but fallen. He regarded himself as God, but he is not God. God is God. All evil is perverted goodness. Think of an evil we see around us happening. For example, a man rapes a woman. You say that is terrible. But think about it — a man cannot rape a woman unless the man has a desire for sex. And a desire for sex in a marriage is healthy as it is a God-given gift. When a man perverts that desire, he loses control over it. So the man is a healthy male with a God-given desire although he has committed rape. Even rape, a terrible thing, is actually perverted goodness.

This is how you can get a sense of proportion. You are not carried away by whatever is pushing you down day by day. Whatever you see — corruption, war and so on — look upon them as perverted goodness, distorted goodness. Thank God, evil is all like grass and will all be destroyed.

In contrast, righteousness is like a tree. Think of an apple tree. You can count the number of seeds in an apple, and every apple seed contains the capacity to become an apple tree. So the apple seed contains many apples. The apple may have only so many seeds but what is important are the seeds.

A fruit is special; it bears seeds. There are some seedless fruits. Most fruits have seeds; we value fruit more when it bears seeds. Righteousness bears fruit. Righteousness can reproduce itself. You can never know how much goodness can come from one act of righteousness. Grass is not like fruit. Grass can only be reproduced by conscious planting.

Then the psalm goes on to say:

> *But you, O Lord, are exalted forever. For surely your enemies, O Lord, surely your enemies will perish; all evildoers will be scattered. You have exalted my horn like that of a wild ox; fine oils have been poured upon me. My eyes have seen the defeat of my adversaries; my ears have heard the rout of my wicked foes.* (vv. 8–11)

So this is what happens to grass. Do not be afraid of grass. Being destroyed is the fate of all grass.

However, we rejoice in the fact that we can bear fruit. A symbol for those of us who stay near the equator is the coconut palm tree. The wonderful thing about the palm tree is its steadiness. It moves when the wind moves it from side to side. The fruit it bears can fill your hunger; if you are thirsty, the water in the coconut can quench your thirst and the tree leaves you can use to make the roof of your house.

Are you and I like the palm tree? If you are, verses 12–15 say that

> *The righteous will flourish like a palm tree, they will grow like a cedar of Lebanon; planted in the house of the Lord, they will flourish in the courts of our God. They will still bear fruit in old age, they will stay fresh and green, proclaiming, "The Lord is upright; he is my Rock, and there is no wickedness in him."*

So, the secret is not just to live a long life but a righteous life planted in the house of the Lord. Many people in the world are not "planted in the house of the Lord". When we are planted in the house of God, we are nourished by God and sustained by Him in all that we do. Jesus provides the analogy that He is the vine and we are the branches.

The tree roots make the tree tall. You are rooted in Christ. You are rooted in God's Word. You are rooted among God's people. The primary root is in Christ, in God's Word. Are we branches? A branch is something that extends out, bearing fruit. As a tree reaches out further, the more branches it will have. It is the vine which sustains you. Jesus is the vine. Without the vine, the branches cannot exist. We are not the real branches. The real branches (the Jews) are Abraham's descendants. Many of them do not believe in Jesus. We (the Gentiles) are grafted onto the vine. So, be all the more careful. God who removes the natural branch (the Jews) can also remove you.

Never take your faith for granted. The Holy Spirit must continue to anchor you and rejuvenate you. Try to read the Bible daily. The Bible has 33,000 verses. It comes to a hundred verses a day. You can read the Bible through in one year. We are tall trees. But if we are not sustained by God's Word, we will be like grass trodden on by other people. If we grow into a palm tree, we will be so much taller than the grass. God builds His people through God's Word. Trust God. Through God's Word, He will make you a tree.

▪ ▪ ▪

Questions for Reflection

1

What are the circles of activity that are diminishing in my life?

2

What are the circles that have the potential to grow?

3

How does the act of praise start circles that can grow?

4

Why are we more like a tree than grass?

5

What sustains a tree in its growth?

Dr Lee Soo Ann's insights are based on his many years in Christian and academic leadership. Currently a senior fellow in the Department of Economics and the NUS Lee Kuan Yew School of Public Policy, he was also Professor and Dean of Accountancy and Business Administration (1980–1985) and General Secretary of the Bible Society of Singapore (1990–2003). Author of several books and many articles on Singapore, Dr Lee is currently a preaching elder of Prinsep Street Presbyterian Church, President of the Bible Society of Singapore and Advisor to Presbyterian Community Services. His email address is <leesooann@gmail.com>.

LIVING LIFE IN CHAPTERS

William Wan

I have a confession to make. For the longest time, both when I was serving in the church and when I was practising as a lawyer, I avoided politicians. Even so, I prayed very much for them.

I also have friends who have become politicians. But there's this feeling that I must distance myself from them, even though I know them, because there is just this discomfort with them. But God has a very humorous and strange way of getting me to work with politicians in this season of my life. And I have discovered that many of them are just wonderful people, many of them love the Lord and many of them are serving with their hearts. That is really amazing.

So, this is my "confession". But you know, this is one aspect of living through "seasons of life". God opens our eyes to certain things. We are always learning new things including the mysteries of God's workings.

My Journey

Today, I want to share with you about my journey. First, a little bit about myself. I have three children whom God has blessed. I have been a pastor for a long time. Imagine raising three kids and trying to put them through universities in Singapore, or overseas for that matter. It is not easy. What I share today, I do so authentically and sincerely with all praise going to the Lord.

Indeed, God has been good. My three children were educated overseas because we lived abroad for more than 20 years. My oldest child, Li-Ann, went to Eastern University, USA, where I was a visiting professor. She received a subsidized education, earning a degree in psychology, and did her professional degree at Hahnemann College of Medicine in Philadelphia (now Drexel College of Medicine). She now practises art therapy in Media, Pennsylvania. She is married to Danny, an architect, and they have two children — Ava, who is 17, and Juli, 16.

We have a second daughter, Li-Lynn, who went through a period of rebelliousness. When she was 16, we were in the United States. One day, she came up to me and said, "Dad, I'm 16. I want to have my independence. I want to move out of this house, I want to go and be on my own." I said, "You're only 16." Her response was, "According to the law, I'm an adult now." To cut to the chase, she asked for a bus ticket to return to Canada where she was born. In Toronto, she was part of the drug scene for seven years.

When she rebelled, we felt so helpless. All we could do was to get down on our knees and pray, and we resolved to love her unconditionally. God brought her back. Christian parents like us are not spared the pain of parenting. You may read her story here: <asianbeacon.org/the-prodigal-daughter>.

Today, Li-Lynn has a PhD from Dalhousie University. She is a professional potter and sole proprietor of Water Dragon Pottery (facebook.com/waterdragonpottery). She also teaches history at her alma mater. Her son, Lucas, is 19 years old and in his second year at her alma mater studying engineering.

Our youngest, Le-Ben, now 35, has a PhD in genetics and an MD from the University of Pennsylvania. He is married to Janet, a museum conservator. They live in New York where he practises psychiatry. All told, he spent 15 years studying, from an undergraduate at UPenn, to completing his residency in psychiatry at Mount Sinai Hospital.

One day, my wife and I sat down and did some quick calculations. It dawned on us that if we were to spend our own money to put our three children through their studies, we would have to be very rich parents to have done it. So, how did we do it? Truly, God provided. At various stages of their studies, they were recipients of some kind of grant, scholarship or whatever. This highlights a very important lesson for me — God takes care of His servants. I think that there are many pastors who can testify that God indeed provides; He is awesome.

Let me now read Hebrews 11:8–10.

> *By faith Abraham, when called to go to a place he would later receive as his inheritance, obeyed and went, even though he did not know where he was going. By faith he made his home in the promised land like a stranger in a foreign country; he lived in tents, as did Isaac and Jacob, who were heirs with him of the same promise. For he was looking forward to the city with foundations, whose architect and builder is God.*

Obedience to God

Based on this passage, I would like to talk about my journey, focusing on three aspects. The first is about obedience to God. Abraham obeyed God. Abraham did not know where he was going. He did not know how and why God would call him, but he heard the voice of God and he just went. That is obedience!

When I became a Christian in 1961, I was in Secondary 1. Three years later, I was baptized. About that time, we started the youth fellowship that became Bartley Christian Church. I was a founding member. It was my distinction to be the first person in that church to go to Bible college, and I eventually returned to pastor the church.

I pastored that church twice. The first time, I was teaching at Discipleship Training Centre (DTC). The church was worshipping in four or five centres. So, in the late '70s, we built the first church. God had led me to think of consolidating the church because we did not have our own property. Eventually, we bought the land, and we pulled everybody together and populated that church. I pastored it for three years concurrently with my teaching ministry at DTC, and being founding General Secretary of the Evangelical Fellowship of Singapore. Burned out, I then left for Canada and did not come back until the mid '90s. In the mid '90s, I came back to be the senior pastor of a much enlarged Bartley Christian Church with two centres, one at the old premises on Bartley Road and another at Pasir Ris (now RiverLife).

The moving out of Singapore and the coming back were never planned. There was nothing in my mind to say that at a certain point in time I would be in Canada or the US. I just moved along. When I was called back to pastor Bartley

Christian Church I had, by any human standards, a successful ministry. At that time, I was senior pastor of a growing cross-cultural multi-racial church in Washington, DC. I was also teaching at the university. My kids were growing up nicely. And then I received this insistent call from Bartley, for the longest time, saying, "Come back." Little did I know that this second coming back, so to speak, would last for only a little over two years.

Many of you would have heard about it. There was conflict and I was actually fired. The Board of Elders gave me 24 hours' notice — the founding pastor of the church fired by his own church at 24 hours' notice. I was deeply hurt. As a lawyer I wanted to sue them, but as a Christian pastor, I could not. Some people thought I came out to start a new church. I did not. In fact, I did not call a single person to leave the church with me. They left on their own accord. Hundreds left. I had no choice but to hang around for one more year to pull the church together. It was a very painful time. I was so wounded and yet I had no choice but to pastor the other wounded ones as well.

The good news is that three years ago, we were reconciled. The church had its 50th anniversary, and they apologized publicly. In fact, I have been invited to preach at Bartley Church several times since. A brother recently remarked, "You look so relaxed nowadays!" There are reasons for that. It is very hard to be so relaxed when you carry this burden, this hurt. And so this is in itself a testimony of reconciliation.

When God calls us and puts us through the grind, it is not always about blessings and more blessings. Blessings can be in disguise. Blessings can come through pain, through betrayal, through defamation, through all kinds of stuff. Even today, there are churches that will not invite me to preach because of what happened at Bartley. I just heard about that recently. What can I say? Nothing except, "God, you take care of me, and I trust you." When we are called, like Abraham, to obey Him, to believe in Him, it is all about God-centredness. If we are centred on God, I have discovered, He will take us through blessings up on the hill as well as blessings in the valley.

It is not true that blessings only come in good things. Blessings can come in terrible things. Because of what happened at Bartley, I had to go back and practise law after pastoring the church for a year. It was not easy returning to practice after more than two decades away from Singapore. In all, I spent almost ten years in legal practice. The first five years I could not preach anywhere; I was so hurt. I simply disappeared from the Christian scene. I was not involved in much except for going to church. And then God started healing me, and about five years later I started to preach again. It was during my time in law practice when God opened many different doors. Then I opted for early retirement at 60 and spent four years running a psychometric company. It was when I was on holiday in New York that I got a call asking me if I would come back and run the Kindness Movement.

If I had not left Bartley Church, I would have continued to be a pastor today as never in my life did I think that I would go back to practise law. I thought I was done with law after I left in the mid '70s. I stopped practising law in 1975 and I thought, "That's it!" But God put me back in the practice of law and brought me to this point where I am serving our nation through the Kindness Movement. God's blessings can come in different forms. So that is the first lesson I learnt — it is about being God-centred.

Obsession with Heavenly Things

The second point about the passage is that we have to be not only obedient, but also obsessed. Obsessed with the heavenly place, obsessed with spiritual things, obsessed with a home that is better than this home. Not obsessed with possession, but obsessed with the fact that we are not going to be here forever.

What does that mean? For me, the implications are very simple. Whatever God tells us to do, we must be willing to do. It's not about our career; it's not about our wealth. I have found myself, in a very strange way, able and willing, not because I'm better than you or more spiritual than you, but because of the sense of willingness to obey God; an obsession that there is a better place prepared for me. I left law twice, and each time I was doing well. It's not a case where I have nothing better to do and I decided to do ministry. The second time I left my partnership as a senior partner, I actually upset my managing partner a lot. For six months he refused to talk to me because he felt that I abandoned him. But we are also reconciled.

The first time I left Leong Kwok Yan, I felt really bad. Leong Kwok Yan is still in practice. He is a fine Christian brother. We came out and set up our practice together, and then within a few years I left him on his own. I clearly remember Kwok Yan saying to me, very kindly, "William, you know I would rather that you stay and build up this practice. We are doing very well. But between God and me, God must have the priority. If you believe that God called you, I can't keep you." That's how godly this man is. So I left Kwok Yan and went off and prepared for the ministry, then came back to teach at Discipleship Training Centre (DTC).

So, you see, whilst money is useful — I would love to have more money because it can do some wonderful things — somehow, it never really kept me in legal practice, but God has provided. In 1975 when I left my practice, I owned a landed property measuring 6,000 square feet. I sold it in 1981 for very little. By 1982, land prices had soared! When I came back to Singapore, that land and house was worth millions of dollars. I did not feel that it was a disaster as God had provided all my needs. Not my wants, but my needs. What I'm really saying is, somehow because of my obsession with heaven, earthly things — not that they are not important, we need money to function, to do things — pale in significance to what I see in my vision, a much better place. And that was Abraham's vision as well. A city not built by human hands, but whose architect is God. I look forward to that city. I live my life longing for that city. I thought I would pass away by the time I turned 60. But now, I have got extra years.

On my birthday, I like to visit a cemetery, especially when I am in the West. Do you know why? I like to look at the epitaphs. I like to look at who these people were. Lord so-and-so, Sir so-and-so. The Queen's Counsel, the King's Counsel. Politicians, prime ministers, wealthy people. They all end up in the same place. It reminds me of a few things. Firstly, my mortality. I'm not going to be here forever. Secondly, I will likewise go to a little hole in the ground. Or in Singapore, a little urn on the shelf or in a niche. Nothing more, nothing less. It doesn't matter how clever you were, how rich or how powerful. God is fair; it's all exactly the same. It is what happens beyond that counts. I am reminded to be humble, because there is nothing to be arrogant about. Just when you think that you have become famous or succeeded in life, then you have got to go there. It is good for your soul to remember that we are made of dust and to dust we shall return.

I love to sing, "This world is not my home, I'm just passing through".[1] That means we open our palms and say to God, "God, everything I have is Yours. Everything. I came into this world with nothing. You put them in my hands. If You need to take them for whatever reason, take them. They are not mine." And that is also why I could move in and out of law practice. I can move in and out of anything. It does not matter. For me, it is not a career. And so I tell people I live my life in chapters. Some people may misunderstand me, thinking that I am a rolling stone that gathers no moss. I don't believe this is the case. I believe that in every chapter God has something for me to do and I give a hundred and ten per cent to what I do; but when it's time to move on, I move on. I do not try to remember the past too much, because I look forward to the present and the future.

Take the Prison Fellowship for example. The Prison Fellowship as an organization was actually started by Rev Henry Khoo, Elder Seet Poon Soo, Elder PJ John and me more than 40 years ago. Before that, it was a chaplaincy ministry conducted by Rev Khoo Siaw Hwa, the father of Henry Khoo. Before that, there was no Prison Fellowship. I registered it as Christian Rehabilitation Ltd. That was the period when Neveille Tan and Tony Ng were converted. Some of you may know them. They were our first early trophies of grace. After that I left Singapore and disappeared for a long time.

Then, two years ago, they asked me to come back and become chairman again of Prison Fellowship — after a 40-year gap. I share this to reiterate that whatever we do, once it is done, we give it back to God and pray that God will bless the labour of those who come after us. I don't have a need to feel that I must be holding on to it, because it is the Lord's. It does not belong to me. The same thing happened with the Lawyers Christian Fellowship. Our Lawyers Christian Fellowship was initiated by Francis Lee and me way back when we started practice in 1973. Now, someone else leads the work. I do not feel like I need to hold on to it. But God brought me back to speak at some of the dedication meetings.

"I believe that in every chapter God has something for me to do."

One of the things that I have discovered, especially in church work, is that sometimes people stay too long in a place and refuse to let go. It can be very dangerous. God wants to rejuvenate and refresh us. So because I feel that my life is lived in chapters and I just believe that God wants me there for a time to serve, it is okay for me to let go and move on. I thought for the longest time that I had moved on from Bartley Christian Church until they insisted I came back. At that time when they fired me, I thought I had made my biggest mistake — I should have just moved on and never come back. But now as I look back, God had a purpose too, in my coming back and being fired. It is all about God's sovereign purpose. Romans 8:28 and Ecclesiastes 3:11 remain my favourite texts on God's sovereignty.

So I focus my attention on heaven. I'm obsessed with heaven. And therefore this life and everything that has taken place is a preparation for the best reserved for me in heaven. I am packed to go. I am travelling light. I am prepared to serve as He calls me at any given time, and I am ready to move on at a moment's notice.

Being Other-Centred

The last point from the passage is about being other-centred. Abraham was called to be a blessing to the world. The covenant in Genesis 12 is very clear, "Through you and your descendants I will bless the world" (my paraphrase). To love our neighbours is the way God uses us to bless the world. These days I am not very much involved with Christian ministry other than the Prison Fellowship and preaching in churches. And I still write for the *Asian Beacon* magazine, which was started by Rev Ben Sawatsky. In 1969, I was pastor of an Evangelical Free Church and Ben Sawatsky was a missionary in that church. *The Beacon* was actually an American magazine for the Evangelical Free Church. *Asian Beacon* was started as an Asian version of the American *Beacon*. I was privileged to be on the original editorial board. Here again, I left *Asian Beacon* for the longest time but recently, they asked me to write for them on a regular basis. God has His own way of bringing things back together.

Besides writing for *Asian Beacon* and preaching in churches, I am not involved in other Christian ministries. I feel that in this chapter of my life, helming the Kindness Movement is an opportunity for me to engage the communities and the secular world, so to speak. And so I spend a lot of my time doing that. The Kindness Movement consumes most of my time now. I am also involved in the Scouts' Council and am on the board of the National Kidney Foundation. Also, I have just been appointed as chairman of the Ethics Committee for the new Farrer Park Hospital. All these secular platforms provide me wonderful ways to engage people.

When I was a senior partner in a law firm about 20 years ago, I was asked if I would consider becoming a Nominated Member of Parliament. I said no for various reasons, partly because I did not think I had a cause to champion in Parliament. When I started at the Kindness Movement I was asked again and I said yes, because I thought I could champion kindness and seniors' causes. But they found that I was a civil servant, because we were still part of the Ministry of Culture, Community Development and Youth then. More recently, I was asked by three separate groups of people and I let my name stand because now the movement is officially not part of the ministry. I went to the Selection Committee and was not selected. I think I know why, but that is perfectly all right. I believe in the sovereignty of God and I wrote to thank the committee for their decision.

You can see that my life in this season is mostly about engaging our society. I feel very strongly that Christians must reach out and be engaged outside the four walls of our churches. Let me illustrate what I mean. In 1971, I published my first book, *Total Evangelism,* intended for Varsity Christian Fellowship as a training manual for evangelism. Following that, the book was used by Youth for Christ and in other places, with seminars organized to promote evangelism. And so often when I was promoting evangelism in the church context, I would ask people how many of them have good friends who are not Christians by a show of hands. There were very few. Most Christians could identify Christians as their good friends, and very few non-Christians as their good friends or best friends. And I said that that was not very good, because you have to make friends with people who are not Christians. And because *Total Evangelism* was about friendship evangelism, if you do not reach out to your friends, and you do not have friends who are non-Christians, how are you going to reach them?

That occurred to me when I was pastoring churches in the US, Canada and Singapore. So I would tell my congregation that the first thing they should be committed to, in terms of time, is worship — to dedicate Sunday for worship, or if they go for Saturday service, Saturday for worship. Then, they should be part of a small group, and a prayer meeting if they can. Then I would say, "The rest of your time, please go and engage the community. I do not want you in church. Get out." And that is still what I am saying today. We need to love our neighbours as ourselves. How do we do that? Get engaged in your community. There are so many ways in which you can get engaged.

That is why Life Anew (which is now 70×7) was birthed by Prison Fellowship as a charity with an Institution of Public Character (IPC) status. As an IPC, we can raise funds from public foundations and the public and give them tax benefits. Why was Life Anew created? The Prison Fellowship focuses on evangelism. The authorities understand that. So, the way it works is that if you are a prisoner, you have to fill up a form to say that you are a Christian. Only on that basis would you be allowed to go to chapel, and on that basis would our volunteers be able to connect with you. If you are Muslim or Buddhist, we cannot touch you. That is fair enough. Now, the question for us is then how do we reach the offenders and the families who are not Christians?

So we set up Life Anew. It is the social welfare arm of prison ministry, and our objective is not evangelism. Our objective is to meet needs — whether social, financial, family, emotional or psychological needs, counselling needs, family financial assistance, children needing tuition, care and so on. We created Life Anew to reach offenders and their families without regard to race and religion. That is community engagement. As we befriend them and help their families, we hope they will see us as people who love them. And if they want to know the gospel, there's nothing to stop them from asking us to share our faith with them. So again, the community engagement aspect is brought into the Prison Fellowship.

Let me now share with you two of the books I have written. The first is *Pastoral Reflections,* which I wrote when I was helping a church in Batu Pahat, Malaysia. I published it to raise money for an Early Intervention Centre for children with Down's syndrome and autism initiated by the church. The other is *More Pastoral Reflections,* which I wrote just before I became the Kindness Movement's General Secretary. I give this away to the people with whom I work as a way of sharing my beliefs through my reflections. This way, they will know me better, especially my motivation as a Christian.

My Bucket List

In closing, let me say that I believe in a holistic lifestyle. By that, I mean we need to be spiritually, mentally, emotionally and physically fit. I believe that to be useful to the work of the Lord, it is of utmost importance that we keep well. I am grateful that I have been keeping well by the grace of God. There are health issues beyond our control, of course. But where we have control, we need to be disciplined to develop and maintain good habits. These include healthy eating and sleeping habits, regular exercise and finding time for rest and recreation.

When I reached 60 years of age, I decided to make a random and spontaneous "bucket list". This comprises things I would like to do that require some physical challenges, and do not take too much time in executing them. The bucket list is also an incentive for me to keep fit so that I can achieve them without too much trouble. To that end, I have completed a number of challenges on my list after my 60th birthday. They include skydiving, snipe racing, scuba diving and rock climbing. I have also made trips to less-travelled places like UNESCO Heritage Sites along the Silk Route and the former Soviet Republic.

I live to celebrate the goodness of God and to serve wherever He leads me. I seek to bloom where He plants me. And I look forward to another world beyond this, to "a city with foundations, whose architect and builder is God" (Hebrews 11:10). And it will be my reward to hear Him say, "Well done, [my] good and faithful servant" (Matthew 25:23).

▪ ▪ ▪

Questions for Reflection

1

Why is it so difficult to trust and obey God in the context of modern living?

2

If we believe that "heaven is a wonderful place, filled with glory and grace",[2] why are we so reluctant to leave this earth?

3

How does believing in Romans 8:23 and Ecclesiastes 3:11 help us to deal with tragedies and other negative experiences in our journey?

4

What are some practical ways we can show that we truly love our immediate neighbours as we do ourselves?

5

Discuss the implications of living our lives "in chapters" in relation to the idea that "a rolling stone gathers no moss".

Dr William Wan is a lawyer, pastor, academician and psychometric analyst. He has worked in these capacities in Singapore, Canada and the US. Currently, he is the General Secretary of the Singapore Kindness Movement and Pastor Emeritus of Hope Presbyterian Church. William writes a column for Asian Beacon *and has contributed many articles to various publications including* Impact, Church and Society, Law and Justice in Singapore *and* The Law Gazette. *His email address is <william_wan@kindness.sg>.*

RETIRING OR RE-TYRING

Wong Kar Fatt

When I was asked to speak about active retirement, I got very worried. This was because I have never heard anybody talk about retirement. I know there are books written on it. I looked at them for help. In the end, I felt the best thing for me to do was just to share my personal journey and some of my own ideas on what retirement means to me.

At this point in time, I think most of us are in the same phase of life, where we are no longer gainfully employed. Some of my friends will say that they are semi-retired. That is still not retirement! If you are still obliged to work for a living, even if only to support half or a quarter of your expenses, some of what I share will not apply to you, as you are still bound by obligations to do certain things. By "not gainfully employed", I mean you are at a phase where you have a lot of flexibility with your time and money, and you are seeking fulfilment of a different kind or indeed, different challenges. If you are at this phase of your life, then we are on the same page.

I have this problem when I meet my ex-colleagues. I tell them, "I'm no longer working". Their immediate reaction is, "What's wrong with you?" People don't like the idea of not working and doing something else. I find this mindset quite unacceptable if we are to embrace life at another level. There is another part of our life that holds so much potential for meaningful living and with so much to do. I call it "the next phase"!

Hence, I want to embrace another mindset. Are we retiring and putting ourselves out of circulation? Or are we "re-tyring"? There is some negative perception when we talk about retiring. When we retire, the perception is that we take ourselves out of circulation, we are no longer useful to society and family, our physical and mental capacities grow weaker and our social standing and self-esteem take a beating. In the midst of all this, we end up wondering whether we are on the wrong track.

I reject this perception. I therefore would rather talk about "re-tyring". Just like old tyres, some of us are worn out emotionally, physically or mentally. We feel very worn out and feel that we are no longer able to run like we used to. But it is precisely at this point that we should equip ourselves. When we enter this phase of life, we have to equip ourselves and be ready to race again. This time, to be even more energized and refreshed than we could ever imagine. Here, I will share some of the things that I do now, having "re-tyred" myself.

The first thing is to discard the notion that retiring means taking yourself out of circulation, like an old man. We do not ever want to feel that we are in the stage where we just sit around and wait for things to happen. That will indeed be pathetic. Rather, I would prefer to take the mindset of a re-energized man, a man who does not feel like he is "over the hill". A man who thinks that this is the phase where he can harness all his life experiences acquired over the years for the betterment of others and as a result, enrich his own life. If we think of ourselves this way, we will remain active. We will not feel like men who are out of circulation.

The Lord has given us a life that is useful throughout our entire lifespan. There's never a part that's useless. Look at the Old Testament. Look at Caleb. How old was he when he asked God to let him claim a mountain? He was 80 years old! What about Moses or Abraham? All the amazing things that happened to them were at an age when many of us would regard ourselves as "out of circulation".

We have to think about the next season, in terms of spiritual renewal and formation. In the previous season, we may have spent a lot of our lives working in the corporate world. We ended up with very little time to think about spiritual formation, to think about God and to think about a part of ourselves, that can be very hollow at times.

"Spiritual renewal" is needed because the part of us that has to do with our relationship with our Lord Jesus has been neglected due to various priorities in the earlier phase of our life. So we need to start with getting our relationship with our Lord Jesus Christ on the right track. Note that the focus here is not just on learning and studying the Word, but also on our relationship with Jesus. This relationship is that part of us which needs time to nurture. It requires us to actively posture our souls toward the Person of Jesus Christ as revealed through His Word in the Bible.

Next, "spiritual formation" takes us into a period of feeding our souls, in the way you involve yourself in ministry and as you grow in maturity. In this season, we will have many opportunities to intentionally engage in spiritual formation, as we have more flexibility with our time. We must be willing to come out of our comfort zones to face new outlooks and challenges.

Many of us have been so caught up in the corporate world that when the time finally comes to step out, we think it is too big a risk. I am not advocating that we become reckless. We are at the point where our life experiences have enabled us to have a wider perspective and the ability to take more things in our stride and say: "This is out of my comfort zone, but I am willing to try." This is when we can ask the Lord to give us the opportunity and see how He will work in our life. Indeed, this is the time when we must trust God and ask Him to show us where He wants us to go next. Abraham came out of his comfort zone (his homeland) when the Lord called and was given the opportunity to be part of God's divine plan to build a new nation of people.

We must seek to be re-energized through proactive activities and involvement in our circles of church, family and social network. Never neglect your networks, because we live our lives within these networks. We should never be disconnected, but instead be constantly aware of our social environment and what is going on around us.

To let you know where I am coming from, let me share a bit of my personal journey. I am 61 years old now, have one wonderful wife, three amazing kids and two grandchildren. I worked for 27 years as a banker, six years as a corporate consultant and subsequently as Group CEO of eight companies before I retired six years ago. I have been in church leadership since the 1980s and I was a member of Mount Carmel's first Session.

For 12 years, from 2001 to 2012, I served as an elder in church. I have had two heart attacks and was "awarded" nine medical heart stents for these two episodes. Yes, it is a Singapore record! I did not realize this until my cardiologist told me, "You have the most heart stents in Singapore." I am not proud of it but what can I do? It has already happened. I have also torn two ligaments in my left leg playing badminton when I fell twice on the same leg. Despite all this, I can still praise the Lord because I have been in excellent health since 2003. Just last week, I went for my tenth-year medical check-up. According to the medical records, I have been down with flu only once in the last ten years. It is really amazing how the Lord, by His grace and mercy, has protected me all these years!

I want to share with you two truths that have shaped my life's perspective. As disciples in Christ, we have an inheritance that is rich beyond our imagination for the rest of our lives. What do I mean by that? Let us look at Psalm 16:5–11 (NIV 2011),

> 5*LORD, you alone are my portion and my cup;*
> *you make my lot secure.*
> 6*The boundary lines have fallen for me in pleasant places;*
> *surely I have a delightful inheritance.*
> 7*I will praise the LORD, who counsels me;*
> *even at night my heart instructs me.*
> 8*I keep my eyes always on the LORD.*
> *With him at my right hand, I will not be shaken.*
> 9*Therefore my heart is glad and my tongue rejoices;*
> *my body also will rest secure,*
> 10*because you will not abandon me to the realm of the dead,*
> *nor will you let your faithful one see decay.*
> 11*You make known to me the path of life;*
> *you will fill me with joy in your presence,*
> *with eternal pleasures at your right hand.*

What a wonderful model for us to follow for the rest of our lives! Here we talk about our "lot" (v. 5). What is our "lot"? It is our relationship with Jesus Christ. Christ Himself has enabled us to live out our different life experiences. Different! No two people can have exactly the same journey. We have our unique skill sets developed after so many years of working, as well as our natural talents. We also have spiritual gifts, at least one that the Lord has given to each of us. It is unique to each of us in our personal contexts.

Spiritual gifts are given to us to fulfil His purpose and used only for His glory. It is up to us to sit down and think about our "lot" in life. What are the talents, gifts and opportunities that Jesus Christ Himself has given us? What does God want you to do for Him? Yes, we enjoy ourselves but we must remember — ultimately, it is His purpose that matters. That is the picture that shapes my perspective for the way forward.

The second picture to have in our minds is "the seasons in our lives". In Ecclesiastes it says that there is a time for everything and a season for every activity under the heavens. There is a time to be born and a time to die, a time to plant and a time to uproot, and it goes on. The bottom line is, God, in His own time, has made everything beautiful. Ask yourself, which season are you in?

I resonate with Søren Kierkegaard who said, "Life can only be understood backwards; but it must be lived forwards." Each of us has a past that can shackle us and slow us down. We must learn to release the parts that shackle us and say to the Lord: "I have learned my lesson, please release these 'shackles' so that I can move forward, and in so doing, harness my life experiences to live intentionally." Our lives cannot be lived in default mode, waiting for things to happen! Our lives must have a purpose and a direction that are aligned to God's will.

> "God, in His own time, has made everything beautiful."

I am a wildlife and bird photographer, or at least I aspire to be. I joke with some of my friends that I want to be a National Geographic photographer. My wife often remarks that I am ridiculous. One day, I will submit some of my photographs to National Geographic, and if they are accepted, it will be great. This prospect alone has truly energized me. I constantly challenge myself to reach that standard of capturing the beauty of nature!

I know that every season has its own beauty. Even winter! I am planning to go to Hokkaido in the middle of winter, when it's -30 or -40 degrees. The wildlife is so different during that season, when there are migratory birds coming from the north, and there is much beauty there. What I am saying is that whatever season of life you are in, there is beauty in it that the Lord wants to show us. I believe that there is always something about you that is unique, and that you can share with others to bless them.

How then shall we live? The next point aligns very nicely with the objective of Carmel Men for Christ.

We must be involved in the community life and mission of the church. Community life is where you come to worship and relate to your brothers and sisters in Christ. But there is so much more to that! There is a mission of the church that we should be involved in! The mission is to evangelize to the lost and make disciples, but we must also watch our prayer life and personal walk with the Lord, lest we get too caught up in activities. When misfortunes come our way, it is our personal walk with the Lord that will allow us to keep moving forward and say, "I still have joy and peace in the Lord."

We should adopt a routine, so we never let ourselves say, "What do I do next?" And in maintaining this routine, it is always good to have somebody to be accountable to for our time, the way we behave and our lifestyle. Some call these friends "soul mates". We must have an accountability group with preferably members of the same gender. Sometimes our spouses cannot keep track of us, but our brothers can, and tell us straight in the face: "Brother, you're out of line." We need to make sure we have this in our lives.

John Wesley once said:

> *When a man becomes a Christian, he becomes industrious, trustworthy and prosperous. Now, if that man, when he gets all he can and saves all he can, does not give all he can, I have more hope for Judas Iscariot than for that man!*

Rather strong words! We are at a stage and season in our lives when we have a lot of things and acquired a lot of things. But do we give? Not just of our money, but also our time and life experiences.

The disciple of Christ is able to enjoy fellowship with His master and also the fruits of his labour. This includes the privilege of blessing others. Whether or not you are employed, there must be opportunities to bless others in the community.

The last point I would like to make — and this is the part I enjoy the most — is that it is all right to play! We must stay engaged in our lifelong passions or interests that refresh and energize us for the rest of our lives. The key words are "refresh" and "energize". Do things that energize you! I have five hobbies but I do not indulge in them all at the same time. I like golf, fishing, nature photography, gardening and Chinese brush painting. Every time I encounter an opportunity to do any of these, I feel excited and get energized in the process. It "re-creates" me.

Some of us may have only one hobby, which is fine if that is what energizes you. But be careful. We must not let our hobbies take our attention away from what is most important in life. We are disciples of Christ, first and foremost. It's all right to play, even though many of us feel very guilty playing. I felt guilty for the first few years, playing while most of my peers were still working.

Lastly, we need to watch our spiritual and physical markers. If any of us needs help with spiritual direction, do not hesitate to seek help from your church leaders and pastors for prayer and guidance. The Lord places us in His community for that purpose when we need spiritual counsel.

The next part is regular medical check-ups. This is not optional! We have to go through with it. Our human bodies suffer physical disability and impairment through wear and tear. Regular check-ups are important, because it helps us to catch many things before it is too late. After 50, we should have regular check-ups every six months, for we never know what will happen to our body.

In closing, let us look at Ecclesiastes 3:11–13 (NIV 2011),

> *He has made everything beautiful in its time. He has also set eternity in the human heart; yet no one can fathom what God has done from beginning to end. I know that there is nothing better for people than to be happy and to do good while they live. That each of them may eat and drink, and find satisfaction in all their toil — this is the gift of God.*

Are you enjoying His gift?

■ ■ ■

Questions for Reflection

1

What are the challenges facing you as you begin life as one who has retired from gainful employment?

2

The church community offers a wide variety of opportunities for ministry at various levels of engagement. Are you availing yourself to such opportunities as you seek God's purpose for the next phase of your life?

3

Have you considered the possibility of seeking a "soul mate" (other than your spouse!) who can help you in your personal growth through mutual encouragement, prayer support and sharing of aspirations and hurts?

4

What part of your life experiences, skill sets or talents can you use now to bless others in a ministry in the church?

5

Do you find yourself energized and invigorated with any particular type of ministry in the church? If so, are you giving yourself the opportunity to explore that as your focus in future years?

Wong Kar Fatt worked as a banker with various local and foreign banks for most of his corporate working life. A lay leader at Mount Carmel Bible-Presbyterian Church, he has served in several key leadership positions in church since 1977. In the 1980s, he was one of the pioneer leaders who set off to start a new work at Mount Hermon Bible-Presbyterian Church. Kar Fatt stepped up to the plate in 2001 to lead the Board of Elders and did so for 12 years before stepping down in 2012. Since then, he has been involved in the church's men's ministry, helping to facilitate fellowship and bonding amongst the brothers through forging personal friendships or "soul mates". Kar Fatt's family — his mother, three children and grandchildren — all worship in Mount Carmel, and epitomizes the "generational membership" phenomenon emerging in Mount Carmel. His email address is <frederickkf410@gmail.com>.

VITAL RESILIENCE: HOW SAMUEL FINISHED WELL

David W. F. Wong

In the desert of Arizona, an American philanthropist embarked on an unusual project.[1] He financed the building of a biosphere, a living space completely cut off from the rest of the world. Behind its airtight glass walls, a community of researchers live, self-sufficient with plants and animals, food and water, all within the sphere. If successful, such a community could be replicated in outer space.

The success of the project remains in doubt, but some findings prove interesting. For example, certain species of trees thrived in the biosphere. One of them, the cottonwood tree, grew to an enormous height. However, on closer study, the trunk was found to be extremely weak. Without air currents in the biosphere, the tree did not develop strength needed to withstand winds. It had height, but not resilience.

Resilience is vital to finishing well. No one can close well without developing strength of character, tested through difficult times. A tall tree without a strong trunk will fall at the slightest storm. Prominent leaders have fallen, and the core of their characters has been found wanting. Those who stand firm to the end are the ones who have weathered storms and developed resilience.

One such leader is Samuel. In his role as priest over the people, he experienced one let-down after another. Disappointments could have turned him into a cynic. His mentor, Eli, disappointed him. His own sons disappointed him. The people he led disappointed him. His protégé, Saul, disappointed him.

How did Samuel navigate through these disappointments without falling prey to disenchantment? How did he keep on course when those close to him failed to live up to expectations?[2]

A Failed Mentor

Samuel and Eli provide a study in contrast. Eli fails through fatal indulgence; Samuel succeeds though vital resilience. The poor model in his mentor could have disillusioned Samuel. As a child, he was left with Eli. He grew up with Eli, and from him, learned all about religious duties and service for God. Yet in the same household, Samuel saw the two sons of Eli, Hophni and Phinehas, abusing their privileges as priests. Worse than that, he saw Eli doing nothing to correct them.

Samuel was also privy to the divine judgement befalling the household of Eli. In fact, the word of the Lord was communicated through Samuel to Eli.[3] How did Samuel view his mentor and the disaster soon to overtake him and his family? No doubt, Samuel prayed. But did he pray believing that the calamity could be averted? Or was he resigned to a worst-case scenario, seeing no change in the behaviour of both mentor and his sons?

In my years in the pastoral ministry, I have heard many reasons given by people why they leave a church. One is, "I can no longer respect the pastor." On the surface, it sounds like a good and valid reason. How could a person remain in a church when he no longer accepts the ministry of someone he no longer respects?

However, the reason raises several questions. I would ask the person: Have you spoken to the pastor on the matters that undermine your respect for him? To what extent should a pastor be free from faults to win your respect? Are you placing the burden of your decision on someone else other than yourself?

In instances where a pastor or leader has committed a clear breach of integrity and is unrepentant about it, such a reason would be in order. But what if it is a matter of personal grievance or a judgemental spirit? Samuel had every reason to give up on Eli, but he did not. He could have become disillusioned with the priestly ministry, but he did not.

One reason could be that he knew as well as any other parent how difficult it was to raise children. His own sons, Joel and Abijah, went astray, like Eli's Hophni and Phinehas.[4] How tragic that history should repeat itself from one priest to another! Matthew Henry comments on Samuel,

> *He is not reckoned to be past sixty years of age, now, perhaps not so much; but he was a man betimes, was full of thoughts and cares when he was a child, which perhaps hastened the infirmities of age upon him. The fruits that are the first ripe keep the worst. He had spent his strengths and spirits in the fatigue of public business, and now, if he think to shake himself as at other times, he finds he is mistaken: old age has cut his hair.*[5]

"The fruits that are first ripe keep the worst." Prodigious leaders who excel before their time, ahead of their peers, fall into such a danger. Yet I believe Samuel managed to keep himself — but he could not keep his sons. They turned bad. As such, he could hardly stand in judgement of his mentor. One thought that should hold us back from a judgemental spirit is: How would I have fared if I were in his or her position?

At one of Haggai Institute's leadership seminars, a participant became stridently critical of those from his country who had attended a seminar. They had made a commitment to go back and train others, but, "I have seen these people. They had come back and done nothing". I made a note of his criticism. A year after he himself had gone home, I did a check on him and found that he was no better.

Samuel never stood in judgement of Eli. If anything, he resolved not to fail his mentor. He remained faithful to God till the end. He did not allow his walk with the Lord to be determined by the bad example of others. Neither did he shift the blame of his own turn of events to another's failure to live up to his expectations. Leaders lead by their good example, rather than be led by others' bad example. They look to the Lord rather than to man. What was said of Samuel when he was a child was true of him in his life: "The LORD was with Samuel as he grew up, and he let none of his words fall to the ground."[6]

Rejection, a Bitter Pill

Apart from the poor example of Eli, Samuel had to contend with the people. They came to him one day and asked for a king to rule over them. Samuel saw this as a rejection of his leadership. Such rejection could have ended his ministry to the people. Yet, Samuel made it clear that he would continue to pray for them.

Rejection by people is a hard pill to swallow, especially so when the leader has given his best, and believes that the people once loved him and followed him. Moses faced it in the desert soon after delivering the Israelites from slavery in Egypt. Jesus heard the crowd shouting "Hosanna!" one day, and "Crucify him!" the next. Unpleasant as it may be, rejection can help build resilience.

For Samuel, it helped him see the distinction between what he is doing and what God is doing. God assured him, "… it is not you they have rejected, but they have rejected me as their king."[7] Understanding the difference helps us not to take rejection personally. When a leader has worked hard, built an enterprise and owned the work, any criticism is taken as a personal snub. A work can begin with the people needing the leader, and end with the leader needing the people.

> "Samuel had to reckon with the painful truth that his time had come and gone."

Some political leaders, having served with distinction in the early years of their tenure, refuse to step down. "The people still need me," they reason. Some pastors in extended pastorates, with long years of service, argue the same. The truth may be that they need the people. Leaders enjoy the adulation of their followers, take pride in them like trophies and become addicted to the power and prestige the people give them. It is hard to step down from the pedestal.

Samuel had to learn that he was not the one leading the people. God was their leader. They were rejecting God's leadership when they rejected his. Samuel had to accept that he was only an intermediary, and as such, a dispensable component of the equation. When the people asked for a king, God told Samuel to accede to their request, but not without first warning them of the consequences. God took responsibility for granting them their desire. Samuel was, after all, only God's spokesman.

The people presented a valid reason for their desire to have a king. Samuel's sons were corrupt and they did not want to live under their priesthood. Such a reason must have stung the elderly priest, though he could take comfort in that he himself finished well. When he asked the people if he had done anything wrong, they gave him a clean bill of integrity.[8] Nevertheless, Samuel had to reckon with the painful truth that his time had come and gone. Much as he would like to see it happen, his sons could not carry on his legacy. Every leader has to accept the limitations of time, health and unforeseen circumstances.

Part of being resilient is knowing when to step aside. Not every battle has to be fought. I once asked a leader who had led his denomination ably for 12 years, during which he instituted many reforms, "What are some lessons you learned in the process?" The first he offered was, "Choose your battles." I took that counsel to heart. Soon after, I met opposition to an idea I had proposed for a church. I had given the idea much thought, and saw the resistance as an unwillingness to change. More than that, I felt my credibility being challenged.

After a few sleepless nights, I decided that it was a battle not worth fighting. Perhaps the timing was not right. Perhaps I had not communicated the rationale clearly. The people had rejected the idea, not me. On hindsight, I am glad I stepped back and did not make it an issue. If I had donned combat gear and charged head-on, I might have forced the idea through, but the collateral damage would have outweighed the benefit.

Resilience incorporates a crucial time element. It sees the big picture because it allows for the passing of time. When Samuel promised the people that he would not stop praying for them, he was looking into the future. He knew that they were going to need it. Impatience wants it now. Resilience, with its twin virtue, patience, is prepared to wait. Not every impulse needs to be met, nor every challenge a fight. Rejection touches a raw nerve, but when accepted and viewed in perspective, builds resilience.

Protégé Turned Threat

Rejection by people is one thing; what about rejection by God? Samuel saw it in his protégé, Saul. God cast him aside. Of all of Samuel's disappointments, this must be the hardest to bear. He found Saul when he was yet an unknown entity, anointed him king in secret, and introduced him to public life.

When anointed, Saul did not think himself worthy of the honour: "But am I not a Benjamite, from the smallest tribe of Israel, and is not my clan the least of all the clans of the tribe of Benjamin?" When presented to the people, Saul drew cynicism from some: "How can this fellow save us?"[9]

From such unpromising beginnings, Samuel would watch Saul rise to the occasion. In a moment of national crisis, Saul rallied the people and routed the Ammonites. With the resounding victory, he secured his leadership as well as his kingship. Samuel called on the people to recognize Saul as king, which they did in a grand celebration. It must have been the high point of Samuel's life.

The sense of achievement on the part of Saul cannot be compared to that of Samuel. The pride of the parents at the graduation of their son or daughter is always greater than that of the graduate. So it must be for a mentor who sees someone he has identified, affirmed and believed in, finally honoured and recognized. It is from this height of Samuel's priestly career that we best understand his disappointment when Saul careened out of control in a downward spiral.

It started when Saul usurped the priestly office by offering sacrifice in preparation for the battle against the Philistines. Samuel saw what was at stake, and pronounced Saul unfit as king. Soon afterwards, another opportunity presented itself to Saul when Samuel sent him to battle against the Amalekites. Did Samuel think Saul might redeem himself? If so, it turned out to be a futile hope.

After the battle, Saul presumed to offer sacrifice from the sheep and cattle of the Amalekites when he had been told in no uncertain terms to destroy them and everything else. Both events took place at Gilgal, and each was clearly an act of disobedience against God. Samuel was convinced that the character flaw in Saul was permanent and incorrigible. The account concluded on a grim note, "Until the day Samuel died, he did not go to see Saul again, though Samuel mourned for him."[10] Later, God had to interrupt Samuel's brooding to get him going again: "How long will you mourn for Saul, since I have rejected him as king over Israel?"[11]

As mentor, Samuel seemed to be of two minds about Saul. On the one hand, he mourned for him. Saul was no doubt still on his prayer list. Perhaps the priestly intercessor could not figure out how the choice of Saul could have been wrong. He grieved over Saul. On the other hand, Samuel refused to see Saul. What Saul had done must have hurt Samuel deeply. The priest had invested his reputation, his hopes and the people's future in the first king of Israel — only to see the whole process go awry. Anger and sorrow left Samuel ambivalent.[12]

When God's call came for Samuel to go and anoint another king, fear struck him: "How can I go? Saul will hear about it and kill me."[13] Saul was no longer Samuel's understudy, but a threat to his life. Hence the anointing of the next king was done in utmost privacy. Even then, Samuel showed that he had not learned his lesson. When he saw Eliab, he immediately thought he would be king. But God corrected Samuel, "Do not consider his appearance or his height, for I have rejected him. The LORD does not look at the things man looks at. Man looks at the outward appearance, but the LORD looks at the heart."[14]

Did Samuel still think that a king should be tall and handsome, like Saul? (Saul had been described as "an impressive young man without equal among the Israelites — a head taller than any of the others".[15]) Obviously, Samuel still had the memory and image of Saul lingering in his mind. Lest we judge Samuel harshly, we are all also slow learners. For Samuel, his residual feelings for Saul might have gotten ahead of his priestly duty for God and nation. He had to let go of the past, unlearn the human tendency to judge by appearance, and learn God's way of looking at people.

Through his disappointment with Saul, Samuel emerged no doubt with some emotional scars. His experience with Saul was a betrayal of sorts. Such betrayal can devastate us and turn us into cynics, or it can sober us and help us grow in discernment and maturity. For all the let-downs Samuel faced — with his mentor, his sons, the people and his understudy — he emerged resilient. When we last see him marching off to Ramah, he left behind a young shepherd boy whom he had freshly anointed as a future king.[16] Samuel did not live long enough to see it, but he finally found someone who lived up to expectations.

▪ ▪ ▪

Questions for Reflection

1

List the significant people in Samuel's life. How was each of them a disappointment to him?

2

Think about a disappointment with someone in your life. How did it affect your life and your relationship with the Lord?

3

Why did the people reject Samuel's leadership and ask for a king? Were their reasons valid? How should we take rejection by people?

4

Both Samuel's mentor Eli and understudy Saul turned out bad. If you were in Samuel's shoes, how would the let-down by each of them affect you?

5

To finish well, we need to be resilient. How was "vital resilience" exemplified in Samuel's life? How can we demonstrate it in ours?

Rev Dr David W. F. Wong served as the home-grown pastor of Mount Carmel Bible-Presbyterian Church for 17 years before answering a call from Haggai Institute to pioneer a leadership training centre in Hawaii in 1994. After a fruitful stint there, he returned to Singapore in 2006. He is now senior pastor of Zion Bishan Bible-Presbyterian Church. David writes a column for the Impact *magazine and has authored more than a dozen books, the latest being* The Narrow Road: Turning Neither Left Nor Right *(2015). His email address is <owlnook@yahoo.com.sg>.*

ENDNOTES

The Three Calls of Life

Tan Soo Inn

[1] Miller McPherson, Lynn Smith-Lovin, and Matthew E. Brashears, "Social Isolation in America: Changes in Core Discussion Networks over Two Decades," *American Sociological Review* 71 (2006): 353–375, qtd. in John T. Cacioppo and William Patrick, *Loneliness: Human Nature and the Need for Social Connection* (New York, NY: W. W. Norton & Co., 2008), 247.

Male Spirituality

Robert Solomon

[1] Keith Drury, *Money, Sex and Spiritual Power* (Fishers, IN: Wesleyan Publishing House, 1992).

[2] Sheila Cassidy, *Sharing the Darkness* (Maryknoll, NY: Orbis Books, 1991).

[3] "Two Sexes 'Sin in Different Ways'," *BBC News*, http://news.bbc.co.uk/2/hi/europe/7897034.stm, last modified 18 February 2009, accessed 15 December 2015. The report was based on a study done by Father Roberto Busa, a Jesuit scholar.

Your Past Will Always Haunt You! Unless You Recover

John Ng

[1] First published in Issue 105 of *Metatrends: A Leadership Publication of Meta.*

[2] Daniel Siegel, *Mindsight: The New Science of Personal Transformation* (New York: Bantam Books, 2011), xiii.

[3] Ibid.

[4] Siegel, *Mindsight*, ix–x.

[5] Daniel Siegel, *The Developing Mind: How Relationships and the Brain Interact to Shape Who We Are*, 2nd ed. (New York: Guilford Press, 1999), 13.

[6] Siegel, *The Developing Mind*, 33.

[7] The Arbinger Institute, *The Anatomy of Peace: Resolving the Heart of Conflict* (Oakland, CA: Berrett-Koehler Publishers, 2008).

[8] Siegel, *Mindsight*, xi–xii.

[9] Robert Schuller, *Turning Hurts into Halos* (Nashville, TN: Thomas Nelson, 1999), chapter 5.

[10] Siegel, *The Developing Mind*, xv.

My Halftime Journey

Lee Han Kiat

[1] Diagram from Bob Buford, *Halftime: Moving from Success to Significance* (Grand Rapids, MI: Zondervan, 2008), 107.

[2] Halftime Institute, *The Halftime Roundtable Member Guide* (Dallas, TX: Halftime Institute, 2010).

Turning the Hearts of Fathers and Children Towards Each Other

David Ang

[1] "Singapore Dads for Live Movement," *Wikipedia*, https://en.wikipedia.org/wiki/Singapore_Dads_for_Life_movement, last modified 6 December 2014, accessed 10 December 2015.

[2] Ibid.

What Is Your Long-Term Goal in Life?

Hsieh Fu Hua

[1] Viktor Frankl, *Man's Search for Meaning* (New York: Touchstone Books, 1984).

[2] Thich Nhat Hanh, *Living Buddha, Living Christ* (New York: Riverhead Books, 1995).

God in the Marketplace: Challenges Faced

Philip Ng

[1] C. Peter Wagner, *The Church in the Workplace: How God's People Can Transform Society* (Ventura, CA: Regal Books, 2006).

[2] Wagner, *The Church in the Workplace*, 75.

[3] Rik Kirkland, "Faith and Fortune," *Fortune Magazine*, 9 July 2001.

[4] Ibid.

[5] Marc Gunther, "God and Business," *Fortune Magazine*, 9 July 2001.

Forty Years and Counting

Lim Hua Min

[1] Reproduced courtesy of Phillip Securities.

[2] See Charles Handy, *The Age of Unreason* (Boston, MA: Harvard Business Review Press, 1991).

[3] Jim Collins and Jerry Porras, *Built to Last* (New York: HarperBusiness, 1994).

[4] Jeremy Rifkin, *The Empathic Civilization* (New York: Penguin, 2009).

[5] Sir Fred Catherwood, *The Christian in Industrial Society*, 3rd ed. (Leicester, England: Inter-Varsity Press, 1980).

Serving God Full-Time in the Marketplace

Timothy Liu

[1] The Marketplace Christian Network (marketplacechristian.net) is a ministry founded in 2001 to help every Christian see their work as full-time ministry and to adopt the workplace as their mission field.

[2] The Graduates' Christian Fellowship (gcf.org.sg) was founded in 1955 by a group of young university and polytechnic graduates, with the firm belief that "to whom much is given, much is required" (see Luke 12:48). GCF seeks to serve God with their education and professional training to serve students, church and society.

[3] The Lausanne Committee for World Evangelization (lausanne.org) is a global movement that started at Lausanne Switzerland in 1974, which was attended by 2,400 world leaders, with a rallying call to bring the whole gospel, by the whole church, to the whole world.

Challenges and Issues Being Salt and Light in the Marketplace

Gregory Vijayendran

[1] Rick Warren, *The Purpose Driven Life* (Grand Rapids, MI: Zondervan, 2012).

[2] "'You've got to find what you love,' Jobs says," *Stanford Report*, 14 June 2005, http://news.stanford.edu/news/2005/june15/jobs-061505.html.

[3] Ibid.

[4] *Chariots of Fire*, directed by Hugh Hudson (1981; Los Angeles, CA: Twen-

tieth Century Fox).

[5] C. S. Lewis, *Mere Christianity* (San Francisco, CA: HarperOne, 2009).

[6] Gene Edwards, *A Tale of Three Kings* (Carol Stream, IL: Tyndale, 1992).

The Bible as History

Ernest Chew

[1] E. H. Carr, *What is History?* (London: Macmillan, 1986), 17.

[2] Herbert Butterfield, *Christianity and History* (London: G. Bell & Sons), 107.

[3] Gordon Fee and Douglas Stuart, *How to Read the Bible for All Its Worth* (Grand Rapids, MI: Zondervan, 2003).

[4] Walter Kaiser Jr., *The Old Testament Documents: Are They Reliable and Relevant?* (Downers Grove, IL: InterVarsity Press, 2001).

[5] F. F. Bruce, *The New Testament Documents: Are They Reliable?* (Grand Rapids, MI: William B. Eerdmans Publishing, 2003).

[6] John Oswalt, *The Bible Among the Myths: Unique Revelation or Just Ancient Literature?* (Grand Rapids, MI: Zondervan, 2009).

[7] Richard Bauckham, *Jesus and the Eyewitnesses: The Gospels as an Eyewitness Testimony* (Grand Rapids, MI: William B. Eerdmans Publishing, 2006).

[8] Søren Kierkegaard, *Purity of Heart is to Will One Thing* (New York: HarperOne, 2008).

[9] Robert Solomon, *Reflections on Time & Eternity* (Singapore: Armour Publishing, 2012).

The Origin of Man

Aw Swee Eng

[1] In publishing this article, the editors are mindful that there are committed Christians who do not subscribe to the "young earth Creationism" approach and may not share the author's views.

[2] Richard C. Lewontin, "Billions and Billions of Demons," *The New York Review of Books*, 9 January 1997.

[3] Statement on Teaching Evolution, National Association of Biology Teachers. Adopted by the Board of Directors, 15 March 1995 and revised October 1997.

[4] Jacques Monod, interview with Laurie John, *The Secret of Life*, Australian Broadcasting Commission, 10 June 1976.

[5] Stephen Jones, Robert D. Martin and David R. Pilbeam, *The Cambridge Encyclopedia of Human Evolution* (Cambridge: Cambridge University Press, 1994).

[6] Roger Lewin, *Bones of Contention: Controversies in the Search for Human Origins, 2nd ed.* (Chicago, IL: University of Chicago Press, 1997).

[7] Marvin Lubenow, *Bones of Contention: A Creationist Assessment of Human Fossils* (Grand Rapids, MI: Baker Books, 1992). Phillip Johnson, *Darwin on Trial* (Downers Grove, IL: InterVarsity Press, 1991); *Reason in the Balance* (Downers Grove, IL: InterVarsity Press, 1998); *Defeating Darwinism* (Downers Grove, IL: InterVarsity Press, 1997).

[8] Phillip Johnson, *Darwin on Trial.*

[9] As quoted in Marvin L. Lubenow, *Bones of Contention: A Creationist Assessment of Human Fossils* (Grand Rapids, MI: Baker Books, 2004), 328–329.

[10] Ibid.

[11] Bill Gates, *The Road Ahead* (New York: Viking Penguin, 1995).

[12] John S. Mbiti, *African Religions & Philosophy* (Oxford: Heinemann, 1969). 204-205.

[13] Edgar A. Truax, "Genesis According to the Miao People," *Acts & Facts* 20 (4), www.icr.org/article/genesis-according-miao-people.

[14] Ibid.

[15] Ibid.

[16] Ibid.

[17] Ibid.

[18] *Memoirs of a Geisha,* directed by Rob Marshall (2005; Los Angeles, CA: Columbia Pictures).

[19] David Van Biema, "Can You Believe in God and Evolution?", Time, August 15, 2005.

Towards a Better Understanding of Mandarin-Speaking Churches in Singapore

John Chew

[1] Zhang Weiwei, *The China Wave: Rise of a Civilizational State* (Hackensack, NJ: World Century Publishing, 2012).

Running the Race Marked Out for Us

Ho Peng Kee

[1] Charles Colson and Nancy Pearcey, *How Now Shall We Live?* (Carol Stream, IL: Tyndale, 2004).

[2] Norman Geisler and William Watkins, *Worlds Apart: A Handbook on World Views, 2nd ed.* (Eugene, OR: Wipf and Stock Publishers, 2003), 11.

[3] Brian Walsh, "Worldview," in *The Complete Book of Everyday Christianity,* eds. Robert Banks and R. Paul Stevens (Singapore: Graceworks, 2011), 1151.

[4] Ibid.

[5] Ibid.

[6] James Sire, *A Universe Next Door: A Basic Worldview Catalog*, 5th ed. (Downer's Grove, IL: InterVarsity Press, 2009).

Navigating Life's Transitions

Andrew Goh

[1] RiverLife Church TV, "Breakfast with Jesus," http://bit.ly/BreakfastwithJesus.

Living Life in Chapters

William Wan

[1] Albert Brumley, "This World Is Not My Home," Albert Brumley and Sons, 1964.

[2] O. A. Lambert, "Heaven Is a Wonderful Place," in *The Kids Praise Album!*, Sacred Songs, 1965.

Vital Resilience

David W. F. Wong

[1] This article appears as a chapter in *Finishing Well: Closing Significant Chapters of Life* (Singapore: Finishing Well Ministries, 2006).

[2] 1 Samuel 2:12–17, 22–25

[3] 1 Samuel 3:11–18

[4] 1 Samuel 8:1–3

[5] Matthew Henry, *Matthew Henry's Commentary on the Whole Bible, Vol. 2* (Peabody, MA: Hendrickson Publishers, 1991), 250.

[6] 1 Samuel 3:19

[7] 1 Samuel 8:7

[8] 1 Samuel 12:3–5

[9] 1 Samuel 9:21; 10:27

[10] 1 Samuel 15:35

[11] 1 Samuel 16:1. See also 1 Samuel 15:10–11 when God told Samuel of Saul's disobedience. This troubled Samuel so much that "he cried out to the LORD all that night".

[12] See a parallel situation with David and Absalom in 2 Samuel 13:39; 14:24. The king longed for the son but refused to see him.

[13] 1 Samuel 16:2

[14] 1 Samuel 16:7

[15] 1 Samuel 9:2

[16] 1 Samuel 16:13. The shepherd boy was of course David, whom Samuel met again in 1 Samuel 19:18 when David fled from Saul and sought refuge in Ramah.

ABOUT THE EDITORS

Ho Peng Kee co-leads CM*f*C with Kheng Hai and heads Mt Carmel's prayer ministry. A keen sportsman, he is married to Choy Ping, and they have three daughters.

Lim Kheng Hai is a pastor at Mt Carmel. He oversees the Care Group ministry and the Saturday Evening Service. A former polytechnic lecturer, Kheng Hai has a Doctor in Ministry with a focus on leadership. He is married to Gek Lang and they have three children and a grandson. He enjoys solitude and travelling, and has written a book, *Living Well*.

Siew Kim Siang diligently summarises CM*f*C's monthly talks for publication in the church bulletin. He is a church elder and is involved in the Mandarin worship service. Kim Siang has a Master in Christian Studies from the Biblical Graduate School of Theology (BGST). An active recent retiree, he is now studying to be an accredited trainer with the Singapore Workforce Development Agency. God has blessed him and his wife, Suzannah, with three children and four grandchildren.

Yeo Siew Yam oversees the sound system and recording of CM*f*C's monthly talks. A church elder, he chairs the Standing Committee and heads the Education for Christian Formation ministry. Siew Yam is a serious student of the Bible and has completed several courses at BGST. He is married to Poh Leng and they have three children.